A 1980s
CHILDHOOD

A 1980s
CHILDHOOD

A 1980s
CHILDHOOD

DEREK TAIT

AMBERLEY

First published 2019

Amberley Publishing
The Hill, Stroud
Gloucestershire, GL5 4EP

www.amberley-books.com

Copyright © Derek Tait, 2019

The right of Derek Tait to be identified as the Author
of this work has been asserted in accordance with the
Copyrights, Designs and Patents Act 1988.

All rights reserved. No part of this book may be reprinted
or reproduced or utilised in any form or by any electronic,
mechanical or other means, now known or hereafter invented,
including photocopying and recording, or in any information
storage or retrieval system, without the permission in writing
from the Publishers.

British Library Cataloguing in Publication Data.
A catalogue record for this book is available from the British Library.

ISBN 978 1 4456 9241 8 (paperback)
ISBN 978 1 4456 9242 5 (ebook)

Typeset in 10pt on 12pt Minion Pro.
Typesetting by Aura Technology and Software Services, India.
Printed in the UK.

Contents

	Introduction	7
1	At Home	9
2	School	13
3	Toys and Games	20
4	Outdoor Activities	41
5	Childhood Illnesses	44
6	Fashion	47
7	Sweets and Chocolate	50
8	Radio	54
9	Television	59
10	Movies	94
11	Comics and Books	115
12	Music	131
13	Technology	156
14	Christmas	161
15	Notable Events	164
16	Memorable Personalities of the 1980s	180
	Acknowledgements	190
	Bibliography	191

Contents

Introduction

The 1980s was the last full decade before the internet was introduced in the early 1990s. Its introduction led to a totally different way of life for both adults and their children. It's hard nowadays to imagine a time when there was no internet, no digital technology and few mobile phones. A time when there was only three television channels (until Channel 4 began in November 1982), no Sky Television (first introduced in the UK on 5 February 1989) or Freeview and, at the beginning of the decade, few video recorders and certainly no CDs, DVDs, iPods or digital cameras. It was probably the last decade when children fully explored their surroundings, spending their days and summer holidays outdoors, building dens, climbing trees, playing football or cricket, roller skating, enjoying hopscotch or riding bikes. However, it was also a time of Gameboys, the Rubik's Cube, Sony Walkmans (first introduced in the late 1970s), vinyl records, music cassettes, music centres, ghetto blasters, keyboards, the advent of the home computer and the Sinclair C5.

It was a decade full of innovations in music, fashion and technology. It produced some of the best-loved bands and chart hits as well as some of the most fondly remembered television programmes and movies.

Popular television programmes of the time included *Grange Hill* (who can forget Tucker Jenkins?), *Worzel Gummidge* (starring Jon Pertwee), Jim Henson's *Fraggle Rock*, *Super Gran* (starring Gudrun Ure and Iain Cuthbertson), *Doctor Who* (featuring Tom Baker, Peter Davison, Colin Baker and Sylvester McCoy), *Blue Peter* (with Simon Groom, Peter Duncan and Sarah Greene), the Australian soap *Neighbours* (starring Kylie Minogue and Jason Donovan), the latest chart hits from *Top of the Pops* and madcap action in the American action-adventure series *The A Team* (starring George Peppard as Colonel John 'Hannibal' Smith and Mr T as B. A. Baracus among others).

Well-loved movies included *The Empire Strikes Back* (1980), *Raiders of the Lost Ark* (1981), *E.T. the Extra-Terrestrial* (1982), *Return of the Jedi* (1983), *Gremlins* (1984), *Ghostbusters* (1984), *The Terminator* (1984), *Back to the Future* (1985), *Stand By Me* (1986), *Aliens* (1986) and *Batman* (1989).

Music ranged from The Specials, Madness, Ultravox, Duran Duran, Wham! and Spandau Ballet to The Smiths, Prince, Michael Jackson, Kylie Minogue, Pet Shop Boys and Lisa Stansfield.

This book does its best to jog the memories of anyone who lived through the decade, recalling the good times as well as the bad times, crazy fashions, toys, music, television and film and the general day-to-day life of the 1980s.

1

At Home

At the beginning of the 1980s, Margaret Thatcher was the Prime Minister of the United Kingdom and Elizabeth II had been Queen since 1952. Life had been gradually changing over the years but the 1980s would see major differences. At the start of the decade, many people owned their own homes, however, even more were still living in rented accommodation. When Margaret Thatcher became Prime Minister in May 1979, she introduced legislation which allowed people to be able buy their council houses. The Right to Buy was passed in the Housing Act 1980. This meant many more people became property owners.

Compared to what is familiar today, homes then were very different without many of the things that we now take for granted such as home computers, games systems, mobile phones, microwaves and flat-screen televisions to name just a few. Most homes were heated by a gas or electric fire in the front room and, unlike in the previous decade, few people heated their homes with coal fires, although there were still many about.

Most men worked from 9am to 5pm and the decade also saw many more married women returning to paid employment to help to pay for extras such as a new mortgage, a car, technology and family holidays. The home received several callers during the day. Before 9am, the milkman, postman and paperboy would all have visited. Many people had their newspapers delivered to the door by their local newsagent and expected to read them over breakfast before setting off to work. It was the same with the post, which was delivered twice daily by a smartly dressed postman. The milkman arrived, in many cases, long before the family arose, arriving on an electric milk float loaded with bottles of milk that were delivered to their customers' doorsteps ready for their morning breakfast.

Most children set off for school either on foot, if they lived nearby, or caught the bus if the school was further away. It was far less common for children to arrive at school by car. A school day started at 9am and continued until 4pm. The curriculum included subjects such as maths, English, geography, history, chemistry, physics, woodwork, technical drawing, physical education (PE), games and domestic science (cookery).

Many more children played outside, building dens in the summer months, climbing trees, riding their bikes or scooters, playing games such as 'it' (also called 'tag') or hopscotch, taking part in war games or pretending to be He-Man, She-ra and Skeletor, happily fighting their friends while shouting, 'By the Power of Grayskull!' worried that anything they got up to might get back to their local beat constable or, worse still, their headmaster. In the winter months, conkers were collected, bonfires were built on Guy Fawkes Night and sledges were constructed in areas where there was heavy snow.

At the start of the decade, wooden surround televisions were found in the main living room, with push button controls (there were few remotes) and often a table top aerial which had to be moved around the room to get a decent picture. Some people had televisions in their bedrooms but these were mainly portables with small 13-inch screens. However, as the decade moved on, more bedrooms and children's rooms had their own television sets.

Homes in the early 1980s didn't have many of the electrical gadgets and technology that, today, we take for granted. At the start of the decade, few homes had video recorders, games systems, microwaves or home computers. By the end of the decade, all this had changed greatly.

Homes in the early 1980s still contained many aspects of the previous decade including wallpapers featuring floral patterns, with others featuring bold designs and woodchip, which could be painted a variety of colours. Borders became popular, usually featuring bright colours and patterns as well as a range of floral designs. Artex walls and ceilings had first become popular in the 1970s but the trend carried on well into the 1980s including plaster swirls and stippling, which conveniently covered any cracks or holes. Its drawback was that it proved almost impossible to remove when fashions changed.

Peach coloured schemes, with brightly coloured carpets and rugs, adorned many homes. Paint techniques were used to enhance walls including sponging and rag rolling, which produced a mottled effect that proved to be highly popular. Pine tables and chairs were also sought after as were MFI, build-it-yourself, flat-packed wall units and furniture. Mahogany furniture was also very fashionable.

By the mid-1980s, Laura Ashley fabrics became popular with soft furnishings, wallpaper and lampshades featuring matching designs. Later in the decade, black was seen as ultra-modern and many homes had black corner units, shelving units, video recorders and TV stands. Television casings changed from wooden-surrounds to more up-to-date black plastic housing. Music centres also adopted the same popular black casing. Red and black plastic accessories and colour schemes became fashionable in the later 1980s including red framed pictures of sports cars and other popular prints supplied in great abundance by high street stores such as the ever-popular Athena. Black ash furniture also had a high appeal in the latter part of the decade. Chintzy curtains featuring red, blue and yellow patterns adorned windows complete with fanciful, colourful tie-backs and pelmets.

Many houses were still quite draughty at the beginning of the decade with older, wooden or metal framed, single-glazed windows. Aluminium double-glazed windows had been introduced in the late 1970s but these really took off in the 1980s as more and more homes had their windows replaced not only for warmth but also to cut out noise. White plastic frames replaced the older metal ones.

In 1980, many homes now had their own telephone although there were still a great many people without a home phone. In 1982, just over 50 per cent of homes in the UK had a phone. Many of these were still the heavy, dial-type, phones popular well into the 1980s although push-button phones were later introduced. Before 1980, all telephones in the home were rented from the GPO (General Post Office). British Telecom was formed in 1980 and continued to lease phones to householders until 1981 when they first offered phones for sale. New telephone plugs and sockets were introduced, which enabled phones to be easily disconnected and replaced. Before this, telephones were wired directly to the socket and only an engineer could change them. Push-button trim phones took over from the dial type and later cordless home phones were introduced that allowed their owners to wander freely around the house without being connected to the phone's base by a lead.

In the kitchen, a whole range of gadgets became the norm during the decade. Microwaves had first been introduced in the UK in the late 1970s but became far more popular during the 1980s. Pinging meals in seconds, rather than waiting for them to cook slowly in a conventional oven, seemed very convenient and a range of microwave meals were soon introduced. Breville sandwich toasters were also well-used items in the kitchen of the 1980s, allowing users to make tasty, hot, sealed sandwiches with a variety of fillings including cheese, ham, and egg as well as sweet ingredients such as jam. The difficulty of cleaning the appliance after the sandwich was made probably led to its downfall, with it eventually being relegated to the back of the cupboard. Other gadgets associated with the kitchen during the decade included portable chicken fryers, deep fat chip fryers, mixers and whiskers, while a hostess trolley in the dining room was said to offer effortless entertaining because the various compartments kept food hot; and teasmades in the bedroom made getting up in the morning a bit easier.

Many children's bedrooms of the 1980s, for the first time, had their own televisions, often colour portable sets, which were later used in conjunction with the latest video game consoles, home computers and video recorders. Watching *Tiswas, The Multi-Coloured Swap Shop, Saturday Superstore* or *Going Live* in bed was seen as the ideal way to spend a Saturday morning after a week at school. Posters adorned the walls of children's bedrooms during the decade and these would have included pop stars, television celebrities and footballers, some taken out of *Jackie, Look-in, Shoot!* or other comics and magazines of the day. Pace posters had proved very popular throughout the 1970s and early 1980s and featured pop stars as well as television and movies stars.

Home life changed greatly over the following decades and today children spend a lot more of their time indoors, engrossed by the tools of the digital age; wide-screen televisions, mobile phones and, of course, home computers. Gone are the days of milk floats, early arrivals by the postman, beat policemen patrolling the streets, dogs wandering freely wherever they wanted, children playing unsupervised outside for hours on end, building dens and generally exploring the surrounding area. For children, the 1980s was a more innocent, untroubled time without modern technology, a more carefree life which today is lost forever.

2

School

A school day in the 1980s began at 9am. It was less common, at the time, for parents to drive their children to school; children were expected to find their own way to school. Walking to school had its benefits; you could meet your friends on the way, swap cards and stickers or visit the local newsagent for sweets or comics. Groups of friends met on the bus too.

The school day started in the playground, often with a whistle being blown to get everyone into class. Most infants and junior schools would make their pupils form an orderly straight line, and there would be no talking, before they were led off into their classes.

The first event of the day was the morning assembly, which was presided over by the head teacher. Prayers were said before a hymn was sung, quite often 'All Things Bright and Beautiful'. After that, the head would discuss the school events and deal with any problems such as children misbehaving or being late. The morning assembly was very Christian-based, as was religious education, with the main events in the religious year being Easter and Christmas. As well as the morning hymns and prayers, there would also be Bible stories told in class, especially leading up to Easter and Christmas. The Christmas preparations would also include the school's nativity play.

Teachers in the 1980s could be quite strict with the cane being given to anyone (usually boys) who stepped out of line. It could also be given to children for talking in assembly or in class, or for running in the corridor, fighting or other misbehaviour although 'lines' were often given for lesser misdemeanours. Lines involved writing the same thing over and over again, up to 100 times, and usually involved writing something such as 'I shall not talk in class.' All teachers were referred to as 'Sir' or 'Miss' although the teacher/pupil relationship was more relaxed than it had been in previous decades. Teachers were allowed to give children the cane until 1987 when a law was passed to abolish the practice.

The morning assembly usually lasted for half-an-hour before pupils were led off to their classes. Children would normally be called by their surnames both when the register was called and in the classroom and pupils would have to reply with 'Yes, sir!' or 'Yes, miss!' In infants and junior school, most children had one teacher who covered all subjects which were usually maths, English, history and geography. There would also be some artwork involved and a regular fitness regime with the PE teacher. Cross country running also played a part as did country dancing, in which both girls and boys had to take part.

Maths included learning multiplication tables, which would be tested in class, fractions, binary numbers, long division and multiplication, logarithms and algebra. English involved handwriting, reading and sentence structure. History often covered the history of the British monarchy. Nearly all schools by the 1980s had their own television sets which were wheeled into the classroom on a large metal trolley, which, later in the 1980s also included a VHS video recorder.

Physical Education, or PE, involved changing into a PE kit which consisted of a white T-shirt, shorts and black gym shoes. Activities included climbing ropes, walking on parallel bars, vaulting the horse (a huge wooden contraption) and catching a medicine ball that was so heavy it could easily knock any child off his feet. Games involved playing football, rounders and cricket and taking part in the annual sports day. Some schools even had their own swimming pools but they would be unheated and covered in ice during the winter. Many other schools took their pupils by coach to a local pool that was miles away where they could not only swim but practise their diving from one of the many boards. Swimming lessons began with teaching the pupils how to swim and once that was achieved, there were competitions. The usual length of the pool was 10 metres and anyone who completed the distance would be awarded a certificate which would usually be given out by the head teacher during the next assembly.

Many pupils in the infants and juniors schools sat at small wooden desks facing forwards, relics from previous decades. The wooden lid of the desk, which was usually covered in the carved names of former pupils, lifted up and inside it were stored all the books needed for the day, as well as hidden items such as marbles and paper aeroplanes, etc. This was fine in junior school when children had one classroom and one teacher but when they later went to secondary school, all books and other items had to be carted from one room to another. At the corner of the wooden desk was a hole for an ink pot but this came from another age. By the 1980s, children at junior school were expected to use pencils while older children at secondary school could use fountain pens and, later, biros. Biros had been invented several decades previously but weren't allowed to be used until later years so most kids returned home, after a day writing with a leaky ink pen (they all leaked) covered in ink all over their hands.

Desks at secondary school were more modern, tubular metal with green vinyl tops, replacing the older wooden desks. Secondary schools included a range of extra subjects such as chemistry, physics, biology, woodwork, metalwork and languages which included French, German and Spanish. Many schools had a language lab were children sat in a booth with a pair of headphones and answered questions fed to them in a foreign tongue.

New exercise books would be handed out to every pupil so that they could complete their work in them. These would be expected to be covered with brown paper or similar (wallpaper was popular) and there would be trouble if an exercise book was found to be uncovered. A whole range of 1980s whacky wallpapers were used including hideous floral patterns. The reason for covering books was never very clear. Ring binders were decorated with stickers from Smash Hits or Panini stickers of footballers. This was through choice, however, and not on the instruction of the teachers. Pencil and pen cases were artistically decorated with the owner's favourite band, drawn in pen when lessons became too boring. Many kids had a 1980s chunky pen which had about seven refills in its casing and when one was depressed it was able to write in various colours.

Any other books issued such as reading books or books on one of the subjects taken, such as maths, chemistry or physics, were also expected to be covered. Some books were quite heavy and, especially in secondary school, had to be carried home then brought in whenever they were needed. Gradually more and more schools began providing lockers.

School uniforms were worn at many schools and these usually consisted of dark trousers, white shirt, school tie, jumper and blazer for boys and a similar uniform with a skirt for girls. Long socks were worn by both and the phrase 'pull your socks up' was often heard from teachers. Other schools abandoned the school uniform altogether, leading to school photos featuring a range of colourful 1980s fashions.

Some older boys would be made prefects and their duties would be to look after (or tell off) younger children, stop them talking in assembly and stop them running in the corridor. Some schools had a book in which the children's misdemeanours would be recorded and then read out in assembly by the head teacher. This could lead to lines, detention or, sometimes, the cane. The cane was often given for the silliest offences.

In the morning, there would be a break when all the children would run out into the playground to play games like 'it' (or 'tag') or, for girls, hopscotch or skipping. If it was raining, the class would stay indoors and maybe read comics such as *Look and Learn*.

Many classes had a tuck shop which was usually run by the well-behaved kids (the ones who could be trusted with the money). Snacks that they sold included chocolate and sweets (including penny chews), Smith's crisps (including Snaps Tomato flavour for 10p a bag), KP peanuts and Rich Tea biscuits. Also available were cans of sweet fizzy drinks including Orangeade and Coca-Cola. Often the money raised went towards the school's funds.

School computers were few and far between but most schools had a BBC Microcomputer, helpful for some school work, which also allowed pupils to play a game called *Granny's Garden* which featured a wicked witch complete with a spooky soundtrack. Unlike today's machines, computers in the 1980s seemed to take forever to load up a game, or anything else, and an endless series of funny noises were heard while it carried out the process. It was all worth the wait though to play the unresponsive low-graphic game which was as exciting as most school computers got at the time.

In longer dinner breaks, children would play football and also games such as British Bulldog, He-Man and Skeletor or re-enact the Second World War. Popular playground games included Hide and Seek, It (or tag), What's the time, Mr Wolf? and Ring a Ring o' Roses.

One of the most exciting games to play was British Bulldog. The game was extremely popular and consisted of two teams who stood on either sides of the playground. Kids would have to run from one end to the other and the boys in the middle had to try and catch them. It could get quite aggressive at times but no one came to much harm. The winner was the last person remaining uncaught.

Occasionally, a fight would break out and everyone would gather around to cheer one side against the other. After a while, a dinner lady or teacher would eventually break up the fight.

Hide and Seek involved one person covering their eyes and counting while their friends ran away and hid, waiting for the seeker to come and find him.

Choosing someone to be 'tag' or 'it' involved picking someone by chanting:

Eeny, meeny, miny, moe,
Catch a tiger by the toe.
If he hollers, let him go,
Eeny, meeny, miny, moe,

and slowly counting along the group. The poem also featured various other words instead of 'tiger'.

Another way of picking someone was by using the chant, 'One potato, two potato, three potato four, five potato, six potato, seven potato, more.'

Children playing 'Ring a Ring o' Roses' would gather in a circle and chant,

'Ring a ring of roses.
A pocketful of posies,
Atishoo, Atishoo,
We all fall down!'

The game has been played around the world for hundreds of years and many people link it to the plague, although many others dispute this and say the symptoms such as sneezing and a red circular rash (the ring of roses) are not those of the bubonic plague.

What's the time, Mr Wolf? involved one player taking the part of Mr Wolf, who would stand opposite the other players, facing away from them. The players would then chant 'What's the time, Mr Wolf?' and Mr Wolf would reply with a time. If it was '3 o'clock', the players would take three steps closer. In response to the chant, Mr Wolf could also answer, 'Dinner Time' which would then allow him to try and catch one of the players so they, in turn, became the new 'Mr Wolf'.

Girls would have a long skipping rope and would chant as other girls skipped in and out of it. Hopscotch would also be played with a grid marked out on the floor in chalk.

There were many other playground games some more popular in certain parts of the country than others.

Marbles was a game for the summer months and conkers was played in the autumn. Every boy had a collection of conkers and finding a horse chestnut tree was like finding the Holy Grail. Each conker would have a string fed through it and children took it in turns to hit the other person's conker until one of the conkers broke. A point was given to the person with the surviving conker. Soaking a conker in vinegar would harden it and give it a better chance of winning. Older conkers were also harder so keeping one for a year gave a boy a better advantage the following year.

All boys played marbles and had their own collection which they had either won or bought from the local sweet shop. Marbles could be bought in small bags. Some were prized more than others depending on their size and colour. Depending where you lived, ordinary sized marbles were sometimes called 'alleys' and larger ones were called 'stumpers.' Large ball bearings were much sought after and were worth more when playing. To play, a shallow hole would be dug in the mud and players would compete against opponents until one had lost all his marbles. At the end of the term, the boy with the most marbles would often shout 'scrambles' and throw them one by one for other boys to run after and collect.

Many children collected stickers which were often swapped in the playground. Panini stickers were mostly football stickers, of footballers with dodgy haircuts, which were hugely popular, but there were also stickers from popular television series such as *Star Trek, ThunderCats, ALF* and *Masters of the Universe* as well as from movies including *Flash Gordon, Ghostbusters, Batman, Return of the Jedi* and *The Empire Strikes Back.* Topps released their own sticker sets which included stickers from *E.T. The Extra-Terrestrial* as well as *Garbage Pail Kids.* There were also *Smash Hits* stickers as well as ones featuring dinosaurs and Barbie. All were stuck in special albums.

Bubble-gum cards were also traded in the playground. These included sets from *The A-Team, Dune, Superman II, Batman, ET* and *Terminator 2* as well as cards of Michael Jackson and Duran Duran.

School dinners were still an option in the 1980s but many kids now brought their own packed lunches, which included items such as sandwiches, Smiths crisps, Wagon Wheels, 54321 bars and drinks such as Capri-Sun or Um-Bongo. Plastic lunch boxes carried all you needed to get you through the day and these included pictures of popular crazes of the moment including *My Little Pony, Ghostbusters, Batman, Transformers, Masters of the Universe* and *MASK.*

At Christmas time, a special Christmas meal would be laid on. Some schools for younger children had their own class parties complete with jelly and blancmange.

School trips were occasionally organised and usually involved a subject taught in class. Many trips were to historical locations such as National Trust properties or historical areas near to the school.

Before everyone broke up for the summer holidays, which caused much excitement, the school would organise its annual Sports Day. All children were expected to take part and their parents would come to watch. Events included running, baton racing, high jump, long jump and swimming.

Each end of term brought a school report which was handed to a pupil to give to his or her parents. The envelope came sealed but many children read theirs before they got home. The school report recorded how the child had done over the term. Few were glowing and many carried the comment: 'Could do better!' Once parents had read the report, a slip at the bottom had to be signed by one of the parents to say that they'd seen it.

Schools would also have regular jumble sales and fetes to raise money, usually just before the spring, summer and Christmas holidays. Children would be asked to donate something such as old toys or comics and parents would be asked to donate tins of food and other items. Entry tickets were issued which were sold, often by the pupils, to friends and relatives. Sometimes there was a prize for the pupil who sold the most. Jumble collections were also arranged and children were encouraged to knock at the doors of strangers to ask for anything suitable. During the harvest festival, parents were asked for tins of food which were later donated to the local church to be distributed among the elderly.

Christmas was a great time in the classroom. Decorations would be made and games played on the last day of term. Some schools even allowed pupils to bring in a toy. Bible stories were read, which all added to the excitement of the occasion. Many children took part in the school nativity play and parents were asked to make costumes and were invited to watch. There were also organised carol services in the area and, if you were in the school choir, you were asked to sing at the local church.

Although teachers were still strict, many weren't as strict as the teachers had been in previous decades. Classes were still well-controlled though and any unruly behaviour wasn't tolerated. Any misbehaving child would find themselves facing the wall, with their hands on their heads or out in the hallway. Some would be sent to the headmaster's office to await the cane.

Homework included, to start off with, spelling, handwriting skills and learning fractions and multiplication tables. Tests, both written and verbal, would be held in the classroom the next day with the teacher firing questions at his pupils much to the embarrassment of many.

The CSE (Certificate of Secondary Education) was introduced in the 1960s and continued until 1987, and provided a qualification for all school leavers. The GSE (General Certificate of Education or O-Level) was only taken by the minority of school children so as a result, many, before the CSE being introduced, left with no qualifications. The CSE was graded from 1 to 5. The highest grades being equivalent to O-Level passes.

Fridays would finish with an end of the week assembly with more prayers and hymns to be sung. An end of term assembly would also be held before school breaks. School holidays were much looked forward to by every child and included three weeks off at Easter, six weeks off for the summer and three weeks off for Christmas.

A school day ended at 4pm when all children rushed out of the classroom to get home as quickly as possible to watch their favourite television programmes and to have their tea and, if it was summer, to quickly get out again to meet their friends and play football or build dens. At the time, most couldn't wait to leave school but, today, many remember it as one of the best times of their lives.

3

Toys and Games

The decade featured lots of well-loved toys and games. Many electronic toys were introduced during the 1980s as well as a variety of clever and simpler toys. Some toys such as Action Man, Meccano, Sindy and Lego had been around for decades but other toys and games are specifically thought of as 1980s innovations such as the Rubik's Cube, Simon, Atari and Cabbage Patch Kids.

Below are just some of the favourite toys and games of the decade.

Action Force figures were first marketed in 1982 by Palitoy. They were introduced because of the fall in popularity of their previously bestselling toy, Action Man. Also, smaller action figures, such as those released in connection with the Star Wars franchise, were selling well and Action Force was issued in competition to these. The figures included historical war soldiers such as Commandos, Desert Rats and Stormtroopers as well as Marines, frogmen, parachutists, pilots, Arctic teams and naval assault. There were also various vehicles and other items issued which included Jeeps, a snowmobile, an Action Force base and a deep sea diver platform. In

A Palitoy Action Man, one of the best-loved toys for boys in the 1960s and 1980s.

1983, the characters appeared in the comic *Battle* (later called *Battle Action Force*) which continued until 1986 with the closure of Palitoy. However, in 1987, Marvel released an *Action Force* comic, which continued until 1988.

Action Man was launched in 1966. Palitoy had the licence to copy the incredibly popular GI Joe doll, which was hugely successful in America. The company, which was based in Coalville in Leicestershire, produced the action figure to be sold in Great Britain and Australia. The doll was much sought after by boys and came with a huge range of accessories. The first figures available featured a soldier, sailor and pilot. They came with painted-on hair in either blonde, auburn, brown or black. In the early years, the toys competed with the all-British Tommy Gun, which was manufactured by Pedigree Toys who also produced the Sindy doll. The Tommy Gun toy was of a higher quality than Action Man but by 1968, it could no longer compete and disappeared in the same year. Outfits for Action Man included those of soldiers, pilots, astronauts, footballers and adventurers. They also came with rafts, tanks and motorbikes. Boys everywhere in the 1960s took their Action Man out to play with them, dropping him from high windows on home-made parachutes or playing mock battles with their friends in their gardens. The toy was extremely popular and lasted into the 1980s by which time it had moveable eagle eyes, gripping hands and flocked hair. A talking version was also available. Television adverts at Christmas showed Action Man having great adventures incorporating the many extras that were available. This guaranteed that every boy would want an Action Man and everything that went with him on 25 December. The toy was relaunched by Hasbro in 1993, restyled and with new facial features, but it was never quite the same.

Action Transfers first appeared in the 1960s and continued well into the 1980s. The rub-down transfers included people, animals, vehicles, weapons, explosions as well as popular characters from cartoons, television and movies. During the 1980s, these included transfers from *Return of the Jedi* as

The Atari Video Computer System became hugely successful in 1980 when the arcade game Space Invaders was released for the machine.

well as *Battlestar Galactica. Superman II* transfers were issued with packets of Shreddies in the early 1980s and *ET* transfers were given away free with the cereal in 1982. Action Transfers were originally made by Letraset, the makers of instant lettering transfer sheets. The first Action Transfers were produced in 1969.

The Atari video computer system (the Atari 2600) originally came out in 1977 and it popularised the use of hardware incorporating microprocessors with games contained on ROM cartridges. When *Space Invaders* was released for the Atari in 1980, the machines became hugely successful. The original Atari VCS came with a brown wood veneer, two joystick controllers and the games *Combat* and *Pac-Man*. In the 1980s, Activision started producing games for the console including the ever-popular *Pitfall!*, one of their best-remembered games. With the success of the Atari, both Mattel Electronics and Coleco released their own games consoles in 1982. Coleco's console featured all-time favourites *Donkey Kong* and *Sonic the Hedgehog*. In the same year, Atari invested in two new games, *Pac-Man* and *E.T. the Extra-Terrestrial*, which proved unsuccessful for the company and partly led to the video game crash of 1983. Poor third-party games led to the console's downfall. However, by 1983, over 10 million consoles had been sold making it, at the time, the most popular home games console. Other games produced for the Atari included *Air/Sea Battle, Asteroids, Missile Command* and the ever-popular *Space Invaders*. Activision also made a range of compatible games and these included *Tennis, Freeway* and *Stampede*.

A-Team playsets proved highly popular with children who enjoyed the action-packed television show. The toys included figures of H. M. 'Howlin' Mad' Murdock, B. A. Baracus, John 'Hannibal' Smith and Templeton 'Faceman' Peck, as well as A-Team vehicles. An *A-Team* playhouse as well as backpacks and lunchboxes were also produced.

Baby Alive was a doll which could be fed, given drinks and ultimately wet itself. It was first manufactured by Kenner in 1973 and continued to be popular for the next few decades. The doll came with food packets, the contents needed to be mixed with water before it was fed to the doll, which also came with a bottle, nappies and feeding spoon. The doll was powered by a battery and later models could talk.

Barbershop was a toy made by Palitoy which incorporated Play-Doh. By cranking a handle, hair grew on the included Fuzz family and this could be shaped, styled and clipped.

Barbie dolls were first manufactured by Mattel in America in 1959 and proved hugely popular with girls in the following decades. To date, over a billion dolls have been sold worldwide making the doll one of the most popular toys of all time. The doll came with a range of accessories including clothes, a spa, a pool, a pink scooter and a piano. In the 1980s, a pony, a star traveller home, a dog and a townhouse were also available as well as a Barbie make-up set. In 1987, Barbie began to appear in animated films, television specials, video games and music and still remains hugely popular today.

Big Badge Factory allowed children to make their own 2-inch badges using a range of eighteen designs and pictures included with the toy. By using the big badge 'whomper', the badge could be pressed together and then worn.

Binatone's black-and-white TV game was very basic but still very popular. Games included Tennis, Squash, Squash Practice, Football, Target Practice and Shooting. It came with two hand controllers as well as a plastic pistol.

Buckaroo was first produced by Ideal in 1970 but its popularity has continued ever since. Players take turns to place items on a plastic mule without causing the spring-loaded mule to buck up and throw everything off. The loser is the first person who causes the mule to throw off all the accumulated items which include a saddle, a bedroll, a canteen, a cowboy hat, a crate, a frying pan, a guitar, a holster, a lamp, a rope, a shovel and a rope.

Buck Rogers playsets included a range of action figures as well as a command centre, spaceships, robots, a walking Twiki and a full-size Buck Rogers helmet. Corgi also produced various die-cast versions of the Starfighter.

Cabbage Patch Kids became the must-have toy of 1982 and featured on many children's Christmas lists. A shortage of the toy led to fights at some toy shops when they were released in the US. The dolls were produced by Coleco between 1982 and 1988 and by Hasbro later in the 1980s. The Jesmar Toy Company produced the dolls for the European market. The dolls consisted of a large, round vinyl head with a soft fabric body. All the dolls were slightly different from each other and came with their own individual birth certificate.

Care Bears were first manufactured as a soft toy by Kenner in 1983. Before that, the Care Bear image had been used on greetings cards in the US. They came in a variety of colours and proved hugely collectable. To date, there are 218 different bears available. They appeared in two TV specials during the decade including *The Care Bears in the Land Without Feelings* (1983) and *The Care Bears Battle the Freeze Machine* (1984). There was also a *Care Bear* television series between 1985 and 1988, as well as three feature films which included *The Care Bears Movie* (1985), *Care Bears Movie II: A New Generation* (1986) and *The Care Bears Adventure in Wonderland* (1987).

CBS ColecoVision games console came with a variety of games on a cartridge as well as an accelerator and steering wheel. Games included *Donkey Kong* (which came with the system), *Smurf, Zaxxon* and *Turbo*.

Chemistry sets were still as popular in the 1980s as they had ever been although, surprisingly, earlier sets in previous decades had contained substances such as cyanide, uranium and even sulphuric acid. The Chemistry 4 set sold during the 1980s included equipment for 104 experiments. Microscopes could be bought separately.

Colour with Yarn, from Fisher Price, allowed its user to create pictures of birds and flowers using a yarn pencil and various pieces of coloured yarn. It came complete with a plastic pick, a peel-and-stick picture and a frame to put the finished artwork into.

Corgi Toys first appeared in the UK in 1956. Some of their best-selling cars appeared in the 1960s including James Bond's Aston Martin DB5, the Batmobile, the Thrush Buster from the *Man from Uncle* and the classic car from *Chitty Chitty Bang Bang*. James Bond's DB5 remains the best-selling toy car ever. All cars and vehicles from Corgi sold worldwide. Corgi Toys were produced by Mettoy who had been trading since 1933 and had previously mainly produced tinplate. Corgi produced a range of vehicles including popular cars, lorries, vans and tractors, etc. Their most popular vehicles were ones relating to film and television. Corgi's catalogue from 1980 showed some of the many vehicles they had for sale at the time including the pink van from *Charlie's Angels*, Starsky's red-and-white striped Gran Torino complete with *Starsky and Hutch* figures, Kojak's Buick Regal with Kojak and Crocker figures, *The Professionals'* Ford Capri complete with Bodie, Doyle and Cowley figures, The Saint's white Jaguar XJS and Dan Tanna's red Ford Thunderbird from the show *Vega$*. Also featured in the catalogue were vehicles connected to James Bond, Buck Rogers, Spiderman, Superman and Batman as well as a range of non-TV and movie related vehicles such as fire engines, police cars, ambulances, buses, lorries (advertising Weetabix, Coca-Cola and other brands) and racing cars as well as a range of everyday cars and vehicles.

Cyclograph was produced by Parker and allowed its user to produce various designs and patterns using a collection of plastic wheels and circles. It was very similar to *Spirograph*.

Domino Rally from Action GT allowed players to set up elaborate patterns with the 400 dominos included and watch them tumble as the final domino is pushed.

Dukes of Hazard playsets included a range of items including action figures of the main cast with various vehicles including the General Lee, a police car. There was also a Barnbuster set which featured General Lee stunt vehicles, a toy barn and barrels for the car to crash into. Speed Jumper was another *Dukes of Hazzard* stunt toy featuring various cars and ramps.

Duplo Bricks were larger Lego-type bricks for smaller children. Sets available in the 1980s included various building sets to make houses, garages, cars and trains.

Etch-a-Sketch was introduced in 1960 and allowed children to draw on a screen by turning two dials at the bottom of the screen to create pictures. By turning the screen upside down and shaking it, the picture would disappear and then another drawing could be created. The product was hugely successful and sold worldwide. Its popularity continued over the decades and is still sold today.

Evel Knievel and related toys had first become popular in the 1970s but their appeal continued well into the 1980s. Toys available included an Evel Knievel 7-inch figure complete with a gyro-powered motorbike, which could perform wheelies and mid-air somersaults.

Fun Around Faces allowed players to make hundreds of comical faces by placing human and animal faces into the console and watching the faces change as a handle was cranked.

Ghostbusters merchandise included action figures of the main characters from the hit movie as well as vehicles (the Ecto-1), a fire station (the home of the ghostbusters), a Ghost Zapper which projected ghost images and emitted an electronic sound when a trigger was pulled to zap the ghosts. Also available were backpacks and a child-size proton pack, complete with a Nutrona Blaster and a ghost seeking meter.

Girl's World featured a scale model of a woman's head, complete with long hair, and came with various accessories including curlers, a hairbrush and lipstick and eye shadow in several colours allowing its owner to practice make-up skills on the head, after which the colours were easily wiped off so they could be reapplied.

The *Grandstand Kevin Keegan 4800 Colour Video Game* connected straight to the television socket of the TV and allowed users to play six different games – soccer, tennis, practice, squash, rifle 1 and rifle 2 – and featured realistic sounds. It came with two hand controls and a plastic rifle.

Gummi Bears were plush colourful soft toys based on the characters from *Disney's Adventures of the Gummi Bears*. The toys were made by Fisher-Price and included Tummi Gummi, Cubbi Gummi, Grammi Gummi, Zummi Gummi and Sunni Gummi.

Horror Make-Up was manufactured by D. Decker Ltd and allowed its users to apply horrific *Frankenstein*-like make-up using the exclusive ingredient 'Flex Flesh'. The box carried images of a boy complete with hideous injuries and stated, 'Transform yourself into hundreds of horrible creatures'.

Impossiball was produced by MB Games and was similar to the Rubik's Cube. Unlike the cube, it was ball-shaped and had twenty movable parts of different colours which had to be arranged in the right order. The original Impossiball was designed by William O. Gustafson in 1981 and was sold worldwide from 1984 onwards.

Intellivision from Mattel Electronics was a game console that gave a 3D effect. It came complete with a soccer game cartridge. Other games available included *Auto Racing*, *Armour Battle*, *Skiing*, *Space Battle*, *Star Strike* and *Triple Action*.

Jaws was manufactured by Tyco in the 1970s and 1980s. It was similar to Buckaroo and featured a shark with an open mouth on which the players had to place various objects before its jaws tightly snapped shut. The plastic blue-coloured objects included a bone, a gun, a skull, a bag, a glove, a broken wheel, an anchor as well as other seafaring-connected items. The box featured a terrifying picture of the shark from the successful movie *Jaws*.

Ker-Plunk was the hit of the year when it first came out in 1967. It was produced by MB Games and featured a tube with intercrossing sticks with marbles above them. The aim of the game was to pull out the sticks without the marbles falling. Any marbles that fall were kept by the player who pulled out the stick. Once the last marble had fallen, players counted how many marbles they had and the winner was the player with the least.

Lego had been a hugely successful toy for children for many years. The interlocking bricks were first made in 1949 and, since then, over 560 billion Lego parts have been produced. Lego allowed children to build whatever they wanted including cars, trains, castles, etc. Sets were released featuring a variety of themes including Vikings, dinosaurs, the Wild West, undersea exploration, pirates, space and many more. A Lego set fuelled a child's imagination. Over the years, the sets have become more advanced and include various characters as well as motors, switches and cameras. Lego sets in the 1980s included helicopters, motorised cars, space cruisers, satellite launch centres, fire stations and post offices, beach buggies as well as basic sets.

Magna Doodle was very similar to Etch-a-Sketch and featured a magnetic screen which allowed its user to make various drawings using a special pen. Games such as noughts and crosses as well as messages could also be written on the toy. It later appeared regularly on the hit American television show *Friends* in Joey and Chandler's apartment and featured various comical notes. The toy was manufactured by Tyco.

MASK, launched in 1985, featured a selection of action figures, an animated television series, videogames and comics. The toys were produced by Kenner and, as well as moveable figures, there were vehicles including a stunt jet, a race car, a transporter and several motorbikes. A backpack was also available.

Masters of the Universe merchandise included figures of He-Man, Skeletor, Orko and Kobra Khan as well as models of Snake Mountain (Skeletor's stronghold), Castle Grayskull, Panthor (Skeletor's evil battle cat), a Dragon Walker, a Night Stalker and a Battle Bone's collector's case. Other figures were also available as well as a storybook, complete with audio cassette and a VHS video of the cartoon.

Matchbox cars were first introduced in 1953. They were so named because they came in boxes similar to those that contained matches. Matchbox was a brand produced by Lesney which was founded by Jack Odell, Leslie Smith and Rodney Smith. A model of Queen Elizabeth II's Coronation Coach became Lesney's first toy to sell more than a million. The first Matchbox product was designed by Jack Odell. Odell's daughter attended a school which would only allow children to bring in toys small enough to fit in a matchbox. Odell scaled down Lesney's red and green road roller and the toy became the prototype for Matchbox's first 1–75 vehicle. Soon, it was joined by a dumper truck and cement mixer and the three toys became the beginning of the Matchbox range. Other models were soon added to the range including cars such as the Ford Zodiac, MG Midget and Vauxhall Cresta. At first, all models were based on British cars but as the company grew, European and American cars were also included. Their reasonable prices meant that most boys in the 1950s, 1960s and the 1970s had a collection of Matchbox cars. In June 1982, Lesney became bankrupt but the Matchbox brand continued after being sold to Universal Toys and David Yeh. Jack Odell continued to market Matchbox Yesteryear-type vehicles under the brand name Lledo. Matchbox became Matchbox International Ltd and by 1985, the toys were being manufactured in China.

Meccano was invented by Frank Hornby in 1901 and was originally called 'Mechanics Made Easy'. The toy consisted of small metal strips with holes, plates, pulleys, gears, and nuts and bolts. The toy was seen as educational as well as fun but very soon demand started to exceed supply so Hornby set up a factory in Liverpool to cope with the additional manufacturing needs. The kits became more and more popular and were soon on sale around the world. By 1907, Hornby had registered the name Meccano and seven years later, an additional factory was opened in Liverpool to keep up with demand. By the 1950s, Meccano was a well-loved toy but, because of the Second World War, production was interrupted when the factory at Binns Road in Liverpool was used to help the war effort. The Korean War in 1950 also disrupted production because of metal shortages but, by the mid-1950s, production was back to normal. Children loved playing with Meccano in the 1960s, 1970s and 1980s and what they constructed was limited only to their imagination. Cranes were a popular item to construct, as were cars, boats and aeroplanes.

Mini Arcade Games became incredibly popular during the 1980s and some of the most fondly remembered included *Astro Wars* (a space game with five lanes of action), *Atomic, Caveman, Crazy Climber, Crazy Kong* (based on the ever-popular *Donkey Kong* arcade game), *Invader from Space, Kevin Keegan's Big Game, Master Challenge, Missile Invader, Munchman, PacMan2, Scramble* (a 5-phase action space game), *Space Flight* and *Turtles.* Many were produced by Grandstand, Parker, Ideal and Entex.

Mr Frosty, produced by Playskool, allowed its user to make mouth-watering ice crunchies and drinks using a snowman-shaped plastic dispenser.

Mr Men Slide Projector, made by House Martin, featured all the favourite characters from the books on slides which could be shone on a bedroom wall using the red plastic projector.

My Little Pony toys were produced by Hasbro and first appeared in 1981. The little ponies came in a range of colours and included Twilight Sparkle, Fluttershy, Rainbow Dash, Pinkie Pie, Applejack, Sunset Shimmer and various others. As well as the toys, there was also various accessories produced including backpacks, umbrellas and shoes. A cartoon series was also produced as well as a weekly comic. During the 1980s, over 150 million My Little Pony toys were sold.

Paul Daniels Magic Set included 100 different magic tricks designed for children of eight years and older. The popular television show helped promote the set and it proved very popular with budding magicians.

Perfection involved putting the correct shapes into holes in the time allowed. As with Mr Pop, if the task wasn't competed in the allotted time, all the pieces would shoot out and the contestant would have to start again.

Philips G7000 Home Video Computer Game System came with a keyboard and two hand controllers. Included in the package was a game called *Satellite Attack* which, like all other games for the machine, came on a cartridge. Other games that could be bought for the system included *Space Monster, Munchkin, Music, Golf, Cosmic Conflict* and *Monkeyshines.*

Racing tracks, similar to Scalextric, had been well loved for decades. In the 1980s, Ideal produced a *Dukes of Hazzard* version complete with the General Lee and the Hazzard County Sheriff's car. Meanwhile, Matchbox produced the Matchbox PT6000 Race and Chase which included 14 feet of track and two cars with working headlights. Similar racing tracks included Aurora's Police Stop, Mattel's Hot Wheels and a Trans-Am's Firebird Challenge Race Set. All were powered by transformers and came with hand-held controllers.

Rambo merchandise in the 1980s included a range of action figures and vehicles as well as plastic knives, electronic UZI guns, machine guns and high-powered water pistols. Although the movie was for adults, the character proved very popular with boys and toys related to the character were much sought after.

Roller skates were liked by both boys and girls although girls were more often seen skating along the pavements outside people's houses. The metal roller skates were adjustable in the middle so that they could fit any shoe size.

Rom, The Space Knight, from Parker Brothers, was a silver-coloured battery-operated electronic robot toy which featured flashing red eyes, electronic noises and accessories such as an energy analyser and a neutraliser, which had flashing lights and made a zapping noise. The hugely popular character was also featured in a Marvel comic. In the UK, ROM was licensed to Palitoy as part of the Space Adventurer line connected with Action Man.

Rubik's Cube was one of the most original and fondly remembered toys of the 1980s. It was invented by Ernő Rubik in 1974. Rubik was an Hungarian sculptor and professor of architecture at the time. His idea was licensed to Ideal Toys in 1980 and won the Best Puzzle German Game of the Year special award in 1980. The original Rubik's Cube had six faces covered by nine stickers. They featured the colours red, blue, orange, green, white and yellow. Turning the cube produced a mixture of colours and the ultimate aim of the toy was to get every side the same colour by twisting and turning the cube. They proved hugely popular and to date over 350 million cubes have been sold worldwide.

A Saturn giant walking robot, complete with firing missiles, popular during the 1980s.

The Rubik's Cube, an iconic toy of the 1980s, was invented by Ernő Rubik in 1974. Licensed to Ideal Toys, it won the Best Puzzle German Game of the Year award in 1980.

Scalextric was sought after by every boy. Television and adverts in comics and magazines made the racing track and cars look like something from Le Mans. With dual controls, boys were able to race their cars around the track at speed while trying their best to beat their opponent. The race usually ended with one car, or both, spinning off the track. Scalextric sets were also popular at amusement arcades and holiday camps but there was a great thrill having one of your own and being able to race a range of sleek sports cars at home.

Simon was a brightly coloured electronic game which created a series of noises and lights which the user had to memorise and copy the order in which they appeared in.

Sindy first appeared in 1963 in the UK and was manufactured by Pedigree Dolls and Toys. The fashion doll came with a range of clothes and accessories and proved hugely popular with girls. In the 1960s and 1970s, it became one of the best-selling toys in the UK. In 1978, the toy was introduced into the US market but was withdrawn in 1980 when its then owners, Marx, went into receivership. During the 1980s, millions of pounds were spent promoting the toy with new fashion lines, one gown was designed by the Emanuels (Elizabeth Florence Emanuel and her then husband David, who were famous for designing Princess Diana's wedding dress) shortly after Mattel had released evening gowns for Barbie designed by Oscar de la Renta. A *Sindy* magazine was launched, which competed with the American *Barbie* magazine, and in 1987, the doll was redesigned by Hasbro followed by £1.5 million advertising campaign. In its first 40-year period, almost 100 million Sindy dolls were sold in Britain alone.

Slinky was a huge coiled spring that became very popular after a television advertising campaign. It suddenly became the toy to have. Its main feature was that it could walk downstairs on its own which, at the time, seemed amazing. However, although very popular, it was soon discovered that it did little else. Most Slinkys eventually ended up twisted and unusable. A smaller version called Springy was later released but was never as popular as the original.

Soft toys were very popular and many featured characters from well-loved television shows including *Rupert, Danger Mouse, Dusty Bin, Roland Rat* and *Orville the Duck*.

Space Hoppers seemed fantastic things that you could sit on and bounce all around your front room and garden. Television adverts made them look incredible and able to bounce great heights. In reality, it was hard to get them to bounce a few inches off the ground but they were still great fun. Some kids would even have races on them, which would only end when a hopper caught something sharp and ended up punctured.

Spirograph was first sold in 1965 by Denys Fisher and it allowed you to make weird and wonderful colourful patterns on a sheet of paper. It consisted of plastic rings with gear teeth. Holes in the rings allowed pens to be used to make a variety of geometric shapes with fantastic results. It sounds very basic nowadays but kept children amused for hours.

Star Wars merchandise included plastic figures of all the main characters, produced by Palitoy, as well as a Millennium Falcon, a Snowspeeder, an X-Wing Fighter, a Tie-Interceptor, a Scout Walker, a Rebel Transport space ship and an AT-AT (All Terrain Armored Transport). More toys were released as the decade moved on including an Ewok village and Rancor Monster.

Stock Car Smash Up by Denys Fisher, featured two racing cars that came with plastic straps which fed through the cars and, when pulled, powered the vehicle which was then aimed at the opponent's car. Various parts of the car were designed to fall off when they hit. An advertising campaign resulted in the cars becoming very popular and many other rip-cord cars were later introduced.

Stretch Armstrong was originally manufactured between 1976 and 1980 but has since been reissued and still proves hugely popular today. The 15-inch blonde wrestler doll was made from latex rubber filled with gelled corn syrup, which allowed it to be greatly stretched before returning to its original shape. Pulling the characters arms to great lengths has proved hugely popular with young boys over the years.

Stretch Hulk proved very popular in the 1980s during a period when Stretch Armstrong wasn't available. It worked in an identical way to the earlier Stretch Armstrong doll. Other similar stretch toys included Elastic Batman, Stretch Monster, Elastic Donald Duck, Fetch Armstrong (Stretch Armstrong's dog) and Super Morphman.

Subbuteo, the table-top football game, was originally sold in the late 1940s but came immensely popular in the 1960s. Competitors flicked their players to score goals. Teams were available in a variety of football strips and included many accessories such as linesmen, stands and crowds, policemen and eventually even a streaker. A 1988 TV mini-series, *Playing for Real*, told the story of a fictional Subbuteo team called Real Falkirk and starred Patricia Kerrigan as its player-manager, which shows how popular the game remained into the late 1980s.

ThunderCats merchandise included plastic action figures of the main characters from the show including Lion-O, with weapons; Battle-Matic arm and secret power ring, and a figure of evil Mumm-Ra, complete with swords and power ring. There were also *ThunderCats* satchels available as well as a Sword of Omens, a child-size replica of Lion-O's powerful sword.

Tin Can Alley was a target game where cans were shot off a wall using a full-size brown plastic electric rifle. The television advert featured well-known Hollywood Western actor Chuck Connors.

Transformers merchandise included various vehicles which converted into highly sophisticated robots. They were first introduced in 1984 and originated from Japan before being manufactured in the US and UK by Hasbro. The toys featured in a highly successful cartoon series as well as in several comic books and later spawned a successful series of movies. The toys proved hugely popular.

Victoria Plum featured in a successful series of books written by television journalist Angela Rippon. Soon after, Telitoy and Dakin produced a range of dolls. Other popular Victoria Plum items, at the time, included bedspreads, pencil sets, lunch boxes, annuals and jigsaws.

Viewmaster, made by GAF, was a plastic viewer that allowed its owner to view, in 3-D, round cardboard wheels that featured transparencies featuring a range of subjects. Many were educational and featured places at home and around the world. There were also others that featured popular television shows such as *Top Cat, Star Trek* and William Tell. The Show Beam Projector was produced by Viewmaster in 1980. It featured a portable hand-held projector which used small film cartridges to project images. Each cartridge contained 30 full-colour 2D images. In 1981, GAF sold the rights to the Viewmaster but it continued to be produced under several different brand names including Tyco and Mattel. In 1984, a talking Viewmaster was produced but didn't catch on and soon disappeared. Popular Viewmaster reels in the 1980s included *Ulysses 31, The Dark Crystal, Doctor Who* featuring Tom Baker, *Terrahawks, The Dukes of Hazzard, Transformers, The A-Team, Mork and Mindy* and *Metal Mickey*.

Weebles first appeared in 1971 but continued to sell well throughout the 1980s. The small plastic egg-shaped characters could be pushed but always returned to their original position, leading to the popular advert catchphrase, 'Weebles wobble, but they don't fall down'. There were many accessories which accompanied the Weebles including a haunted house, a tree house, a camper, a Tarzan set-up, a marina, a circus and a fun house.

Wisecracking *A.L.F.* was manufactured by Coleco and was based on the popular television series. The 17-inch plush cuddly toys could speak several phrases including 'I'm a people alien' and 'No problem'.

Wuzzles were plush colourful soft toys which came complete with a twenty-four-page story book. The 12-inch high toys included the characters Hoppopotamus, Bumble Lion, Butter Bear and Eleroo.

Board games

There were endless board games produced in the 1980s and all were extremely popular. New ones came out every year, just in time for Christmas. Some are fondly remembered although others are probably long forgotten. Board games such as Cluedo, Monopoly and Mouse Trap are still played today but not in the great numbers that they once were. Here are a few of the most popular board games during the 1980s.

Alligator involved players feeding food to hungry alligators while taking junk from their mouths. The first to get rid of all their food was the winner however, the alligator was liable to snap at any moment.

Balderdash was first released in 1984 and involved bluffing and trivia. The game was based on a classic parlour game called Fictionary.

Battleship, from MB Games, featured plastic battleships which players placed in certain positions on their own individual board. Their opponents had to guess the ships' positions to sink them and ultimately win the game. For decades, children had played the same game using their fathers' pools coupons but the board game made it more interesting by using plastic battleships and counters. An electronic version was released in 1982.

Beetle originated as a British party game using pen and paper but a plastic version was later produced by Milton Bradley. The game involves rolling a dice and the winner is the first person to construct a complete beetle. The numbers on the dice relate to various parts of the beetle. The game has been around in various forms since 1927, was popular in the 1980s and in some areas is still used today as a church fundraiser.

Beware the Spider had players using a special fork to remove creatures trapped in a web without touching it. Any contact with the web made the spider leap out.

Blockbusters was based on the television game show hosted by Bob Holness. The game, manufactured by Waddington's, included a honeycombed plastic grid across which players had to make an unbroken connection between their two outside colours. White played vertically and blue played horizontally. By answering questions, on supplied cards, the players' letters were placed in the grid.

Bob's Full House was based on the popular game show hosted by Bob Monkhouse between 1984 and 1990. Players had to answer questions and mark off numbers on enclosed bingo cards. The winner was the first to complete their card.

Chess, still as popular today, was seen as a game of skill and patience moving pieces one by one until an opponent was beaten by being trapped in the checkmate position. There were undoubtedly many games of chess played in the 1980s although younger children might have considered it too highbrow and boring and, for them, draughts was far more fun.

Cluedo was produced by Waddington's and was first available in 1949. The game featured six characters including Miss Scarlett, Colonel Mustard, Mrs White, Reverend Green, Mrs Peacock and Professor Plum. The aim of the game was to get around the board, which included several different rooms of a mansion, collecting clues while trying to deduce who murdered the game's victim, Dr Black. The idea for the game was devised by Anthony E Pratt who was a solicitor's clerk from Birmingham. It is also still played today.

Connect Four, manufactured by MB games, was a game for two players whose aim, using red and yellow counters, was to complete a line of four pieces either vertically, horizontally or diagonally.

Contraption involved players opening and shutting gates to let their marbles in and out of a cog-based apparatus. The first person to trap their marbles in the highest gear won the game.

Crossfire, a goal-shooting game, involved firing ball bearings to knock a puck into an opponent's goal. The game was first manufactured by Milton Bradley in 1971 but continued to be popular throughout the 1980s.

Cup Final was similar to Palitoy's Striker although much inferior. It featured two teams, in red and blue, with each team having three plastic players. Their kicking action was operated by a button at the back of the player. A goalkeeper at each end operated on a lever which allowed it to try and save incoming goals.

Deflection involved players dropping coloured counters into a rack made of sliding strips. As the counters dropped through slots in the rack, the players took it in turns to move the strips back and forth, trying to make their tokens fall into the highest scoring sections of the bottom tray.

Demon Driver from Parker Games allowed its user to use gears, control speed and overtake cars in both lanes against the clock. If there was a crash, a red light would flash and a buzzer would sound and the lap would be over.

Dizzy Dizzy Dinosaur was a game for two to four players. Each player started with five cavemen who are moved individually along the board after a roll of the dice. If a dinosaur face shows up, the player has to wind up the plastic dizzy dinosaur and let him go. Any caveman knocked over by the dinosaur has to return to the beginning. The winner was the first player to get all of his five cavemen to the centre of the board.

Donkey Kong, based on the popular arcade game, involved players dodging barrels and fireballs, thrown by an irate gorilla, as they tried to rescue a fair maiden. The board game wasn't as popular as the electronic versions later released for home gaming systems but still sold well.

Don't Get in a Flap! involved contestants keeping up with a motorised disc dealer. Each player had different shapes on their quarter of the board and had to obtain all the correctly fitting discs before their opponents could do so. The game was similar to the best-selling board game Perfection.

Downfall from MB Games was a game of skill which involved two or more players turning cogs to try to drop their counters in the right order to win. The aim of the game was for one side to get all of their discs to the bottom before the other team succeeded in the task. It was similar to Connect 4 and Deflection.

Dungeons and Dragons, over the years, has become the world's most popular role playing game with over 20 million people having played the game at one time. It was originally invented in the 1970s but gained great popularity during the 1980s. The game involves adventures and campaigns with players using figures including dragons and other creatures, ultimately controlled by a dungeon master. More serious players also wore costumes relating to the characters they were playing.

Family Fortunes was based on the popular television series starring Les Dennis. Players answered questions with answers based on official surveys which led to them winning cash, the object of the game being to win the most money.

Fireball Island featured a plastic tiki icon which was placed in the centre of a raised moulded, 3D board, where it is able to rotate freely. The object of the game was for players to move their explorer pieces up the side of a mountain following paths and travelling through caves with the aim of reaching the top of the mountain to retrieve a giant ruby. Fireball marbles travelled from the volcanic vents on the mountain and from the icon which knocked the players over hindering their way to the top.

Frustration was one of the most popular games of the 1960s when it was first released and is still available today. It featured a pop-o-matic dice roller. Each player got their own coloured pawns and each pawn had to travel around the board to win the game. The winner was the player with all their pawns on the finish lane.

Game of Life required participants to adopt various roles in life and overcome their problems. An elaborate board led contestants through the many twists and pitfalls of life and the winner used his skill and luck to win.

Game of Knowledge was a game for two to ten players and featured various trivia questions on cards included with the game. Each card has two questions, one of which was for players aged ten to fifteen, and a different question for players ages sixteen and over.

Ghost Castle first came out in 1985. Made by MB Games, it was based on the US board game Which Witch?, released in the US in the 1970s. It was also very similar to the game Haunted House which was popular in the UK during the 1970s. The 3-D game featured four rooms separated by cardboard walls which were fixed in place by a central plastic chimney. Players navigated through the house on a roll of the dice.

Go For Broke was a game for two to four players. The roll the dice then move game starts after each player receives one million dollars from the bank. The winner is the first player to spend all of their money and go bankrupt. Players can gamble money at the racetrack, the casino or play the stock market as well as make donations to charity.

Grabbin' Dragons released in 1982 was a game for two to four players which involved players using their individual dragons to collect the most magical ring by pulling the creature's tail. Players hurry to hook rings on to their dragon's tongue, and pull its tail to bend its neck and drop the ring into the ring container. Once all the rings are gone, the winner is the person who has collected the most.

Guess Who? was an intriguing game of memory, deduction and identification for two players whose aim was to guess what their opponent's cards show.

Hangman was made by MB Games and featured Vincent Price on the box lid as well on television adverts. The game was first introduced in 1976 but its popularity continued well into the 1980s. The aim of the game was to 'hang' your opponent before they guessed your hidden word.

Hungry Hippos from Parker games allowed players to grab as many balls as possible with their brightly coloured plastic hippos by pushing down their tails to open their mouths. The winner was the contestant who collected the most balls.

It's a Knock Out was a game for two to four players and was based on the popular television show. Six well-known games from the show were included. Several of the games featured included tiddlywinks, target shooting, blow football and bowling.

I Vant to Bite Your Finger involved sneaking through Dracula's graveyard without waking him up. If he wakes, you have to see if he wants to bite your finger.

Knight Rider was based on the popular television show starring David Hasselhoff. A game for two to four players, contestants had to clear up 'Trouble Spots' and collect the most bonus money to win.

Knock 'em Out was a board game issued in 1980 by MB Games. It featured a hexagonal grid in which stoppers were placed to stop the player's opponent from making a straight line with their counters. It was similar to Connect 4.

Lingo was a word game that allowed players to clip together words to make the longest word stick.

Mastermind had nothing to do with the successful BBC television show. The pocket-sized game for two players involved code breaking and came with a small plastic decoding board, code pegs in six different colours and key pegs in black and white. The aim of the game was for the codebreaker to guess the colour and pattern set by his opponent, the code-maker. The game sold well but is mainly remembered for its box which showed a bearded Bond-villain-type man, with his much younger female sidekick.

Mike Read's Pop Quiz was based on the popular Saturday evening BBC panel show. Players had to form a pop group by rolling a dice and collecting

A boy in a Knight Rider pedal car. The television show, which starred David Hasselhoff, and featured KITT, an artificially intelligent car, was highly popular during the decade.

cards featuring various band members, before making a record and being the first to get to Number One in the charts by luck and answering a series of Pop Quiz questions.

Mr Pop! was a game for one or more players where the contestant had to pick a card with a man's face on it and then recreate the face on a plastic board using various pieces supplied such as glasses, noses and moustaches. However, a time switch meant that if the face wasn't completed quickly enough, the plastic head would pop forward and all the pieces would fly out.

Monopoly was created in 1934, although the idea for it went back much further. It was an incredibly well-liked board game in the 1980s, usually played by four members of the same family or with several friends. The board, counters and houses have become iconic over the years and are instantly recognisable nowadays. The counters included a Scottie dog, a ship, an iron, a book, a top hat, a racing car and a thimble. The idea was to make your way around the board, collecting £200 when you passed 'Go', buying property along the way and hoping to avoid being sent to jail. The winner was the person who ended up with all of the money.

Mouse Trap was probably one of the best and most original of all the board games first released in the 1960s. It featured an elaborate mouse trap which was built up piece by piece by rolling a dice and proceeding around the board. The aim was to capture the opponent's mouse under the trap at the end. It is still being sold today.

The Neighbours Game was first released in 1988 and was based on the popular television show. The object of the game was to write an episode of Neighbours in three scenes as you moved around the board. The winner was the player with the most points at the end.

Operation was originally released in 1965 but was just as popular in the 1980s. It was a game of dexterity where body parts had to be extracted from a plastic body without touching the sides and setting off an alarm and lighting up the patient's nose. The players received cash for successful extractions and the player with the most cash at the end of the game was the winner.

Pac-Man was a board game version of the popular arcade game where players had to gobble up the most marbles to win. Players had to beware of ghosts but could defeat them by eating an energiser pellet. The game board featured holes to hold power pellets and energiser pellets' and came with four Pac Man player pieces, two ghost pieces with marbles to represent power pellets and energizer pellets.

Perfection was first released in the early 1970s and the aim of the game was to use dexterity and shape recognition to be the fastest player to fit all their shapes into the matching holes in a pop-up tray while racing against the clock.

Pictionary was a game inspired by the parlour game Charades. The word guessing game was invented by Robert Angel and was first released in 1985. The game is played by teams with several players all trying to identify certain words picked by their teammates by moving a piece on the game board which is comprised from a series of squares. Each square had a letter or shape denoting the type of sketch to be drawn on it. The aim of the game was to be the first team to get to the last space on the board by guessing the word or phrase drawn by their partner.

Quicksand combined quick thinking with quick reactions in a race against time. In the game, players each controlled one of six jungle explorers racing to discover the location of a hidden temple. Included in the game were explorer cards, quicksand cards and wild cards. By playing the cards strategically, you and your opponents, are able to move the six explorers closer towards the temple avoiding the quicksand on the way.

Ratrace was first released in 1967. Players started with £200, a credit card as well as a business in the Working Class (on the outer ring of the board). The objective of the game is to make your way into the Middle Class and eventually to High Society (in the inner ring of the game). During the game you have to run your own business, pay tax, get an education, etc. The winner is the player who manages to collect together £100,000 and retires.

Rings on Your Fingers was a memory game for younger children. The first to collect five rings won the game.

Risk first appeared on the market in 1959. The aim of the game was the conquest of the world, which was achieved on the roll of a dice allowing players to gain reinforcements, control territories on each continent and attacking players using the combat rule of comparing the highest dice rolled for each side.

Scrabble was very popular in the 1980s and is still played today. A variation of the game had been around since the 1930s. The game began to be sold in the UK in 1955 and was manufactured by J. W. Spears. The game involved spelling out words on a grid using tiles with individual letters on them. Each tile carried its own point score and the winner was the person who had the highest score at the end of the game.

Snakes and Ladders involved rolling a dice to proceed to the top of the board. If a player landed on a ladder, he could go up it, but if he landed on a snake's head, he had to go down to the row where its tail ended. The game originally came from India where it was known as Moksha Patam but later made its way to England. Milton Bradley produced a similar game in America called Chutes and Ladders.

Squares was a board game produced by Waddington's. The aim of the game was to claim as many squares as possible. It was described as 'a mind swivelling game of strategy, action and fun'.

Stay Alive from MB Games included plastic slides which gave each player the chance to sink their opponent's marbles while at the same time trying to keep their own marbles safe and therefore be the survivor.

Test Match was a cricket game made by Peter Pan. It featured 'real over arm bowling, genuine battling action and a full team of fielders'.

Tiddlywinks featured small coloured plastic discs which had to be flipped using another disc into a pot. The game was considered a child's game but in 1955, the University of Cambridge introduced an adult game using tiddlywinks with more complex rules, strategy and competition. However, no family playing the game in their house in the 1980s would have been concerned by that! It was just a bit of fun.

Trap Door was a race game where every step potentially contained a trap.

Triominos, from Ideal, was based on the popular game dominos but the pieces were triangular and could be joined on any of the three sides.

Trivial Pursuit was a hugely popular game during the decade and continues to be played today. The game originated in Canada and winning was determined by a player's ability to answer questions about general knowledge and popular culture. The aim of the game was to proceed around the board by correctly answering questions which were split into six categories, with each having a colour to identify it. In the original version, these were Geography (blue), Entertainment (pink), History (yellow), Arts & Literature (brown), Science & Nature (green) and Sports & Leisure (orange).

Twister from MB Games, required players to move their hands or feet onto a different coloured circle on a game mat at the spin of a wheel. The first to topple over was the loser.

Up Against Time was manufactured by Ideal and the aim of the game was to stack barrels and close a gate in the time allowed or the barrels would come tumbling down.

Yahtzee was a five dice game with 'a 1001 ways to win'. There was also a Word Yahtzee which was a challenging letter version of the original game.

Zaxxon from MB Games was another board game based on an arcade version. Players had to seek out and destroy the enemy base.

Today, it's hard to imagine the great popularity that board games once had. Board games are still sold and played today but when there were few computers or other modern devices, and there were limited options on TV, board games were far more widely used and proved great entertainment for families and friends.

4

Outdoor Activities

Running home from school and having your tea as quickly as possible was what most kids did, especially in the summer, so that they could go out and play. Climbing trees, riding bikes, playing on building sites and building dens were popular pastimes for boys. Girls roller skated, played hopscotch and skipped. Children who had them also enjoyed push along scooters, pogo balls and variations of Space Hoppers, which were first made popular in the 1970s.

Building sites were generally unlocked and unfenced so boys could have fun running along walls, shooting tin cans and bottles off them with home-made catapults or generally looking for materials to build a den. Most boys had a den hidden away somewhere, usually in the woods. If there was an empty building site, it was the perfect opportunity to find building materials and some dens could be quite elaborate.

Re-enacting things that had appeared on the television or in films at the cinema was a popular pastime. Boys would pretend to be Luke Skywalker fighting Darth Vader, Indiana Jones or characters from *Ghostbusters*. Boys also pretended to be soldiers, involving battles between the English and Germans. Playing war games usually started with the chant, 'Who wants a game of war' or 'We won the war in 1944' and would continue until enough boys had gathered to play a game. The same process still carried on even in the 1980s. Once enough boys had been found, two people would pick up sides choosing people from the line-up. It wasn't much fun if you were the last boy chosen. Once sides were chosen, everyone would run about pretending to machine gun each other or pretending to throw hand grenades.

The Cubs or the Scouts were very popular and many boys joined while the girls joined the Brownies or the Guides. A scout leader would teach boys things such as orienteering, rock climbing, bird spotting, how to start a fire and a whole range of other activities. Regular camping trips would include singing songs around a camp fire. All would-be Scouts would have to learn their 'allegiance to the Queen' speech and have a uniform complete with shorts, shirt, scarf and woggle. Badges could be earned for different tasks and would be sewn to the sleeves of the scout's shirt.

If there was a nearby park or piece of ground, games of football and cricket would be played especially in the summer months.

Parks would be full of children and the rides would include swings, roundabouts, see-saws and a slide. Some parks also had metal climbing frames as well as concrete tunnels, cars and boats. Others had real full-size steam engines left over from another era (complete with asbestos!). There were no worries about health and safety and the floor of the park was hard concrete. There were many accidents which included falling off the rides or being hit on the back of the head by a swing but, after a few tears, it was all mostly soon forgotten.

Fishing was popular with boys. Some had more expensive rods bought for them on birthdays or at Christmas. Some made their own or used their dad's old heavy wooden rods. If there was a river nearby, a kid could happily spend all day fishing. Quite often what was caught wasn't fit for anyone except the local cat but a lot of the fun was just in the thrill of catching something.

Many children would take out a net and a jam jar to try and catch their own tadpoles. Any nearby stream or pond was the ideal place to search and there would often be a collection in a jam-jar on the kitchen window. Watching tadpoles develop and grow legs was fascinating. Many children returned them to ponds once they had changed into frogs as feeding them was almost impossible.

Dogs roamed freely through the streets, many had no collars or name tags, and would return home only when it was time to eat. Some dogs would become very well-known in an area and would accompany children on adventures in the woods or while building dens which made everything feel very much like the *Famous Five*, the characters in an Enid Blyton series of books which included Timmy the dog. Any dog seen wandering nowadays could be rounded up and taken to the nearest pound but in the 1980s they were everywhere.

Naughtier kids would take part in cherry knocking where one would dare the other to knock on someone's door and they would all run off. There was always the fear of someone calling the police but it never seemed to happen.

With more cars, lorries and vans on the road, collecting number plates became a hobby. It involved having your own notepad to write down as many number plates as you could. In the same way train spotting appealed to some, although this pastime wasn't as popular.

Astronomy was also popular and some youngsters had their own telescopes to watch the night sky. Television programmes and books by Patrick Moore made the hobby well-liked but, with the space programme always in the news, it increased the interest in the stars and planets in the night sky. Most children could find the Plough, more commonly known then as the Big Dipper, which fell in the constellation of Ursa Minor. They also knew the planets, where the North Star was, and various aspects of the moon. Many classrooms had a moon chart on their walls at the time.

As the year came to an end, and the evenings grew darker, outdoor activities involved Halloween at the end of October and Guy Fawkes Night in November. In October, some mothers would carve out turnips (pumpkins were hardly seen back then) which would be lit by candles. Kids would wander the streets with the hope that a passer-by would give them the odd coin. Most children made a Guy in the lead up to Guy Fawkes Night and would sit on street corners with it in the evenings asking 'Penny for the guy, mister?' Most did quite well out of it and the money raised would go towards buying sweets or bangers (a type of firework). The build-up to Guy Fawkes Night also involved finding as much material, mainly wood, to build the biggest bonfire possible. Boys were very adept at this as they already had the knowledge of where to find scrap material to build dens. There would be a competition in the area as to who could build the biggest bonfire. At the time, councils weren't so bothered where bonfires were built and they could be found everywhere. Unfortunately, the day of Bonfire Night always fell within school time and many bonfires were set alight early by unruly kids. If the bonfire lasted until the night of 5 November, families would come out of their houses and all gather around. Some would have fireworks, many of the younger kids would have sparklers and some would cook potatoes and Spanish chestnuts in the embers. The guy, who had made so much money for its owners several days before, would end up on top of the fire. By the end of the evening, everyone would have had a great time and would return home stinking of smoke.

Christmas also brought much outdoor activity, especially on Boxing Day, when everyone would be out, trying out their new bikes, roller skates or any of the other exciting things that they'd been given for presents.

The outdoor life was an exciting one for children in the 1980s and by the end of the decade, there probably wasn't a child in the land who hadn't built a den, climbed a tree or generally enjoyed playing outside.

5

Childhood Illnesses

A huge change took place after the development of polio vaccines. A feared illness in the 1950s and before, polio was practically unheard of in the UK by the 1980s. Mass immunisation using vaccines, developed by Jonas Salk, began in the mid-1950s and brought what was once a dreaded illness that caused temporary or permanent paralysis as well as death under control. Albert Sabin developed an oral polio vaccine which was licensed in 1962. A drop of this type of polio vaccine was given on a lump of sugar.

Every child in a classroom in the 1980s ended up catching anything that was going around at the time. Mumps was an inevitable illness during childhood. It caused swelling to the face as well as fever and headaches. Within children, it generally ran its course over several weeks without any major complications. Chickenpox was another highly contagious disease spread by coughing and sneezing and produced a rash, fever, headaches and aching muscles. German measles (Rubella) caused a rash, fever and swollen glands and was again highly contagious and so easily caught in a 1980s classroom which usually contained more than 30 children.

Measles was very common and caused a fever, cough, runny nose and red eyes. This was soon followed by a rash. The illness was highly contagious and was soon spread. During the 1950s, measles had killed hundreds of people in Britain. The worst epidemic was in 1941 when 1,145 died as a result of contracting the illness. Measles could also lead to loss of eye sight, breathing and neurological problems. Vaccines for measles reduced the amount of reported cases greatly. A vaccine was developed by Maurice Ralph Hilleman who also produced vaccines for mumps, hepatitis A, hepatitis B, chickenpox, meningitis, pneumonia and Haemophilus influenzae. By doing so, he saved millions of lives.

Meningitis was rare but the airborne infection could be fatal to both children and young adults. Penicillin had some effect against the disease.

The BCG (standing for Bacillus Calmette–Guérin) injection was given to all school children and protected against tuberculosis. The programme was effective in eliminating TB in Britain, which had been a highly contagious killer known in previous years as consumption. Resistance to vaccinations has meant new cases reappearing here in recent years.

Many minor illnesses led to days off school such as stomach upsets, headaches and coughs and colds. Many kids were happy to have the time off school and to be pampered by their mothers while they read comics or books. Coughs, colds and flu seemed to be a lot worse for children and many mothers rubbed Vicks VapoRub on their children's chests to relieve congestion and sinus problems. Cough syrups and sweets were used to ease the pain of a sore throat. There were many available and all the products would be advertised on television when the season for getting colds and flu began.

Visitors to school included the nit nurse who would comb children's hair in search of any foreign invaders. There would also be visits from opticians and hearing specialists. The optical test would involve reading from an eye chart and testing for colour blindness by making a child look at pictures made up of hundreds of coloured dots. If they could spot the number within the picture, their eyesight was fine but if not, they were probably colour blind. Kids with lazy eyes were given a pair of NHS glasses with a pink Elastoplast stuck over one lens. Hearing specialists examined ears and then spoke quietly behind a pupil to see if they could hear properly. Nurses also checked for flat feet and verrucas. A later test at school for boys involved them dropping their trousers and coughing. No one was ever quite sure what it was for though!

Besides being worn on NHS glasses, Elastoplast was regularly used for grazed heads, cut knees and hands. Scraped knees were treated with iodine which stung and also stained knees yellow. Bee and wasp stings were often soaked in Dettol which was widely used as an antiseptic not only by mothers but by school dinner ladies and anyone else in charge of children.

Yearly checks with the school dentist were much feared and it seemed that the dentist always found at least one tooth to drill. In the previous decade, any teeth that had to be taken out meant that the child would have to be given gas which was administered with a rubber mask placed over the face. However, by the 1980s, numbing injections were given more readily although their long, sharp needles still made the experience unpleasant. Lucky kids had parents who had their own private dentists which meant a visit to the school dentist was avoidable.

Tonsillitis was a very common condition for children during the 1980s. In previous decades all suffering from it were taken into hospital to have their tonsils removed. However, by the 1980s, the operation became less common although tonsillectomies were still carried out, the only upside being that patients were fed ice cream to soothe the swelling after the procedure.

Appendicitis meant a visit to the hospital for an operation. This could result in bragging rights when the youngster would return to school after having their appendixes out and could show off the scar.

Common accidents involved falling off bikes, falling out of trees or falling off walls. Everything was seen as an adventure and many youngsters somehow managed to split their heads open or break arms and would end up at the X-ray department of the local hospital. There was always a kid in class who would have an arm in plaster which everyone would happily sign their name on. Even the local playground could be a source of accidents and many children were hurt by swings or see-saws. The concrete floors of playgrounds made the damage even worse especially when children fell over or came off something.

Headaches always seemed worse as a child. Treatment included Alka-Seltzer tablets which were dissolved in water. Their slogan was, 'There's nothing like Alka-Seltzer for headaches and indigestion'.

There's no doubt that illnesses seemed a lot worse in childhood but once an immunisation had built up, many illnesses such as measles and mumps were a thing of the past. An inevitable drawback to an adventurous outdoor life was the odd knock, bruise and broken limb but it all, somehow, in hindsight, seemed worth it!

6

Fashion

Clothing fashions varied greatly throughout the 1980s. At the beginning of the decade, there were still aspects of fashions from the 1970s including influences of glam, rock and punk. The 1980s are remembered for big shoulder pads.

Various hairstyles were popular throughout the 1980s. Straight hair for women was popular at the start of the decade, with many of the late-1970s styles still common. However, the perm had become fashionable by 1980. The fashion for 'big hair' that featured heavily in the popular soap operas *Dallas* and *Dynasty* and other US television programmes was copied in towns and cities. Large, high-volume, backcombed, hairstyles, popularised by film, television and pop stars, were iconic during the 1980s as was crimped hair later on in the decade. An excessive amount of mousse and hairspray added to the look. Towards the end of the 1980s, high ponytails and side ponytails together with scrunchies or headbands became common. Men's hairstyles at the beginning of the decade included shorter hairstyles. Sideburns, which had been popular during the 1960s and 1970s, disappeared altogether, as did the popularity for beards although designer stubble became fashionable in the later 1980s, popularised by television shows such as *Miami Vice*. The mullet became fashionable in the mid-1980s to the early 1990s as seen on Mel Gibson in the movie *Lethal Weapon*, Ted Danson in the television show *Cheers*, as well as on an array of pop stars such as Bono, Darryl Hall, Duran Duran and Mark Knopfler.

Top fashion models during the 1980s included Brooke Shields, Christie Brinkley, Joan Severance, Kim Alexis, Carol Alt, Yasmin Le Bon, Kelly Emberg, Elle Macpherson and Paulina Porizkova who reflected the clothes worn throughout the decade. Women's fashion at the start of the decade became more colourful and included long woollen coats, long flared skirts, slim miniskirts, slightly tapered trousers, designer jeans, spandex cycling shorts together with bulky sweaters, jumpsuits, pastel colours, leather trench coats, fur coats, large scarves, leather gloves and dresses worn with either wide or thin belts. Accessories for women included thin belts, knee-high boots with heels, white trainers, jelly shoes, mules, round-toed shoes and boots, jelly bracelets (started by Madonna in 1983), together with small necklaces and watches.

Power dressing was a phrase applied to women in the workplace who dressed in trousers accompanied by jackets with large shoulder pads. Power suits were fashionable in the UK from the early 1980s until the late 1990s.

The aerobics craze which had started in the late 1970s continued into the 1980s and was popularised by Jane Fonda as well as by, in the UK, Diana Moran (the Green Goddess) and Lizzie Webb (Mad Lizzie) on television breakfast shows. This led to a trend for wearing, often brightly coloured, leotards, leggings, sweatpants and tracksuits. Accessories included leg warmers, wide belts and elastic headbands.

Television programmes such as *Miami Vice* and *Magnum P.I.* as well as pop stars such as Michael Jackson and Madonna influenced fashion during the middle of the decade. In the mid-1980s, popular trends included Levi 501s, Hawaiian shirts, shell suits, chunky hand-knitted jumpers, sports shirts, jackets with shorter or rolled-up sleeves as well as cowboy boots.

Other widely worn fashions included Doc Martens boots, parachute pants, and designer jewellery. Digital watches were popular during the beginning of the decade but there was a return to dial-type watches later in the 1980s. Swatch watches became both collectable and fashionable. Glasses with larger plastic frames were popular with both men and woman during the decade (as worn by Christopher Biggins and Sue Pollard) sometimes with coloured frames and later tortoiseshell ones. Ray-Ban Wayfarers became very popular, and were worn by Tom Cruise in the 1983 movie *Risky Business* as well as by Sonny Crockett (Don Johnson) in *Miami Vice*. Their appearance in the show was said to have led to the sale of an extra 720,000 pairs in 1984.

Music influenced fashion too. Heavy metal fashion included long hair, leather biker jackets, cut-off denim jackets, tight worn-out jeans, and white, high trainers and badges with logos of favourite metal bands. Punk meant multi-coloured Mohawk haircuts, ripped skinny jeans, band T-shirts, safety pins worn on denim or leather jackets. The New Romantics had androgynous clothing, including ruffled poet shirts, red or blue hussar jackets with gold braid, silk sashes, tight trousers, shiny rayon waistcoats, and tailcoats all based on those worn during the Regency era. Rockabilly featured a Teddy Boy look popularised by groups such as the Stray Cats, Crazy Cavan, Darts, Showaddywaddy and Shakin' Stevens. Gothic meant dark clothes and hair, sometimes pale make-up, together with Dr Marten boots. Rude boys and skinheads wore clothing including slim fitting mohair, tonic and houndstooth suits as well as basket weave shoes, polo shirts, Sta press trousers, Doc Martens boots, braces, Harrington jackets and pork pie hats popularized by bands such as The Specials, UB40 and Madness. Casuals was a look adopted by ex-skinheads who began dressing in designer clothing and sportswear including Burberry coats, Stone Island, Lacoste, Ben Sherman and Fred Perry polo shirts, tracksuits and bomber jackets. Rap and hip hop led to a look featuring high-priced sports shoes such as Converse, Adidas and Nike trainers, track suits with large chains necklaces as well as bucket hats, oversized jackets and T-shirts and high contrast jackets.

7

Sweets and Chocolate

Television, cinema, comic and magazine advertising all influenced the sweets and chocolates that we bought during the 1980s. There were many well-remembered adverts on the television for chocolate at the time including the Curly Wurly advert featuring Terry Scott as an oversized schoolboy; the advert featuring the Milk Tray man (just like James Bond); the Rolo advert, introduced in the early 1980s with the caption, 'Do you love anyone enough to give them your last Rolo?'; the Milky Bar kid advert with the caption, 'The Milky Bars are on me'; and the Cadburys Fudge advert with the song, 'A finger of fudge is just enough to give your kids a treat'. Topic's well-remembered advert featured the slogan 'A hazelnut in every bite'. And, of course, there was also the Ferrero Rocher advert which took place at the ambassador's reception and carried the caption, 'Monsieur, with these Rocher you are really spoiling us'.

Brightly coloured wrappers and free gifts such as badges were all made to make chocolate and sweets appeal to children. Boiled sweets, bonbons, chocolate mice, liquorice, flying saucers, milk bottles, Dracula teeth, drumsticks, gobstoppers, black jacks and fruit salads were all favourites at sweet shops and newsagents.

Collecting was always very popular with children and trading cards were collected and swapped in the playground. Cards came in packs with a strip of bubblegum. Many featured popular television shows of the day, including *The A Team* as well as pop stars such as Michael Jackson and Duran Duran. There were many trading cards released in the decade that tied in with the latest movies and these included *Star Trek The Motion Picture, ET, Tron, The Black Hole, Dune, The Empire Strikes Back, Superman II, Superman III, Return of the Jedi, Jaws III, Supergirl, Rocky IV, Return to Oz, Batman, Terminator II* as well as many others.

Cards featuring football players and wrestling stars were also very popular.

Bazooka Joe bubblegum was also well-liked and came with a free cartoon comic strip. By collecting the strips, you could send away for a range of products such as jewellery, binoculars and cameras. The gifts looked excellent in the adverts but were all cheaply made abroad and many soon fell apart.

Favourite chocolates of the time included All Chocolate, Peanut and Toffee Treets, which were first introduced in the 1960s. Peanut Treets came in a yellow packet, All Chocolate Treets came in a brown packet and Toffee Treets came in a blue packet. The television advert for the product, first shown in 1967, featured the memorable slogan 'Melts in your mouth, not in your hand'. Treets as a brand was discontinued in 1988 with All Chocolate Treets becoming Minstrels. Peanut Treets were replaced by Peanut M&Ms and Toffee Treets were later called Relays before being discontinued altogether.

Other chocolate brands associated with television adverts included Cadbury's Flake, featuring the Flake girl; Bounty, again featuring a bikini-clad girl but this time on a desert island; and Turkish Delight, featuring a girl in Arab costume with the slogan 'Full of Eastern Promise'.

Animal Bars featured a different animal on each label, and these could be cut out and stuck in a special album from Nestlé. It appealed to the collector inside every child.

Many chocolates and sweets from the 1980s are still around today, including Smarties, Polos, Toffee Crisp, Kit-Kat, Crunchie, Mars Bar, Milky Way, Caramac, Aero, Twix and Maltesers. However, there are lots of fondly remembered sweets and chocolates from the decade that have now long since disappeared or have changed their names. Up until 1990, Marathon was the original name of Snickers but this was changed by Mars so that the bar had the same name all over the world. Below is a list of other fondly remembered sweets and chocolates of the decade which are sure to jog people's memories.

Spangles were distributed in the UK by Mars between 1950 and 1984 before they were discontinued. They made a brief reappearance in 1995. The boiled sweets came in a range of flavours including strawberry, orange, blackcurrant, lemon and lime and pineapple. Later flavours included acid drop, barley sugar, liquorice, peppermint, spearmint and tangerine. For a while, there was a white mint Spangle, with a hole, which was introduced

A Cadbury's Flake, one of the best-selling and most well-known chocolate bars.

A Cadbury's Creme Egg. In 1983, Cadbury buried several 22-carat, 3-inch tall, gold eggs in various locations around Great Britain and offered clues to their whereabouts in a booklet called *Conundrum: The Cadbury's Creme Egg mystery.*

to compete with Polo mints. In a poll, Spangles were voted the sweet that consumers would most like to see reappear.

Cadbury Creme Eggs, still available today, were first introduced in their current form in 1963 when they were called Fry's Creme Eggs. The name was changed in 1971. The chocolate egg contains white and yellow fondant and comes wrapped in silver paper. Today, Creme Eggs are available between New Year's Day and Easter Day but during the 1980s, they were available all year round.

In 1983, Cadbury buried several 22-carat, 3-inch tall, gold eggs in various locations around Great Britain and offered clues to their whereabouts in a booklet written by Don Shaw and illustrated by Nick Price, called *Conundrum – The Cadbury's Creme Egg Mystery.* Chaos ensued with thousands of people joining in the search and randomly digging up the countryside, private land and protected sites. Eventually, after complaints from landowners, the National Trust and other organisations, the promotion had to be abandoned. During the late 1980s, Cadbury Creme Egg digital watches were given away free to people who collected several foil wrappers.

Peanut Boost was formerly known as Starbar and was rebranded in 1985. There was also a caramel and biscuit version issued which, today, is the standard Boost bar. The chunky bar was filled with caramel and crushed roasted peanuts. Starbar is still available in its original version in Ireland.

Caramac was first manufactured by Mackintosh in 1959. The name for the bar came after a completion was held at Mackintosh's Norwich factory, the winning name came from Barbara Herne. The bar, which is still made today, is a yellow colour and consists of sweetened condensed milk, butter, sugar and various flavourings.

Smarties were originally manufactured by H. I. Rowntree & Company in 1937 although the company had been making chocolate beans from 1882. Today, they're produced by Nestlé. For many years, including the 1980s, they came in a tube, complete with a coloured lid with a letter of the alphabet on it. These were originally to encourage children to spell. Since 2005, Smarties have been packaged in a cardboard hexagonal box. The chocolate coated sweets come in eight colours: red, orange, yellow, green, blue, mauve, pink and brown.

Ipso flavoured drops, similar to Tic-Tacs, were sold in the UK during the 1970s and 1980s. They came in four flavours including strawberry, lime, orange and mint. They are remembered for their brick-like packaging which allowed the boxes to fit together. The television advert showed a man on a train platform daydreaming about West Indian and Jamaican dancers while eating the sweets. He was interrupted by a woman warning him that he was about to miss his train. The advert's catchphrase was 'A little refreshment will take you a long way'.

Crunchie, today, is made by Cadbury but was originally first produced in 1929 by J. S. Fry & Sons. The bar features a honeycomb centre surrounded by chocolate. Since the 1980s, Crunchie has been advertised with the slogan, 'Get that Friday feeling'.

Fry's Turkish Delight was first launched in the UK in 1914 and was manufactured by J. S. Fry & Sons. It consists of rose-flavoured Turkish delight covered in milk chocolate.

Cadbury's Fruit and Nut was first produced in 1926. The bar contains raisins and almonds covered in chocolate. An advertising campaign in the 1970s featured Frank Muir singing 'Everyone's a fruit and nutcase' to the tune of the *Danse des mirlitons* from Tchaikovsky's *The Nutcracker*. Today, the bar is more commonly known as 'Cadbury Dairy Milk Fruit and Nut'.

Other well-loved chocolate of the decade, in no particular order, included Cadbury's Whole Nut, Paynes Milk Chocolate Fruit Creams, Cadbury's Wildlife Bar, Mackintosh's Week End, Cadbury's Buttons, Rowntree's Fruit Pastels, Rowntree's Fruit Gums, Cadbury's Starbar, Rowntree Mackintosh's Lion Bar, Cadbury's Roses, Nestle Dairy Crunch, Cadbury's Curly Wurly, Cadbury's Flake, Mackintosh's Golden Cup, Rowntree's Cabana, Nestle Milky Bar, Fry's Peppermint Cream, Fry's Chocolate Cream, Banjo bars, Cadbury's Dairy Milk, Galaxy Ripple, Cadbury's Bourneville Dark, the Wrigley Company's Opal Fruits, the Mars company's Milky Way, Nestle UK's Toffee Crisp, Toblerone, Mackintosh's Quality Street, Galaxy chocolates, Cadbury's Classic Collection Turkish, Cadbury Bar Noir, Nestle Fruit and Nut, Polos, Trebor Mints, Nestle Milk Chocolate, Terry's Waifa, Mars's Twix, Cadbury's Wispa, Mackintosh's Prize, Banjo Coconut, Nestlé's Yorkie, Terry's Bitz, Cadbury's Bar Six, Rowntree's Jelly Tots and Candy Tots, Mars's Marathon (now called Snickers), Fry's Five Centres, Nestlé's Black Magic, Terry's Pyramint, Mint Aero, Chocolate Aero, Cadbury's Fruit and Nut, Refreshers, Roundtree's Rolos, Cadbury's Milk Tray, Mars's Coconut Bounty, Strawberry Bounty, Cadbury's Double Decker, McVitie's Extra Time United, Cadbury's Picnic, Bassett's Liquorice Allsorts, Cadbury's Whole Nuts and Kit Kat.

8

Radio

There were a lot fewer radio stations during the 1980s than there are today. The BBC broadcast on its four official stations but there were also local radio stations as well as the ever-popular Radio Luxembourg and other pirate stations.

BBC's Radio One was the most popular radio station at the beginning of the 1980s. In 1981, the daily line-up included:

5.00 a.m.	Ray Moore (as Radio 2)
7.00 a.m.	Mike Read
9.00 a.m.	Simon Bates featuring events, birthdays and anniversaries on the day through the years as well as *The Golden Hour* and *Our Tune* at 11am.
11.30 a.m.	Dave Lee Travis was moved to the mid-morning slot after passing the breakfast show over to Mike Read.
12.30 p.m.	*Newsbeat* presented by Peter Mayne.
12.45 p.m.	Paul Burnett
2.30 p.m.	Steve Wright
4.30 p.m.	Peter Powell. On Thursdays, the show included a review of the new *Top 30 album chart* as well as *Newsbeat* at 5.30pm.
7.00 p.m.	Paul Gambaccini
8.00 p.m.	Richard Skinner
10.00 p.m. to midnight	John Peel

Mike Read took over the *Breakfast Show* from Dave Lee Travis (2 May 1978 to 2 January 1981) on Monday 5 January 1981. He later presented the Sunday morning show in 1986 before hosting the Saturday morning show in 1987. He famously stopped playing *Relax* by Frankie Goes to Hollywood half-way through during his show, broadcast on 11 January 1984, saying that the lyrics were obscene. He refused to play it again. Despite the BBC banning the record, the song reached number one in the UK charts on 22 January 1984 and stayed there for five weeks. In 1986, the *Breakfast Show* was taken over by Mike Smith and later Simon Mayo.

Other fondly remembered Radio One DJs of the 1980s included Tony Blackburn, Liz Kershaw, Gary Davies, Bruno Brookes, Alan Freeman, Janice Long, Johnnie Walker, Annie Nightingale, Jackie Brambles, Mark Goodier, Richard Skinner, Bob Harris, Andy Kershaw, Adrian John, Adrian Juste, Alexis Korner, Andy Peebles, Pat Sharp, Ed Stewart and Tommy Vance.

During the summer months, the *Radio One Roadshow* toured the country appearing live on the radio during the morning show. In 1981, the roadshow was hosted by several DJs including Dave Lee Travis, Andy Peebles, Simon Bates, Mike Read, Paul Burnett, Tony Blackburn, Peter Powell and Steve Wright. The show included music, requests and live bands together with competitions and giveaways.

Studio B15 was broadcast on Sunday afternoons on Radio One between 1980 and 1983. The show was hosted by Adrian Love and carried interviews, news and contributions from listeners in various phone-ins. One listener asked 'Whatever happened to John Lennon?' which led to DJ Andy Peebles flying to New York to interview Lennon, days before he was tragically killed.

Sunday evenings were unmissable as they featured the chart run-down of the *Top 40* hits presented by Tony Blackburn. All kids did their best to record their favourite tunes on their cassette recorders. Other Sunday shows included the morning show hosted by Tony Blackburn (including *Junior Choice*) as well as shows by Rosko, Adrian Juste and Alexis Corner.

Radio Two during week days featured Colin Berry, Ray Moore, Terry Wogan, Jimmy Young, John Dunn, Ed Stewart, David Hamilton, David Symonds and Brian Matthew.

By the 1980s, in addition to the main BBC stations, there were also many local radio stations as well as the offshore, ever-popular, Radio Luxembourg. Listening under the bedsheets to the poorly transmitted signal became addictive as the station played records that mainstream radio stations weren't allowed to play together with a range of competitions to win holidays, records, radio/cassette players, video game systems as well as other electronic gadgets. With the *Daily Mirror*, Radio Luxembourg ran the popular *Daily Mirror Rock and Pop Club* on Tuesdays, giving away the latest LPs every week. DJs at the station at the time included Barry Alldis, Stuart and Ollie Henry, Rob Jones, Tony Prince (The Royal Ruler), Benny Brown, Ian Brass (Brasso), Mike Hollis and Bob Stewart.

A week's listings of shows broadcast during 1982 included:

Sundays:

7.00 p.m.	*Haunted Studio* with Stuart and Ollie Henry.
9.00 p.m.	Star *Chart and Top 30 UK Singles* with Tony Prince.
11.00 p.m.	*Sunday's Top 20* with Barry Alldis and Rob Jones.
1.00 a.m.	*Earthlink* with Benny Brown.

Mondays:

6.45 p.m.	*Radio Outreach* with John Knight; *Battle of the Giants*; *Top 30 Airplay*; *Top 30 Disco* with Rob Jones and Benny Brown.
1.00 a.m.	*Earthlink* with Barry Alldis.

Tuesdays:

6.45 p.m.	*208 Editorial* with Rodney Collins; *Beatle Hour*; *Daily Mirror Rock and Pop Club*; *Top 30 UK*; *Top 30 Albums* with Rob Jones and Barry Alldis.
9.00 p.m.	*Top 30 UK*; *Top 30 Albums* with Benny Brown.
1.00 a.m.	*Earthlink* with Mike Hollis.

Wednesdays:

7.00 p.m.	*Gold and Games* with Rob Jones and Benny Brown.
9.00 p.m.	*American Top 30* with Bob Stewart.
11.00 p.m.	*Top 30 Easy Listening* with Benny Brown.
1.00 a.m.	*EarthLink* with Mike Hollis.

Thursdays:

7.00 p.m.	*The Number Ones*; *Top of the Pops* with Bob Stewart and Mike Hollis.
9.00 p.m.	*Top 30 Futurist* with Rob Jones.
11.00 p.m.	*Discothèque* with Benny Brown. *Midnight – Spotlight On ...* with Stuart Henry.
1.00 a.m.	*Earthlink* with Stuart and Ollie Henry.

Fridays:

7.00 p.m.	*The Record Journal* with Stuart and Ollie Henry.
9.00 p.m.	*Top 30 Disco* with Tony Prince.
11.00 p.m.	*Top 30 Airplay* with Bob Stewart.
1.00 a.m.	*Earthlink* with Barry Alldis.

Saturdays:

6.45 p.m.	*208 Editorial* with Rodney Collins.
7.00 p.m.	*Street Heat*; *Top 30 Rock Show* with Stuart and Ollie Henry.
11.00 p.m.	*Big L Marlboro Top 20 Country* with Bob Stewart.
12.00 a.m.	*Midnight Memories* with Barry Alldis.
1.00 a.m.	*Earthlink*; *Love Songs* with Mike Hollis.

Many radio programmes which had been broadcast for several decades previously continued into the 1980s. These included:

The Archers (1951–present) was originally listed as 'an everyday story of country folk' and it still continues today, making it the world's longest running radio soap. Set in the fictional village of Ambridge, it told the story of the middle-class farming family, the Archers. It was first broadcast on Whit Monday on 29 May 1950 with five episodes being transmitted throughout the week. The pilot series, created by Godfrey Baseley, was described as 'a farming Dick Barton'.

Two-Way Family Favourites (1945–84) linked families at home with troops serving overseas in the forces. The show was hosted by husband-and-wife team, Jean Metcalfe and Cliff Michelmore, and proved hugely popular. The forerunner of the show, *Forces Favourites*, was aired during the Second World War and featured requests, messages to loved ones and music.

Sing Something Simple (1959–2001) featured melodies from the last seventy years sung by the Cliff Adams Singers and was broadcast on Sunday evenings. It became the longest-running continuous music programme in the world until it was axed in 2001.

Semprini Serenade (1957–82) was a weekday show hosted by Alberto Semprini who opened the show with the lines ʻOld ones, new ones, loved ones, neglected ones'. The show featured themes from films and stage shows as well as old and new tunes.

Your Hundred Best Tunes (1959–2007) was broadcast on Sunday evenings and was hosted by Alan Keith and featured classic music.

Friday Night is Music Night (1952–present) remains the world's longest-running live concert programme. It features a range of music including classical, film, swing, jazz, opera, folk and songs from musicals.

Listen with Mother (1950–82) was broadcast every weekday afternoon at 1.45pm and lasted 15 minutes. Its presenters included Daphne Oxenford, Eileen Brown, Julia Lang, Dorothy Smith and many others. It consisted of stories, nursery rhymes as well as songs, which were regularly sung by

Eileen Browne and George Dixon. The show was aimed at the under-fives and regularly had over 1 million listeners. The theme tune was Gabriele Fauré's *Dolly Suite* and the show began with the words, 'Are you sitting comfortably? Then I'll begin'. It led on to the television version, *Watch with Mother*.

Woman's Hour (1946–present) was hosted by Sue MacGregor (1972–1987) and Jenni Murray (since 1987), and featured items of interest to women including interviews and topical debates. The show still continues today and attracts millions of listeners.

Radio One remained the favourite and most listened to station throughout the 1980s. The following decade saw far more local and national stations hit the airwaves including Virgin Radio (founded by Richard Branson), Heart FM as well as a large range of regional stations including Cool FM, Gemini Radio, Kiss FM, Choice FM, Talk Radio, LBC, Spirit FM and Asian Sound Radio. There were many more. However, today, Radio One still remains the UK's most listened to station.

9

Television

At the beginning of the 1980s, most people owned their own 20-inch colour television although some families still chose to rent from shops such as Rumbelows and DER. Televisions were bulky, came in fake wood surrounds and featured a series of push buttons to change the channels. There were few remote controls so channels had to be turned over manually. Many televisions came with a table top aerial which had to be placed in the best position to avoid distortion. Many houses had roof top aerials.

At the beginning of the decade, there were only three TV channels; BBC1, BBC2 and ITV. Some people had video tape recorders, which had been introduced in the late 1970s, but these were few and far between. It wasn't until 1982 that VCRs really took off properly. A Ferguson VHS video recorder which offered 'video programmability and stereo capability' cost £599, although there were cheaper models available. Eventually, the cost of a video recorder dropped dramatically as they were mass produced.

At first, there were three main formats. These included the Philips Video 2000, JVC's VHS and Sony's Betamax. As the popularity of video recorders grew, VHS and Betamax became the most popular formats with VHS

An early top-loading video cassette recorder. VCRs became hugely popular from 1982 onwards. At the time, a Ferguson VHS video recorder, which offered video programmability and stereo capability, cost £599.

eventually taking the bulk of the market. Original video recorders were all top loaders and came with a digital timer so that programmes could be recorded automatically. Popular size tapes came in 3-hour lengths although 1-hour, 2-hour and, later, 4-hour tapes were also available. When Long Play video recorders were introduced, which played at half speed) people were able to record a maximum of 8 hours on a tape, although the quality wasn't as good as a normal play video recorder. Video tapes were bulky items and occasionally spun out in the machine. Quality was sometimes grainy and tapes tended to deteriorate over time.

Video disc players were also available but these were just for showing films and couldn't record. The Philips LaserDisc was first sold in the US in 1978 and arrived in the UK in the 1980s. The discs were large, the size of a 12-inch vinyl record, and although the quality was better than that of VHS and Betamax, the format never gained the popularity of video tape. A similar system, using a laser beam, was used years later when DVDs took over from video tapes in the 1990s.

Hitachi also issued disc players in the 1980s; it used a stylus instead of a laser beam. Again, the discs were the size of a 12-inch LP record. Although novel at the time, the format never took off and few machines were sold.

Popular television shows at the start of the decade included *Coronation Street, Crossroads, Shoestring, The Professionals, Top of the Pops, Doctor Who, The Goodies* and *The Two Ronnies*.

On 15 September 1984, the Princess of Wales gave birth to her second son, Henry Charles Albert David, more commonly known as Prince Harry. His birth made him sixth in line to the British throne.

One broadcast which attracted a huge television audience was the marriage of Prince Charles and Diana Spencer on 29 July 1981. The wedding took place at St Paul's Cathedral and was watched by an incredible 750 million people worldwide. Street parties were held to celebrate the occasion and endless items featuring the couple's faces were sold including mugs, plates, T-shirts and badges. A second royal wedding took place on 23 July 1986 when Prince Andrew married Sarah Ferguson at Westminster Abbey. This time, over 500 million people tuned in to watch the ceremony.

There were endless memorable television shows broadcast during the decade. Politics played a part in some of the more serious, and depressing, dramas broadcast.

With high unemployment under Margaret Thatcher's government, *Boys from the Blackstuff* (1982) seemed to reflect the current state of the country with the overall difficulty finding work. The drama was written by Liverpudlian playwright Alan Bleasdale and told the story of five unemployed tarmacers desperately searching for employment. The series was based on a previous one-off drama broadcast in 1980 called simply *The Black Stuff*. Although most of the series had been written before Margaret Thatcher came to power, it was seen as a reflection of the desperation felt by many under her government. By the time the show was broadcast, unemployment had reached 3,000,000 people due to economic recession and the restructuring of industry. The drama featured five main characters including, most memorably, Bernard Hill as Yosser Hughes as well as Michael Angelis as Chrissie Todd; Alan Igbon as Loggo Logmond; Dixie Dean, the gang's one time foreman, played by Tom Georgeson; and George Malone, a trade unionist and docker, played by Peter Kerrigan. Yosser Hughes' psychotic behaviour is well remembered, driven mad by unemployment, regularly headbutting people and uttering the phrases 'Gizza' job!' and 'I can do that!' which were mimicked by viewers up and down the land. The series established the career of Julie Walters who played Chrissie's wife, Angie, memorable for shouting at her husband, 'Fight back, Chrissie'. The series proved hugely popular and is fondly remembered today.

With the election of Ronald Reagan in 1981, a fear arose that the world could be on the brink of a nuclear war with the poor relationship between the USSR and America and the escalation of the Cold War. The BBC broadcast *Threads* in 1984 which showed the results of a nuclear war and its aftermath on the residents of Britain. It featured Paul Vaughan as the Narrator; Karen Meagher as Ruth Beckett; Reece Dinsdale (Jimmy Kemp); David Brierley (Bill Kemp); and Rita May (Rita Kemp). The show scared a great many people, some stocked up food in case of a disaster while others built their own nuclear fall-out shelters. The show was widely discussed all around the world but, fortunately, its contents never became a reality.

On a lighter note, there were many less depressing programmes shown during the decade including many popular children's programmes, including one of the best-loved shows of the past few decades, *Blue Peter* (1958–present). During the 1980s, *Blue Peter* was hosted by Sarah Greene (1980–1983), Peter Duncan (1980–1986), Simon Groom (1978–1986), Janet Ellis (1983–1987), Michael Sundin (1984–1985), Mark Curry (1986–1989), Caron Keating (1986–1990), Yvette Fielding (1987–1992) and John Leslie (1989–1994).

Sarah Greene was offered the part as a presenter by the programme's editor, Biddy Baxter. Sara replaced Tina Heath who had been part of the show since 1979. At the time, at the age of twenty-two, she was the show's youngest ever presenter. Her younger sister, Laura, occasionally appeared on the show and later became a weather presenter. After leaving *Blue Peter*, Sarah Greene hosted *Saturday Superstore* with Mike Read and later co-presented *Going Live!* with Phillip Schofield. She married DJ Mike Smith in 1989.

Peter Duncan had appeared in many movies and television programmes before he began working as a presenter on *Blue Peter*. His previous notable TV roles included parts in *The Tomorrow People* (1973–1979), *Space 1999* (1975–1977), *King Cinder* (1977), *Play for Today* (1970–1984), *Warship* (1973–1977), *Oranges and Lemons* (1973) and in the second series of *Survivors* (1975–1977). He also played Jimmy Carter in the popular ITV children's television series *The Flockton Flyer* (1977–1978). His movie appearances included *Stardust* (1974), Kit Nubbles in *Mister Quilp* (1975), the thankless Richard in *The Lifetaker* (1976), and a small part in the film *Flash Gordon* (1980). His willingness to do many of the more challenging ordeals on the show, including running the first London marathon and completing the Royal Marines' Endurance Course, led to his own show, *Duncan Dares,* in 1984.

Simon Groom joined *Blue Peter* in 1978 after a brief stint as a teacher and a DJ. He stayed with the programme for eight years, co-presenting with Lesley Judd, John Noakes, Christopher Wenner, Tina Heath, Peter Duncan, Sarah Greene, Janet Ellis and Michael Sundin.

Janet Ellis joined the show in 1983 after appearing in *Jackanory Playhouse*, *The Sweeney*, *Doctor Who* and *Jigsaw*. She stayed with the show for four years and during that time became the first female civilian in Europe to free fall from 20,000 feet. She famously broke her leg while training. After leaving the show, she hosted the BBC's *Open Air* programme as well as writing a book with co-host and friend Caron Keating called *How to Get Married Without Divorcing Your Family.*

Michael Sundin joined the show in 1984 and stayed for a year. He was a former, actor and trampolinist. Biddy Baxter had invited Sundin to an audition to replace Peter Duncan after seeing him play Tik-Tok in the Walt Disney film *Return to Oz*. After leaving the show, he appeared in the movie *Lionheart* (1987) before appearing in a UK theatre tour of *Seven Brides for Seven Brothers* as well as a tour of *Starlight Express*. He died in 1989, aged twenty-eight.

Mark Curry joined Blue Peter on 23 June 1986 replacing Simon Groom. He spent three weeks in Malawi where he reported on villagers' problems with blindness and chronic eye conditions. When he was two years old, he'd had an eye operation and was therefore keen to raise money for the Blue Peter appeal of 1986 for the charity, Sightsavers. In 1987, he travelled to the Soviet Union for the programme's summer expedition. His co-hosts on the programme were Janet Ellis, Peter Duncan, Caron Keating, Yvette Fielding and John Leslie.

Caron Keating joined the show in 1986 and stayed until 1990. She was the daughter of television and radio presenter, Gloria Hunniford. She presented *The Video Picture Show, Channel One* and the music programme *Greenrock* in Northern Ireland before joining *Blue Peter*. During her time on the programme, she travelled to Moscow in 1987, swam with sharks, abseiled down skyscrapers and stood strapped to a stunt aircraft whilst it performed aerial acrobatics. In 1988, she interviewed Minister Margaret Thatcher on the show. After leaving *Blue Peter,* Keating joined Radio 5 before hosting *A Game of Two Halves* with Mark Kermode. In 1997, she was diagnosed with breast cancer and died in 2004.

Yvette Fielding joined *Blue Peter* in 1987 and, at eighteen, became the youngest presenter on the show. Before appearing on the programme, Fielding appeared in the fondly remembered children's drama *Seaview* (1983–1985) where she played the part of Sandy Shelton, a teenage girl growing up in her parents' guest house in Blackpool. She also appeared in an episode of *Juliet Bravo*. Whilst co-hosting *Blue Peter*, Fielding was awarded the SOS Award for the Most Popular Woman on Television. Her ride on a rollercoaster with Mark Curry was later voted the favourite *Blue Peter* moment of all time by viewers. After leaving the show, she co-hosted *What's Up Doc?*, a children's show shown on ITV on Saturday mornings. Today, she is best known for presenting *Most Haunted*, a show made by Fielding and her husband Karl Beattie's own television production company, Antix Productions.

John Leslie joined *Blue Peter* in 1989 staying with the show for five years until 1994. During his time on the programme, he ran in the London Marathon and abseiled down the BBC Television Centre. He presented *Blue Peter* with Caron Keating, Yvette Fielding, Diane-Louise Jordan,

Anthea Turner and Tim Vincent. After leaving the show, he hosted *Wheel of Fortune* before appearing as a co-host on *This Morning*.

Grange Hill (1978–2008) ran throughout the 1980s and was how most people at school, at the time, nostalgically remember their childhood (even if it wasn't quite like that). Amazingly, the show ran for thirty years. It became one of the most popular children's shows of all time. Fondly remembered pupils include Tucker Jenkins (Todd Carty), Trisha Yates (Michelle Herbert), Alan Humphries (George Armstrong), Benny Green (Terry Sue-Patt), Cathy Hargreaves (Lindy Brill), Pogo Patterson (Peter Moran), Suzanne Ross (Susan Tully), Gripper Stebson (Mark Savage), Zammo McGuire (Lee MacDonald), Roland Browning (Erkan Mustafa) and Fay Lucas (Alison Bettles). There were many more.

Schools all had their own Tucker Jenkins, Alan Humphries, Zammo McGuire and Gripper Stebson (the school bully is never forgotten). Memorable episodes include Tucker Jenkins aborted trip to France, Zammo's drug taking despair, which led to the record *Just Say No*; Bullet Baxter punching bully boy PE teacher Mr Hicks (every school had a PE teacher like Hicks); Gripper Stebson getting his final comeuppance when the bullied kids gang up against him; and Jeremy Irvine drowning in the school pool.

In the *French Trip* episode, Tucker's friend Tommy Watson fails to book onto the school trip to France, so Tucker smuggles him on to the coach without the teachers noticing. Once on the ferry, two French boys chat up Cathy and Trisha while Tucker and Alan Humphries do their best to keep Tommy hidden. When the coach arrives in France, it is searched by a customs official who spots Tommy hiding under the back seat. Tommy is ordered home which means that one of the teachers has to escort him back and the trip is cancelled. However, Miss Lexington contacts the coach firm and instead the class have a trip to Bournemouth.

The Zammo McGuire's heroin addiction story began in series nine and continued in series ten. The storyline revolved around Zammo's addiction to the drug and how its effects altered his relationships with his friends and family. It was very controversial at the time. After much lying and stealing, a memorable final scene sees Kevin and Jackie confront Zammo who scrambles around on the floor of the locker room for his heroin as he's confronted by the police, Mrs McClusky, Mr Kennedy and his mother. In 1986, the cast of *Grange Hill* released a single *Just Say No*, which tied in with Zammo's struggle with drugs. The song reached number five in the charts. The anti-drug 'Just Say No' campaign had been running in the US for several years, headed by Nancy Reagan, and the cast of *Grange Hill* were invited to the White House to meet Reagan.

Episode 4 of the fourth season featured newcomer PE teacher, Mr Hicks. Bad-tempered Hicks pushes Christopher 'Stewpot' Stewart during a swimming lesson causing him to cut his head. Hicks manages to talk his way out of the incident but Stewpot's parents visit the school to complain. From that point onward, Mr Hicks has it in for Stewpot, regularly bullying him. Miss Lexington reports the matter to Mr Baxter who, at first, dismisses the matter but then witnesses Hicks pushing Stewpot to the floor during a lesson. Baxter punches Hicks in the jaw and the teacher is dismissed. The episode is also memorable for introducing Gripper Stebson, Miss Lexington, Matthew Cartwright and Danny Taylor.

Gripper Stebson finally gets his comeuppance in series six in the episode *Repercussions*. After a reign of terror and his continual bullying of Roland Browning and a Sikh boy called Randir, Stebson is confronted in the toilets by a group of boys led by Pogo Paterson. Before a fight can break out, Mr Baxter intervenes and Gripper is ultimately expelled from the school.

Memorable teachers appearing in *Grange Hill* included Mr Bronson (Michael Sheard), a strict disciplinarian complete with ginger wig; Bullet Baxter (Michael Cronin), the no-nonsense PE teacher (every school had one); Mr Sutcliffe (James Wynn), the English and drama teacher, 'Sooty' to the pupils; Mr McGuffey (Fraser Cains), an English teacher with the nickname 'Scruffy; Mr Hopwood (Brian Capron) 'Hoppy', the woodwork teacher; Mrs McClusky (Gwyneth Powell) 'Bridget the Midget', the headmistress; Mr Keating, (Robert Hartley) the maths teacher and deputy headmaster; Miss Mooney (Lucinda Gane) the dizzy science teacher; Mr Griffiths (George a Cooper) the irritable caretaker; and Miss Lexington (Allyson Rees) known as 'Sexy Lexy'. Every school had their own Bronson, Baxter, Sutcliffe, McGuffey and Hopwood in some form or another, so much so, that everyone felt that the show must have been based on their own school.

The popularity of *Grange Hill* led to a spin-off show *Tucker's Luck* (1983–1985), again starring Todd Carty. *Grange Hill* will always be remembered for its accurate portrayal of school days and was one of the best-ever children series, not only of the 1980s, but also of the previous decade and the years following, until the show finally ended in 2008.

Doctor Who (1963–present) was first broadcast on 23 November 1963. It starred William Hartnell as the Doctor, and his first adventure, called 'An Unearthly Child', took him and his granddaughter, Susan, back to the Stone Age. The introduction of the Daleks in the second series of episodes made the show an instant hit. Daleks suddenly appeared everywhere, including in comics, as toys and on ice lollies. In 1966, the Doctor regenerated, and for the following three years was played by Patrick Troughton and later Jon Pertwee.

During the 1980s, the show had four doctors including Tom Baker (1974–81), Peter Davison (1982–84), Colin Baker (1984–86) and Sylvester McCoy (1987–89). Tom Baker had been hugely successful as Doctor Who and Peter Davison was a total change from the Doctor that people had been used to for the previous seven years. The new Doctor travelled with several assistants including Adric (Matthew Waterhouse), Nyssa (Sarah Sutton) and Tegan Jovanka (Janet Fielding), who had also travelled alongside Tom Baker's doctor. Later, his companions included Vislor Turlough (Mark Strickson) and Peri Brown (Nicola Bryant). Although, completely different from Tom Baker, the new incarnation of the Doctor and his subsequent adventures proved highly popular. The era included the reintroduction of many *Doctor Who* favourites including the Master, Cybermen, Omega, the Black and White Guardians, and the Silurians.

Colin Baker took over the role in 1984, appearing in three series. After *The Trial of a Time Lord*, Michael Grade, who wasn't a fan of the show, decided to rest the programme for eighteen months, and Baker was asked to appear in one final story but declined and the Doctor eventually regenerated into Sylvester McCoy, leaving many questions in the *Doctor Who* timeline unanswered. During his time as Doctor Who, Baker was accompanied, again, by Peri Brown as well as by Melanie Bush (Bonnie Langford). Colin Baker was an excellent Doctor Who but his time in the show was spoiled by the dropping of many planned episodes, the postponement of the series and the overlong *Trial of a Time Lord* story.

By the time Sylvester McCoy took over the role in 1987, he was accompanied, again, by Melanie Bush and later by Ace (Sophie Aldred). His first appearance was in *Time and the Rani* showing the seventh Doctor as a whimsical and thoughtful character who was also secretive and manipulative. The Doctor faced his old foes, the Daleks, as well as a Bertie Bassett-like robot, the Kandy Man, in *The Happiness Patrol* which also starred Sheila Hancock. The show suffered in the ratings after being scheduled to run at the same time as ITV's *Coronation Street* leading to the new controller of BBC One, Jonathan Powell, making the decision to end production at the end of the show's twenty-sixth series. For many fans, Sylvester McCoy was their favourite Doctor. However, the show was cancelled in 1989. Although the 1980s saw the demise of *Doctor Who*, he reappeared in a Canadian one-off production starring Paul McGann in 1996. However, it wasn't until 2005 that the Doctor reappeared regularly on BBC One again, this time played by Christopher Eccleston.

Tom's Midnight Garden (1989) was first adapted for the BBC in 1968 and then again in 1974 before the 80s version was broadcast in 1989. It was based on a novel by Philippa Pearce and the drama told the story of Tom Long who is sent away to stay with his aunt and uncle when his brother, Peter, contracts measles. His aunt and uncle live in a flat in part of a big old house without a garden. Their elderly and reclusive landlady, Mrs Bartholomew, lives upstairs. Tom isn't allowed to venture outdoors because he might be infectious. Lying awake in bed after midnight, he hears the communal grandfather clock strike thirteen. On leaving his room to investigate, he finds the back door of the house open and going outside discovers a large sunlit garden. Every night when the clock strikes thirteen, he revisits the Victorian garden and meets with a small girl called Hatty and they become good friends. On further visits, Tom finds that Hatty has grown older. On his final night in the house, Tom takes a trip into the garden but finds that it is no longer there. Before he leaves, the elderly landlady, Mrs Bartholomew, reveals that she is actually Hatty.

Moondial (1988) was a six-part drama broadcast by the BBC. It featured a young girl, Minty (Siri Neal), who goes to stay with her aunt when her mother is hurt in a car accident. Minty explores the nearby mansion and discovers a moondial that allows her to travel back in time. There, she meets two children, Tom (Tony Sands), who lives in Victorian times, and Sarah (Helena Avellano), who lives in the previous century to Tom's. Minty does her best to rescue the children from their unhappy lives. *Moondial* had a repeat in 1990.

The Chronicles Of Narnia (1988–1990) was based on the well-loved books by C. S. Lewis. The BBC series was first broadcast on 13 November 1988 and ran until 23 December 1990. It was based on four of the novels: *The Lion, the Witch and the Wardrobe, Prince Caspian, The Voyage of the Dawn Treader* and *The Silver Chair.* The original story featured Peter, Susan, Edmund and Lucy Pevensie, siblings who find themselves evacuated to the countryside in 1940 to escape the bombing in London. They stay with Professor Digory Kirke. Shortly after arriving at their new home, the children decide to explore their surroundings and Lucy enters a wardrobe and finds herself in a snowy woodland. Whilst there, she meets s a faun called Mr Tumnus who tells her that she is in Narnia. Eventually, Lucy returns home but is ridiculed by her siblings when she tells them where she has been. However, Edmund follows her into the wardrobe and finds himself in Narnia. The tale continues over many years and includes a White Witch, Aslan the lion, several battles, various talking animals and mythical creatures. The series won many awards and the books remain amongst the best-loved children's books of all time.

Rentaghost (1976–1984) was hugely successful and featured the antics of a number of ghosts, all employed by the company, Rentaghost. The ghosts were hired out to perform various haunting tasks. The firm is run by Fred Mumford, who is recently deceased and believes he can find gainful employment for ghosts whose lives were as unsuccessful as his. His recruits include Timothy Claypole, a jester with little knowledge of modern technology, and Hubert Davenport, a gentleman from Victorian times who is often shocked by the modern world. The ghosts run their business from an office in South Ealing, which is rented from the very much alive Harold Meaker. At first, Meaker doesn't realise that they are ghosts but all is revealed in the third episode. Over several series, other deceased characters are introduced including Hazel the McWitch, a Scottish witch; Nadia Popov, a ghost from Holland who suffers from hay fever and disappears whenever she sneezes; and a pantomime horse, Dobbin, whom Claypole brings to life. The show also featured a ghost from the Wild West called Catastrophe Kate. Christopher Biggins played a local entrepreneur, Adam Painting, who was always trying to involve the ghosts in his various businesses. The show's actors and actresses were: Anthony Jackson (Fred Mumford), Michael Darbyshire (Hubert Davenport), Michael Staniforth (Timothy Claypole), Betty Alberge (Mrs Sheila Mumford), John Dawson (Mr Phil Mumford), Edward Brayshaw (Harold Meaker), Ann Emery (Ethel Meaker), Christopher Biggins (Adam Painting), Molly Weir (Hazel the McWitch), Sue Nicholls (Nadia Popov), Kenneth Connor (Whatsisname

Noel Edmonds, presenter of *The Multi-Coloured Swap Shop* and *Top Gear* during the 1980s. In December 1981, Edmonds, Keith Chegwin and Maggie Philbin formed a pop group called Brown Sauce and recorded a single, 'I Wanna be a Winner'.

Smith) and Aimi MacDonald (Susie Starlight). Lynda La Plante, the author and screenwriter, played Tamara Novek, using her acting name, Lynda Marchal. The original theme song was composed and sung by Michael Staniforth who played Timothy Claypole. The show is remembered fondly by many.

Tiswas (1974–1982) was broadcast by ITV on Saturday mornings and was hosted by Chris Tarrant and Sally James and featured Lenny Henry, John Gorman and Bob Carolgees together with Spit the Dog. The show featured sketches, competitions, pop promos and film clips. Popular features included the Phantom Flan Flinger, the *Bucket of Water* song and Lenny Henry's impressions of the newsreader, 'Trevor McDoughnut'. The Cage featured weekly on the show where children and their parents were regularly locked up and doused in water. Chris Tarrant later appeared in an adult version of the show called *O.T.T.* (Over the Top), which was broadcast in 1982.

Multi-Coloured Swap Shop (1976–1982) was the BBC's answer to *Tiswas* and was also broadcast on Saturday mornings between 9.30 a.m. and 12.30 p.m. The show was hosted by the then twenty-eight-year-old Noel Edmonds and also featured Keith Chegwin, Maggie Philbin and John Craven. The programme was broadcast live and featured interviews, cartoons and competitions. Keith Chegwin travelled the country hosting live outdoor broadcasts where children could take along items they wished to swap. News coverage was provided by John Craven, who also appeared in sketches. The first show featured as guests Tom Baker and Elisabeth Sladen from *Doctor Who* and viewers were encouraged to phone in with questions. Every week, celebrities brought in items that viewers could win by answering a question and sending their name and address on a postcard. The winners' names were drawn from a barrel by another celebrity the following week. In December 1981, Edmonds, Chegwin and Philbin formed a pop group called Brown Sauce and recorded a single, *I Wanna be a Winner*, which was performed on the show. The record reached number fifteen in the charts. Popular cartoons featured in the show included *Hong Kong Phooey*, *Valley of the Dinosaurs*, *Battle of the Planets* and *The Great Grape Ape*. The show had a mascot, a purple dinosaur named *Posh Paws,* named by a viewer because it was almost the words Swap Shop back to front. When Swap Shop ended in 1982, it was followed by a succession of similar type shows including *Get Set For Summer* hosted by Radio One DJ Peter Powell, *Saturday Superstore* presented by Mike Read, *Going Live!* and *Live & Kicking*.

Newsround (1972–) was presented by John Craven, who appeared with bulletins specially written for children. The show was originally called

John Craven's Newsround and had its own presenting team including Roger Finn and Helen Rollason, as well as reports from seasoned reporters such as John Humphrys, Michael Buerk and Martin Bell. Just before Craven left the programme in 1989, it was re-titled as just *Newsround*. A further succession of presenters included Juliet Morris, Krishnan Guru-Murthy, Julie Etchingham, Chris Rogers, Kate Sanderson, Matthew Price and Becky Jago.

Going Live! (1987–1993) replaced *Saturday Superstore* and was hosted by Phillip Schofield and Sarah Greene. Other regulars on the show included Trevor and Simon, Peter Simon, Emma Forbes and the puppet, Gordon the Gopher. The show was broadcast between autumn and spring. It featured special guests, cartoons, sketches, games and pop videos. Segments featured in the show included Double Dare; Growing Pains; Live Line; The Press Conference; The Video Vote; Trevor and Simon; as well as outside broadcasts.

The Muppet Show (1976–1981) had been broadcast since the 1970s but the television show continued until the 1980s. The Muppets were originally created by Jim and Jane Henson in 1955. The television show featured the ever popular Kermit the Frog, Fozzie Bear, Miss Piggy, Gonzo as well as many others. In the 1980s, each week featured guest stars who included Roger Moore, Mark Hamill, Steve Martin, Elton John and many other celebrities of the day. Muppet movies were produced in the 1980s including *The Great Muppet Caper* (1981) and *The Muppets Take Manhattan* (1984). In 1983, Jim Henson debuted another popular television series, featuring various Muppet creatures, called *Fraggle Rock*.

Worzel Gummidge (1979–1981) was produced by Southern Television for ITV and starred Jon Pertwee as a mischievous scarecrow. It ran for four series before ending in 1981. The show featured many famous actors including Geoffrey Bayldon as the Crowman, Una Stubbs (Aunt Sally), Barbara Windsor (Saucy Nancy), Billy Connolly (Bogle McNeep), Bill Maynard (Sgt Beetroot), Joan Sims (Mrs Bloomsbury-Barton), Lorraine Chase (Dolly Clothes-Peg), Bernard Cribbins (Jolly Jack), Connie Booth (Aunt Sally II), David Lodge (the Strong Man) and Mike Reid (a fairground owner). The story featured Worzel Gummidge, a scarecrow who lived in Ten Acre Field, the creation of the Crowman, who often visited the nearby village of Scatterbrook. There, he befriends two children, brother and sister John and Sue Peters, who he involves in various scrapes. He has various heads, made of turnip, mangel-wurzel and swede, used when he had to perform various tasks. Worzel also had his own language, Worzelese, and various catchphrases including 'A cup o' tea an' a slice o' cake' and 'I'll be bum-swizzled'. His love interest was Aunt Sally, a vain fairground coconut-shy doll who considers Worzel too common for her although she regularly exploits him. Jon Pertwee released a single in 1980 called *Worzel's Song* which reached number thirty-three in the charts. The series came to an end in 1981 when Southern Television lost its franchise and TVS decided not to continue with the show. There were many attempts to revive in but it wasn't until Worzel found himself in New Zealand six years later, that it made a reappearance.

Worzel Gummidge Down Under (1987–1989) had Worzel following Aunt Sally to New Zealand after she is sold to a museum owner on the other side of the world. Worzel follows her by stowing away on an aeroplane avoiding the clutches of the evil Travelling Scarecrow Maker. The series again starred Jon Pertwee and Una Stubbs with a new cast including Bruce Phillips (The Crowman), Jonny Marks (Mickey), Olivia Ihimaera-Smiler (Manu), Wi Kuki Kaa (Travelling Scarecrow Maker) and Maria James (Eloise). The show ran for two series with a total of twenty-two episodes. The show was broadcast at 11.30 a.m. on Channel 4 on Sunday mornings and although it still had many of the ingredients or the original show, it never gained its popularity.

The Friday Film Special (1985–1989) was broadcast by the BBC and included, each week, a different movie, made by the Children's Film Foundation. Some of the movies shown included *Cry Wolf* (1968), *The Boy Who Turned Yellow* (1972), *Paganini Strikes Again* (1973), *One Hour to Zero* (1976), *Sky Pirates* (1976), *Fern the Red Deer* (1976), *The Glitterball* (1977), *A Hitch in Time* (1978), *Sammy's Super T-Shirt* (1978), *4-D Special Agent* (1981), *Tightrope to Terror* (1982) and *Haunters of The Deep* (1984).

Starting Out (1973–1992) was a series of programmes made for schools by ATV and Central. A total of fifty-six episodes were made and these were repeated until broadcasting ended in 1992. The programmes were aimed at older pupils who were ready to leave school and who would soon be looking for jobs and beginning life as adults. A new series was made every three years to keep the show up to date and relevant to new generations of students.

Break in the Sun (1981), was written by Bernard Ashley and was considered more gritty and controversial than the usual BBC children's dramas of the time. It starred Nicola Cowper as Patsy, a young girl who runs away from home to escape her violent stepfather played by Brian Hall, doing her best to return to Margate, her mother's old home. The show ran for six episodes and the theme, *Reflections,* was composed by John Renbourn.

You Should Be So Lucky (1986–1987) was a children's game show broadcast by the BBC which featured contestants playing on a giant snakes and ladders board. The show was hosted by Colin Bennett in character as Vince Purity. The series ran for twelve episodes.

Maggie (1981–82) starred Kirsty Miller as Maggie McKinley, a Glaswegian teenager who aspired to further education, a career and an independent life away from home. Her parents, played by Michael Sheard and Mary Riggans, had other ideas and wanted her to find secure employment before getting married and settling down. The two series followed Maggie's progress, including her boyfriends and disagreements with her parents, and ended with her having to make the decision whether to go to university or work within the family business. The memorable theme song was written and sung by B. A. Robertson.

Saturday Superstore (1982–87) was broadcast on Saturday mornings and was hosted by Mike Read, Sarah Greene, Keith Chegwin and John Craven. The new show was produced after its predecessor, *Multi-Coloured Swap Shop*, ended when Noel Edmonds left to present *The Late Late Breakfast Show*. *Search for a Superstar* was a regular part of the programme and featured a children's talent show. The winner in 1986 were Claire and Friends with their later chart hit *It's 'Orrible Being in Love (When You're 8½)*. The contest was won by Juvenile Jazz in 1987. The band included Nigel Ipinson, a later OMD and Stone Roses keyboardist. The programme included many celebrity guests including television and pop stars as well as the then Prime Minister, Margaret Thatcher. Other presenters of *Saturday Superstore* included Vicky Licorish (1985–87) and David Icke (1982–85).

Fraggle Rock (1983–87) was created by Jim Henson and featured Muppet-like creatures. It was jointly made by TVS (Television South) with the Canadian Broadcasting Corporation, US pay television service Home Box Office and Henson Associates. The show featured Fraggles, Doozers, Gorgs and Silly Creatures. The Fraggles and Doozers live in caves known as Fraggle Rock, which are filled with many different creatures and features which link to two different areas including the Land of the Gorgs and Outer Space where the 'silly creatures' (or humans) live. The show proved hugely popular worldwide and the colourful creatures also appeared in comics, books and a feature film.

Sesame Street (1969–present), an educational television show produced for children, was originally produced by the Children's Television Workshop, created by Joan Ganz Cooney and Lloyd Morrisett. The show combined live action, sketches, animation and puppetry featuring Jim Henson's Muppetts. Popular characters included Big Bird, Bert and Ernie, The Cookie Monster, Elmo, Grover, Oscar the Grouch, Count Von Count and Kermit the Frog. It has proved hugely successful since the late 1960s.

Byker Grove (1989–2006) first introduced Ant and Dec to the nation's television screens. The series revolved around a youth club in the Byker district of Newcastle upon Tyne. The show was aimed at teenagers and young adults and tackled many controversial subjects including as drug addiction, homelessness, teen pregnancy, homophobia, and abortion. As well as launching the careers of Anthony McPartlin (P.J.) and Declan Donnelly (Duncan), the show also introduced actress Jill Halfpenny, Donna Air, former CBBC presenter Andrew Hayden-Smith and Emmerdale actors Dale Meeks, Charlie Hardwick, Chelsea Halfpenny, Laura Norton and Victoria Hawkins. Ant and Dec, as PJ and Duncan, later released several singles during their time in the show including *Let's Get Ready to Rhumble*, *Better Watch Out* and *We're On The Ball*.

Animal Magic (1962–83) featured Johnny Morris as a zoo keeper at Bristol Zoo. The great attraction of the show was that Morris would do all the voices of the animals. His co-presenters over the years included Gerald Durrell, Tony Soper, Keith Shackleton, David Taylor and Terry Nutkins.

Crackerjack first appeared on television in 1955 and continued until 1984. The show was introduced by the phrase 'It's Friday, it's five o'clock. . . It's Crackerjack!'. It was hosted by Stu Francis from 1980 to 1984. The show consisted of games (with prizes), a comedy double act, music and a short comedy play at the end. The comedy act, Don and Pete (Don Maclean and Peter Glaze), are fondly remembered.

Other programmes for children shown during the decade included *Chock-A-Block* (1981) presented by Fred Harris and Carol Leader as part of the *See-Saw* series; *Finger Mouse* (1985) a spin-off of an earlier series *Fingerbobs* featuring a paper mouse; *Jonny Briggs* (1986–87) about a young boy and his dog Razzle as well as members of his eccentric family; *Jossy's Giants* (1986–87) a football drama featuring the fictional team the Glipton Grasshoppers and its manager, Joswell 'Jossy' Blair; *Record Breakers* (1972–2001) originally hosted by Roy Castle and Ross McWhirter; *Screen Test* (1970–84) a children's quiz show hosted by Michael Rodd, Brian Trueman and Mark Curry; *Simon and the Witch* (1987–88) starring Hugh Pollard, Elizabeth Spriggs and Joan Sims, about a boy who was friends with a witch; *Stig of the Dump* (1981) starring Keith Jayne as a caveman living in an old chalk pit; *Stoppit and Tidyup* (1988) a cartoon narrated by Terry Wogan; *Take Hart* (1977–83) a children's art show presented by Tony Hart; *Terrahawks* (1983–86) a science fiction puppet show created by Gerry Anderson; *The Amazing Adventures of Morph* (1980–81) featuring Tony Hart's playful Plasticine creation; *The Basil Brush Show* (1968–2007) featuring the mischievous fox with a host of celebrity guests; *The Children of Green Knowe* (1986) featuring the story of an old house and its former ghostly inhabitants; *The Flumps* (1977) featuring the adventures of a family of furry characters; *The Littlest Hobo* (1979–85), a Canadian series featuring a homeless roaming Alsatian called Hobo; *The Magic Roundabout* (1965–92), a children's favourite for many years featuring well-loved characters such as Dougal, Florence and Zebedee; *The Moomins* (1977–82), a Polish/Austrian puppet animation; *The Sooty Show* (1955–98) presented by Matthew Corbett and featuring hand puppets Sooty, Sweep and Soo; *Wide Awake Club* (1984–89), broadcast by TV-am and hosted by Timmy Mallett and Tommy Boyd and others; *Thomas the Tank Engine and Friends* (1984–present), the adventures of a series of characterful steam engines created by the Reverend Wilbert Awdry; *Wacaday* (1985–92), presented during the summer holidays by Timmy Mallett; *Why Don't You?* (1973–95), broadcast during the school holidays; *Wizbit* (1986–88), the story of an alien magician which starred Paul Daniels and Debbie McGee; *Wildtrack* (1980), a programme about the wildlife of Britain featuring Tony Soper and Su Ingle; *Shadow of the Stone* (1987), set in the west of Scotland and starring Shirley Henderson in a tale of witchcraft; *Knightmare* (1987–94), a computer-inspired adventure game show; *Monkey* (1978–80), a Japanese drama based on the sixteenth-century Chinese novel *Journey to the West* by Wu Cheng'en; and *The Wind in the Willows* (1983–90), based on the children's novel by Kenneth Grahame.

Favourite cartoons of the decade included *Battle of the Planets*, an American adaptation of the Japanese anime series *Science Ninja Team Gatchaman*; *King Rollo* (1980) narrated by Ray Brooks; *The Smurfs* (1981–89) originally a Belgian comic franchise; *Ulysses 31* (1981) a French-Japanese animated television series; *Danger Mouse* (1981–92) featuring the voices of David Jason and Terry Scott, *Dogtanian and The Three Muskehounds* (1981), *The Snowman* (1982), *The Mysterious Cities of Gold* (1982–83) a Japanese cartoon set in 1532, featuring a Spanish orphan named Esteban; *Bananaman* (1983–86) featuring the voices of Graeme Garden, Bill Oddie and Tim Brooke-Taylor, *He-Man and the Masters of the Universe* (1983–85), *Henry's Cat* (1983–85) directed by Bob Godfrey and featuring Henry's Cat, Chris Rabbit, Mosey Mouse, Douglas Dog, Sammy Snail, Pansy Pig and Denise Duck; *The Adventures of Teddy Ruxpin* (1987–88) an animated television series featuring an animatronic teddy bear; *Inspector Gadget* (1983–86), *Super Ted* (1983–86) including the voices of Derek Griffiths, Jon Pertwee and Melvyn Hayes; *James the Cat* (1984), *Rainbow Brite* (1984–86), *MASK* (1985), *The Jetsons* (1985–87), *Jem and the Holograms* (1985–88), *ThunderCats* (1985–89), *She Ra: Princess of Power* (1985–87), *The Jimbo and the Jet-Set* (1986–87), *My Little Pony 'n Friends* (1986–87), *Real Ghostbusters* (1986–91), *Duck Tales* (1987–90), *Willo the Wisp* (1981–87) with the voice of Kenneth Williams,

Transformers (1984–87), an American animated series featuring robot superheroes; *Chip 'n Dale Rescue Rangers* (1988–90) and *The Simpsons* (1989–present) featuring Homer, Marge, Bart and Lisa.

For small children, shows included *Rainbow* featuring Geoffrey Hayes with George (Roy Skelton), Bungle (Stanley Bates) and Zippy (Peter Hawkins), *Play School* (1964–88), *Jackanory* (1965–96), *Button Moon* (1980–88), *Let's Pretend* (1982), *Munch Bunch* (1980–82), *Noggin the Nog* (1959–80), *Pigeon Street* (1981) featuring the voice of George Layton, *Play Away* (1974–81) presented by Brian Cant, Toni Arthur, Derek Griffiths, Floella Benjamin and Johnny Ball, and *Puddle Lane* (1985–89).

Detective shows included *Shoestring* (1979–80) starring Trevor Eve as a hapless private detective working as a presenter for Bristol's Radio West; *Bergerac* (1981–91) starring John Nettles as a Jersey-based detective sergeant recovering from alcoholism; *The Gentle Touch* (1980–84) starring Jill Gascoine as Detective Inspector Maggie Forbes who was based at the Seven Dials police station in London; *Dempsey and Makepeace* (1985–86) starring Glynis Barber and Michael Brandon; *Juliet Bravo* (1980–85) originally starring Stephanie Turner and later followed by Anna Carteret; and *The Bill* (1983–2010) set in the fictional Sun Hill police station and featuring a host of household names including Christopher Ellison, Mark Wingett, Eric Richard, Kevin Lloyd and Trudie Goodwin.

In 1977, ITV first broadcast *The Professionals* (1977–83) which starred Martin Shaw, Lewis Collins and Gordon Jackson as agents working for the fictional CI5. The stars had already found fame in other programmes. Gordon Jackson was known for his role as Hudson in the popular *Upstairs, Downstairs* (1971–75), Lewis Collins had appeared as Gavin in the comedy *The Cuckoo Waltz* (1975–80) (which also starred Diane Keen and David Roper) and Martin Shaw had had parts in *Doctor in the House* (1969–70), *Coronation Street* and *The New Avengers* (1976–77), with his future co-star Lewis Collins. *The Professionals* was seen as competition to the BBC's hugely popular show *Starsky and Hutch*.

It shared the realism of *The Sweeney* and famously featured Ford Capris as well as other classic 1970s cars including a Ford Granada (Cowley's car), a Ford Escort RS2000 (driven by Doyle) as well as a Rover SD1, a Rover P6, a Princess, a Triumph 2000, a Triumph Dolomite Sprint and a Triumph TR7. The series was criticised for its level of violence, which included shootings and martial arts. Moral crusader Mary Whitehouse called the show both racist and sexist. It ended in 1983 and ITV replaced it with *Dempsey and Makepeace*. The show was remade starring Edward Woodward in the role of Cowley but it wasn't successful.

Shows which had been broadcast for many years previously continued to be aired including *Come Dancing* (1949–98); *The Good Old Days* (1953–83); *This Week* (1956–92); *The Sky at Night* (1957–present), originally presented by Patrick Moore; and, for sports fans, *Grandstand* (1958–2007) with Frank Bough, *Match of the Day* (1964–present) and *World of Sport* (1965–85), with wrestling and football results, hosted by Dickie Davies. Wrestling on television was very popular during the decade and featured on *World of Sport* on every Saturday afternoon at 4pm until the show's demise in 1985. Popular wrestlers of the day included Giant Haystacks, Big Daddy, Catweazle, Pat Roach, Jackie Pallo, Kendo Nagasaki and Mick McManus. The football results always followed the wrestling, a time when all dads carefully checked their pools coupons in the hope that the results would make them rich.

Soaps included *Coronation Street* (1963–present); *EastEnders* (1985–present); *Emmerdale* (1972–present); *Crossroads* (1964–88) complete with Noele Gordon and wobbly sets; *Albion Market* (1985–86); *Triangle* (1981–83) starring Kate O'Mara, Larry Lamb and Michael Craig; *Brookside* (1982–2003) featuring life in a Liverpool cul-de-sac; *Howard's Way* (1985–90); and *Take the High Road* (1980–2003).

EastEnders was introduced in 1985 as a rival to ITV's very popular soap, *Coronation Street*. It introduced to the viewing public a whole range of memorable characters including 'Dirty Den' Watts (Leslie Grantham), his alcoholic wife, Angie (Anita Dobson), 'Nasty Nick' Cotton as well as Dr Legg, Pauline and Arthur Fowler, Lou Beale, Ethel Skinner (complete with her pug, Willy), Pete and Kathy Beale. The youth element of the show was provided by Ian Beale, Mark Fowler, Sharon Watts and Michelle Fowler. Lofty Holloway was introduced soon after that. The show even had its own punk, Mary Smith, complete with daughter, Annie. The show became a huge success and, today, is one of Britain's most popular soaps.

Albion Market was a short-lived soap produced by ITV and although it was expected to do as well as *Coronation Street,* it suffered in the ratings and was soon cancelled. Stories revolved around the Salford-based market but the dull stories and uninteresting characters didn't grip people's interest. *EastEnders*, which was first broadcast in the same year, attracted a far larger audience and *Albion Market* couldn't compete with the BBC's schedule of programmes, especially the ever-popular *Open All Hours* which was broadcast at the same time.

Crossroads was an incredibly popular soap of its time and watched by millions of viewers. The staggered acting, characters forgetting their lines, wobbly sets and overhead microphones appearing in shot, all failed to put viewers off.

Comedies included *It Ain't Half Hot, Mum* (1974–81) starring Windsor Davies and Melvyn Hayes; *Butterflies* (1978–83) with Wendy Craig and Geoffrey Palmer, *Hi-de-Hi* (1980–88) with Paul Shane and Su Pollard; *To the Manor Born* (1979–2007) featuring Penelope Keith and Peter Bowles; *The Two Ronnies* (1971–87) featuring Ronnie Barker and Ronnie Corbett in a series of sketches; *The Goodies* (1970–82) with Graeme Garden, Tim Brooke-Taylor and Bill Oddie; and *'Allo 'Allo* (1982–92) starring Gorden Kaye and Carmen Silvera.

It Ain't Half Hot, Mum had been shown since the early 1970s and continued to be broadcast until the beginning of the 1980s. Windsor Davies appeared as Battery Sergeant Major Tudor Bryn Williams, reluctantly in charge of a Royal Artillery concert party. The show was set in Deolali in India, towards the end of the Second World War. The main characters included Gunner 'Lofty' Sugden, (played by Don Estelle) a very short soldier with a memorable singing voice; Gunner 'Parky' Parkins (Christopher Mitchell) , an eager young recruit; Gunner 'La-de-dah' Graham (John Clegg), an Oxbridge graduate who plays the piano; Gunner 'Atlas' Mackintosh (Stuart McGugan), a very strong short-tempered Scotsman; Gunner 'Nobby' Clark (Kenneth MacDonald), who performs bird calls and does a whistling act; and Gunner 'Nosher' Evans (Mike Kinsey), who does a paper-tearing act; Bombardier 'Solly' Solomons (George Layton), a Londoner, who is a former theatrical agent; and Gunner 'Gloria' Beaumont (Melvyn Hayes), who plays the part of women in the act as there are no female soldiers assigned to the concert party. Michael Bates played Indian bearer Rangi Ram. The show today is seen as racist and homophobic and although it attracted millions of viewers, it suffered the same fate as the Benny Hill Show and nowadays is never repeated in the UK.

Butterflies starred Wendy Craig as Ria Parkinson, a frustrated housewife, who lived a middle-class life with her husband Ben (Geoffrey Palmer), a dentist, and her two sons, Adam and Russell, played by Nicholas Lyndhurst and Andrew Hall. The Carla Lane comedy was hugely successful and Lane followed it up with *Bread* (1986–91) featuring the lives of the Boswell family and starring Jean Boht, Peter Howitt, Nick Conway, Victor McGuire, Jonathon Morris and Gilly Coman.

One of the best-loved comedies of the 1980s featured Maplins Holiday Camp and its various entertainers. *Hi-de-Hi!* was loosely based on the lives of Redcoats working at Butlin's. Jimmy Perry, one of the writers, became a Redcoat at Butlin's in Filey and Pwllheli after being demobilised from the Army and he drew from his experiences to write the comedy. The show had many memorable characters including entertainment manager Professor Jeffrey Fairbrother (Simon Cadell), camp host Ted Bovis (Paul Shane);

chief Yellowcoat/sports organiser/Radio Maplin announcer Gladys Pugh (Ruth Madoc); camp comic Spike Dixon (Jeffrey Holland); chalet maid/ aspiring Yellowcoat Peggy Ollerenshaw (Su Pollard); riding instructor Fred Quilley (Felix Bowness); dancing instructress Yvonne Stuart-Hargreaves (Diane Holland); dancing instructor Barry Stuart-Hargreaves (Barry Howard); children's entertainer William Partridge (Leslie Dwyer) and Sylvia Garnsey (Nikki Kelly). Squadron Leader, the Honourable Clive Dempster DFC (David Griffin) became the entertainment manager in series six to nine of the show.

Other well-loved comedies of the decade included *Blackadder* (1983–89) starring Rowan Atkinson and Tony Robinson; *The Young Ones* (1982–84) featuring Adrian Edmondson, Rik Mayall, Nigel Planer, Christopher Ryan and Alexei Sayle; *Yes, Minister* (1980–82) with Paul Eddington, Nigel Hawthorne and Derek Fowlds; *Spitting Image* (1984–96) featuring the voices of Chris Barrie, Harry Enfield, John Sessions and Steve Coogan; *Game for a Laugh* (1981–85) a practical joke show presented by Jeremy Beadle, Henry Kelly, Matthew Kelly and Sarah Kennedy; *Citizen Smith* (1977–80) starring Robert Lindsay as Wolfie Smith, the leader of the Tooting Popular Front; *Give Us A Break* (1983–84) again starring Robert Lindsay and Paul McGann as a talented snooker player; *Only Fools and Horses* (1981–2003) with David Jason and Nicholas Lyndhurst.

Only Fools and Horses went on to become one of the UK's all-time favourite comedies. The show was written and created by John Sullivan and featured as the main characters market trader Derek 'Del Boy' Trotter (David Jason); his younger brother Rodney Trotter (Nicholas Lyndhurst); and their elderly grandad (Lennard Pearce) living in a flat in Nelson Mandela House, Peckham. When Lennard Pearce died, another character was introduced, Uncle Albert (played by Buster Merryfield). The show regularly drew in audiences of over 20 million. Other characters featured in the show included road sweeper Trigger (Roger Lloyd-Pack); used car salesman Boycie (John Challis); *The Nag's Head* landlord Mike Fisher (Kenneth MacDonald); lorry driver Denzil (Paul Barber); spiv Mickey Pearce (Patrick Murray); and Boycie's wife Marlene (Sue Holderness). Later shows featured Del and Rodney's better halves, Raquel (Tessa Peake-Jones) and Cassandra (Gwyneth Strong). Memorable episodes include 'Yuppy Love' which features a scene where Del Boy is talking to Trigger and falls through an open bar; and 'A Touch of Glass' where Del, Rodney and Grandad are employed to clean chandeliers in a stately home and ultimately end up smashing one before fleeing the scene. John Sullivan had previously created and written the tremendously popular *Citizen Smith*.

There were many more well-loved television comedy shows broadcast during the decade including *Sorry!* (1981–88) starring Ronnie Corbett as mummy's boy Timothy Lumsden; *Executive Stress* (1986–88) with Penelope Keith and Geoffrey Palmer; *The Two of Us* (1986–90) starring Nicholas Lyndhurst and Janet Dibley; *The Gaffer* (1981–83) starring Bill Maynard and Russell Hunter about a small business owner; *Home to Roost* (1985–90) with John Thaw and Reece Dinsdale as a reunited father and son; *Home James!* (1987–90) starring Jim Davidson who works as a chauffeur for businessman Robert Palmer played by George Sewell; *Up the Elephant and Round the Castle* (1983–85) starring Jim Davidson as lovable rogue Jim London; *Duty Free* (1984–86) a comedy set in Spain featuring Keith Barron, Gwen Taylor and Joanna Van Gyseghem; *All in Good Faith* (1985–88) starring Richard Briers as the Reverend Philip Lambe; *Shelley* (1972–92) with Hywel Bennett as a hapless layabout; *The Kenny Everett Video Show* (1978–81) featuring music and sketches including characters such as Sid Snot and Brother Lee Love; *Brass* (1983–90) starring Timothy West and Caroline Blakiston the story of two feuding families, the wealthy Hardacres and the working-class Fairchilds; *Watching* (1987–93) starring Paul Bown and Emma Wray as a mismatched couple; *Kinvig* (1981) starring Tony Haygarth as an electrical repair shop owner visited by an extra-terrestrial (Prunella Gee); *A Fine Romance* (1981–84) a story of an awkward romance, starring Judi Dench and Michael Williams; *The New Statesman* (1987–92) starring Rik Mayall as MP Alan B'Stard; *Copy Cats* (1985–87) a comedy impressions sketch programme featuring Bobby Davro, Gary Wilmot, Jessica Martin and others; *Tripper's Day* (1984) starring Leonard Rossiter as Norman Tripper, a supermarket manager; *Hallelujah* (1983–84) set in a Salvation Army citadel with Thora Hird and Patsy Rowlands; *Me and My Girl* (1984–88) with Richard O'Sullivan and Joanna Ridly playing father and daughter; *That's My Boy* (1981–86) with Mollie Sugden, Christopher Blake and Jennifer Lonsdale; *Beadle's About* (1986–96) with practical joker, Jeremy Beadle; *Russ Abbot's Madhouse* (1980–85) mayhem from Russ Abbot, Michael Barrymore, Susie Blake, Les Dennis, Bella Emberg and Dustin Gee; *Never the Twain* (1981–91) starring Windsor Davies and Donald Sinden as rival antique dealers; *Keep it in the Family* (1980–83) with Robert Gillespie and Pauline Yates; *Fresh Fields* (1984–86) starring Julie McKenzie and Anton Rodgers; *French Fields* (1989–91) again starring Julie McKenzie and Anton Rodgers but set abroad; *The Secret Diary of Adrian Mole* (1985) about a teenager's troubled life starring Gian Sammarco, Stephen Moore and Julie Walters; *A Bit of a Do* (1989) starring David Jason and Gwen Taylor; *Wood and Walters* (1981–82) comedy sketches featuring Victoria Wood and Julie Walters; *The Dick Emery Show* (1963–81) madcap comedy with Dick Emery; *Lame Ducks* (1984) starring John Duttine, Lorraine Chase and Brian Murphy about a group who decide to live away from everyday society; *Are You Being Served?* (1972–85) featuring the staff of Grace Brothers and starring John Inman, Wendy Richard and Mollie Sugden; *Brush Strokes* (1986–91) starring Karl Howman as an amorous wisecracking house painter; *Dear John* (1986–87) starring Ralph Bates, Belinda Lang, Peter Denyer and Peter Blake as a group of single people looking for love; *French and Saunders* (1987–2007) madcap comedy from Dawn French and Jennifer Saunders; *Hale and Pace* (1988–98) with comedians Gareth Hale and Norman Pace, famous for the sketch, 'The Two Rons'; *Last of the Summer Wine* (1973–2010) featuring retired codgers Foggy, Compo and Clegg; *The Mike Yarwood Show* (1982–87), *Naked Video* (1986–91) sketches including Gregor Fisher, Andy Gray, Helen Lederer, Tony Roper and Elaine C. Smith; *Not the Nine O'Clock News* (1979–82) comedy sketches featuring Rowan Atkinson, Pamela Stephenson, Mel Smith, and Griff Rhys Jones; *Open All Hours* (1973–85) featuring stuttering shopkeeper Arkwright (Ronnie Barker) and his nephew and assistant Granville (David Jason); *Red Dwarf* (1988–present) intergalactic fun with Craig Charles (Dave Lister), Chris Barrie (Arnold Rimmer), Danny John-Jules (Cat), Norman Lovett and later Hattie Hayridge (Holly) and Robert Llewellyn (the mechanoid Kryten); *Alas Smith and Jones* (1989–98) starring Mel Smith and Griff Rhys Jones; *Terry and June* (1979–87) featuring the ups and downs of a middle-class couple starring Terry Scott and June Whitfield; *The Benny Hill Show* (1955–89) with sketches and mayhem featuring Benny Hill; *The Comic Strip Presents* (1982–2000) featuring Adrian Edmondson, Dawn French, Rik Mayall, Nigel Planer, Peter Richardson and Jennifer Saunders; *The Laughter Show* (1984–86) a comedy sketch show featuring Dustin Gee and Les Dennis; *The Les Dawson Show* (1978–89) starring Les Dawson and featuring comedy sketches, stand-up comedy as well as guest appearances, dance numbers and musical performance; *The Paul Hogan Show* (1973–84) comedy routines from the Australian performer, originally broadcast on Channel 4; *The Two Ronnies* (1971–87) comedy sketches featuring Ronnie Barker and Ronnie Corbett; *Three of a Kind* (1981–83) starring Lenny Henry, Tracey Ullman and David Copperfield; *To the Manor Born* (1979–2007) starring Penelope Keith and Peter Bowles; *You Rang M'Lord?* (1988–93) featuring Paul Shane, Jeffrey Holland and Su Pollard; *Saturday Live* (1985–88) transmitted live, it made stars of made stars of Ben Elton, Harry Enfield, Stephen Fry and Hugh Laurie and included appearances by Patrick Marber, Morwenna Banks, Chris Barrie, Emo Philips, Tracey Ullman, Craig Ferguson, Craig Charles and many others.

Dramas included *Play For Today* (1970–84); *The Beiderbecke Trilogy* (1984–88) a comedy drama starring James Bolam and Barbara Flynn; *The Tripods* (1984–85) a sci-fi drama written by John Christopher; *The Monocled Mutineer* (1986) starring Paul McGann as a First World War deserter; *Tales of the Unexpected* (1979–88) mysterious stories feature a cast of famous names including Joan Collins, Susan George, John Gielgud, Derek Jacobi and many others and *London's Burning* (1986–2002) a series about firefighting starring James Hazeldine, Glen Murphy and James Marcus.

Brideshead Revisited (1981) was the big hit of 1981 and featured many well-known actors of the time including Laurence Olivier, John Gielgud, Claire Bloom, Jeremy Irons, Anthony Andrews, Diana Quick, Jane Asher and Nikolas Grace. The epic, written by Evelyn Waugh, told the story covering more than twenty years starting in the 1920s and featuring the life and romances of the protagonist Charles Ryder (Jeremy Irons), and his involvement with the Flyte family, well-off English Catholics whose dwelling is a palatial mansion called Brideshead Castle. Ryder has affairs with two members of the Flyte family – Sebastian (Anthony Andrews) and Julia (Diana Quick). The eleven-episode serial proved incredibly popular and ended with Charles returning to Brideshead towards the end of the Second World War.

The Onedin Line ran from 1971 to 1980. It was set in Liverpool starting in 1860 and revolved around a shipping owner, James Onedin, played by Peter Gilmore and his ongoing struggles with the business and his family. Memorable characters included Captain William Baines (Howard Lang), Anne Webster/Onedin (Anne Stallybrass), Elizabeth Onedin/Frazer/Fogarty (Jessica Benton) and Daniel Fogarty (Michael Billington). The show became unmissable Sunday night entertainment and featured memorable theme music, the Adagio *of* Spartacus *and Phrygia* by Khachaturian. Many of the outdoor scenes were filmed in the picturesque town of Dartmouth in Devon.

One of the BBC's most popular dramas was *All Creatures Great and Small* which told the story of a vet and his adventures assisting in a practice in Yorkshire. The series was based on the popular books written by James Herriot and featured Christopher Timothy as the lead character, at the time Timothy was better known for his appearances on television adverts promoting *The Sun* newspaper. Also appearing in the show was Robert Hardy as the abrasive Siegfried Farnon, Peter Davison as Siegfried's younger brother, Tristan and Carol Drinkwater as Helen Herriot. The show ran throughout the 1980s and was hugely successful continuing until 1990.

Dennis Waterman, star of *Minder*, with his wife, Rula Lenska. *Minder* ran between 1979 and 1994 and starred Waterman as Terry McCann, who was employed as a bodyguard to the unscrupulous businessman Arthur Daley, played by George Cole.

Minder (1979–94) starred Dennis Waterman as Terry McCann who was employed as a bodyguard to the unscrupulous businessman, Arthur Daley. The show involved dodgy dealings and much fighting, with Waterman's character usually coming off the worst. The programme was very successful.

Other dramas included *Lovejoy* (1986–94) antiques shenanigans with Ian McShane, Dudley Sutton, Chris Jury and Phyllis Logan; *Porterhouse Blue* (1987) starring David Jason and Ian Richardson; *Rumpole of the Bailey* (1975–92) court-based drama with Leo McKern; *Sapphire and Steel* (1972–82) a sci-fi series starring David McCallum and Joanna Lumley; *Tenko* (1981–84) a Japanese prisoner of war drama starring Ann Bell, Stephanie Cole, Stephanie Beacham, Louise Jameson, Claire Oberman, Jean Anderson and Burt Kwouk; *The Thorn Birds* (1983) set in Australia and starring Richard Chamberlain, Rachel Ward, Barbara Stanwyck, Christopher Plummer and Jean Simmons; *Taggart* (1983–2010) a Scottish detective drama starring Mark McManus, Neil Duncan and Blythe Duff; *Robin of Sherwood* (1984–86) featuring Michael Praed, Jason Connery, Judi Trott and Nickolas Grace; *Death of a Princess* (1980) starring Sawsan Badr, Paul Freeman and Judy Parfitt about the execution of a Saudi Arabian princess; and *Annika* (1984) starring Jesse Birdsall and Christina Rignér about an Isle of Wight deckchair attendant who falls in love with a Swedish student.

TV game shows were hugely popular during the decade. They offered a range of prizes including cash, cars and white goods. Some offered better prizes than others. Many on *Mr and Mrs* won a carriage clock and in the case of *Bullseye*, broadcast from Birmingham, one of the top prizes was a speedboat. The shows were incredibly well-watched and pulled in millions of viewers.

The Sale of the Century ran from 1971 until 1983 and was hosted by Nicholas Parsons. It was described as the 'quiz of the week' and people tuned in to watch three contestants answer questions to compete for a range of prizes. The show was made originally just to be shown on Anglia Television but it gained nationwide coverage and became one of the most popular programmes on television.

The Generation Game (1971–2002) was unmissable Saturday night entertainment and is well-remembered for the prizes on the conveyor belt at the end including such exotic gifts as teasmades and carriage clocks. Bruce Forsyth hosted the show between 1971 and 1977. Larry Grayson took over in 1978, and kept much of the show's appeal and stayed as presenter until 1981.

There was also *Mastermind* (1972–present) originally presented by Magnus Magnusson; *Top of the World* (1982) hosted by Eamonn Andrews; *We Love TV* (1984–86) presented by Gloria Hunniford; *The Wall Game* (1985) hosted by Helen Bennett; and *Blankety Blank* (1979–2016) hosted by Terry Wogan and then Les Dawson.

Blankety Blank was first introduced to audiences on 18 January 1979. It was initially hosted by Terry Wogan and included a panel on celebrities who completed sentences with what they thought would be the most popular answer. Regular panel members included Kenny Everett, Lorraine Chase, Gareth Hunt, Gary Davies, and Cheryl Baker. It was a hit with the viewing public and continued until 1990 with a variety of hosts including Les Dawson and Lily Savage.

Other game shows included *Tarby's Frame Game* (1987–89) presented by Jimmy Tarbuck; *Through the Keyhole* (1987–95) with David Frost and Loyd Grossman; *Wheel of Fortune* (1988–2001) hosted by Nicky Campbell with Carol Smillie; *Fifteen to One* (1988–2003) presented by William G Stewart; Hitman (1989) with Nick Owen; *Whose Line is it, Anyway* (1988–99) presented by Clive Anderson; *You Bet!* (1988) originally hosted by Bruce Forsyth; *Going for Gold* (1987–96) with Henry Kelly; *Countdown* (1982–present), initially presented by Richard Whiteley; *Catchphrase* (1986–present) with Roy Walker; *Give Us a Clue* (1979–92) presented by Michael Aspel and then Michael Parkinson; *Mr and Mrs* (1965–99) originally hosted by Alan Taylor and Derek Batey; *Play Your Cards Right* (1980–2003) hosted by Bruce Forsyth; *The Krypton Factor* (1977–95) hosted by Gordon Burns; *The Price is Right* (1984–2007) with Leslie Crowther; *Bullseye* (1981–2006) with Jim Bowen; *Winner Takes All* (1975–86) first hosted by Jimmy Tarbuck and then Geoffrey Wheeler; *3–2–1* (1978–88) with Ted Rogers.

Family Fortunes was first broadcast in 1980 and continues to be popular today. When it was first shown, it was hosted by Bob Monkhouse. Max Bygraves took over as presenter in 1983 and stayed with the show until 1985.

In 1987, Les Dennis hosted the show and appeared regularly on the programme for the following fifteen years. There were many more game shows on TV.

Daytime shows included *Pebble Mill At One* (1972–86), *Crown Court* (1972–84), *Breakfast Time* (1983–89), *Good Morning Britain* (1983–92), *Kilroy* (1986–2004) and *This Morning* (1988–present).

Pebble Mill at One was broadcast on week days at 1 p.m., transmitted live from the BBC studios at Birmingham. The show was a mixture of live interviews, cookery, music segments and pre-recorded items. Regular presenters included Jan Leeming, Donny MacLeod, Fern Britton, Marian Foster and Bob Langley as well, later, Magnus Magnusson, Alan Titchmarsh, Judi Spiers, and Paul Coia. Editors for the show included Terry Dobson, Jim Dumighan, and Peter Hercombe. The show was axed in 1986 but a similar show, *Daytime Live,* was broadcast in 1987.

In 1977, the Independent Broadcasting Authority had a nine-week trial run of breakfast television programmes, which was shown on Yorkshire Television only. The shows proved so popular that a franchise was issued, which was eventually awarded to TV-am. Due to launch delays with ITV, the BBC was able to launch its own early morning show first. The BBC's *Breakfast Time* began on 17 January 1983 with TV-am's *Good Morning Britain* being first broadcast on 1 February 1983. The BBC show proved more popular at first with its less formal, more relaxed format. The main presenters of the BBC show included Frank Bough, Selina Scott and Nick Ross. Regular guest appearances were made by Russell Grant, presenting an astrology spot, and Diana Moran (the Green Goddess) hosting the keep fit section. Weather reports came from Francis Wilson and Michael Fish, Bill Giles and Ian McCaskill stood in for him whenever he was away. Debbie Rix was the regular newsreader. The show proved hugely popular.

TV-am was originally spearheaded by Michael Parkinson, David Frost (1983–92), Angela Rippon (1983), Anna Ford (1983) and Robert Kee. During April 1983, Nick Owen and Anne Diamond made their first appearances on the show as did Roland Rat. By May 1983, a new look TV-am was launched with Wincey Willis becoming the new weather presenter (taking over from Commander David Philpott) and a host of new segments were broadcast including *History of Today* with Jeremy Beadle, an exercise section with Mad Lizzie, a cooking spot with a retired vicar called 'The Cooking Canon' (Rustie Lee later took over the segment) and news from the fishing correspondent, George Vella, referred to as 'The Codfather'. Newspaper bingo numbers were read out by Nick Owen with Lynda Berry (and later Anne Diamond).

Factual shows broadcast during the 1980s included *Tomorrow's World* (1965–2003) hosted by Michael Rodd, Judith Hann, Kieran Prendiville, Su

Ingle and many others; *The Sky at Night* (1957–present) with Patrick Moore; *Antiques Roadshow* (1972–present) presented by Arthur Negus and Hugh Scully; *Arthur C. Clarke's Mysterious World* (1980); *Arthur C Clarke's World of Strange Powers* (1985) both featuring stories of strange phenomenon; *Comic Roots* (1982–83) featuring the lives of various comedian and including Roy Hudd, Paul Shane, Alexei Sayle and Kenneth Williams; *Countryfile* (1988–present) originally presented by Anne Brown and Chris Baines with John Craven; *Eureka* (1982–86) an educational show presented by Jeremy Beadle, Sarah Greene, Paul McDowell and Wilf Lunn; *Fax* (1986–88) a show answering viewers questions which was presented by Bill Oddie, Wendy Leavesley, Debbie Rix and Billy Butler; *Film* (1971–present) featuring the latest movies and hosted by Barry Norman; *Gardeners' World* (1968–present) presented during the decade by Geoff Hamilton (1979–1996) and Geoffrey Smith (1980–1982); *The Money Programme* (1966–2010) a finance and business affairs television programme broadcast on BBC2; *One Man and his Dog* (1976–present) featuring sheepdog trials and originally presented by Phil Drabble; *Right to Reply* 1982–2001) broadcast by Channel 4 and voicing viewers concerns, notably hosted by Gus Macdonald; *Rough Justice* (1982–2007) a BBC show investigating alleged miscarriages of justice; *See Hear* (1981–present) a monthly magazine programme for deaf and hard-of-hearing; *Timewatch* (1982–present) featuring documentaries on historical subjects; and *Tomorrow's World's* William Woollard. The motoring show *Top Gear* (1977–present) was originally presented by Angela Rippon followed Noel Edmonds (1979–80), Frank Page (1980–88), Sue Baker (1980–91), Tom Boswell (1981–90), William Woollard (1981–91), Chris Goffey (1981–97) and Tony Mason (1986–2000).

Talent shows included *New Faces* (1973–88), presented by Marti Caine, and *Bob Says Opportunity Knocks* (1987–89) hosted by Bob Monkhouse. *New Faces* had originally been broadcast between 1973 and 1978 when it was first presented by Leslie Crowther before being hosted by Derek Hobson. The acts were judged by a panel of celebrity judges which included Tony Hatch, Mickie Most, Clifford Davis, Arthur Askey, Ted Ray and many others. The show was re-booted in 1986 and continued until 1988. The original show produced many household names including Lenny Henry, Marti Caine, Roger de Courcey and Patti Boulaye. However, the re-booted show produced few well-remembered names, the most successful winner being Joe Pasquale. Other well-known contestants over the years included Michael Barrymore, Roy Walker, The Chuckle Brothers, Victoria Wood, Mick Miller, Les Dennis, Showaddywaddy and Gary Wilmot. *Opportunity Knocks* had originally been hosted by Hughie Green between 1949 and 1978. It started on the radio before being transferred to television. The show was hugely popular and had an audience of many millions. It discovered many stars including Paul Daniels, Little and Large, Roy 'Chubby' Brown, Lena Zavaroni, Max Boyce, Pam Ayres and many others. The show was re-booted in 1987 and presented by Bob Monkhouse and broadcast live on Saturday evenings. The winner was decided by viewers who voted for their favourite act by telephone. The show was taken over by Les Dawson in 1990 who, himself, had been a winning contestant during the Hughie Green years

Fashion shows during the decade included *The Clothes Show* (1986–2000) which was originally presented by Selina Scott and designer Jeff Banks and later, Caryn Franklin.

Charity shows included *Children in Need* (1980–present) and *Comic Relief* (*Red Nose Day*) (1988–present).

Band Aid was the idea of Bob Geldof and Midge Ure and brought together pop acts of the day to raise money to help the effort to fight the famine in Ethiopia. *Do They Know It's Christmas?* was recorded at Sarm West Studios in Notting Hill, London on 25 November 1984 and was released the following week. Artists who took part in the recording included U2,

Live Aid at the JFK Stadium in Philadelphia. The benefit concert took place on Saturday 13 July 1985 when over 100,000 people attended.

Status Quo, Spandau Ballet, The Boomtown Rats, Duran Duran, Ultravox, Bananarama, Heaven 17, Kool and the Gang, Paul Weller, Boy George, Sting, Phil Collins, Marilyn, George Michael and Jody Watley. The record went to number one and stayed there for five weeks, selling over 3 million copies. The success of the record led to *Live Aid,* a benefit concert, which took place on Saturday 13 July 1985. It was held simultaneously at Wembley Stadium in London, where 72,000 people attended, and at John F. Kennedy Stadium in Philadelphia, where 100,000 people attended. More than seventy-five acts took part including Elton John, Queen, Madonna, Santana, Run DMC, Sade, Sting, Bryan Adams, the Beach Boys, Mick Jagger, David Bowie, Queen, Duran Duran, U2, The Who, Tom Petty, Neil Young, and Eric Clapton. Prince Charles and Princess Diana opened the event. The live event was broadcast all around the world by satellite and was watched by an incredible 1 billion viewers in 110 different countries. The most memorable performance of the concert came from Queen. Freddie Mercury stole the show performing for 20 minutes going from *Bohemian Rhapsody* to *We Will Rock You* and finishing with *We Are the Champions.* The show was a huge success and raised many millions to help the famine in Ethiopia.

Children in Need (1980–present), broadcast annually by the BBC, raises money for disadvantaged children and young people in the UK. The original show was broadcast in 1980 and raised £1 million in the first year. The programme was presented by Terry Wogan, Sue Lawley and Esther Rantzen and included many regional segments as the whole of the UK took part in fund-raising activities. The show also contained celebrity appearances, music and sketches. The show's mascot, Pudsey Bear, was created by BBC graphic designer Joanna Lane in 1985. Other presenters of the show during the decade included Gloria Hunniford, Sue Cook and Joanna Lumley.

Comic Relief (Red Nose Day) (1988–present) was started by Richard Curtis and Lenny Henry in response to the famine in Ethiopia. The First Red Nose Day on television was held on Friday 5 February 1988 and raised a total of £15 million. Plastic red noses were sold to raise money for the campaign. Over 150 celebrities and comedians participated in the first programme in which Lenny Henry travelled to Ethiopia. The show attracted 30 million viewers.

Australian soaps included *Neighbours, Home and Away, Prisoner (Cell Block H), Sons and Daughters, The Flying Doctors* and *The Sullivans. Neighbours* first hit British screens on 27 October 1986. The show proved more popular in the UK than it did in Australia. The programme initially appeared as part of BBC's revamped daytime programming and was broadcast twice a day, in the morning and repeated at lunchtime. Then the daughter of Michael Grade, the current controller of the BBC, suggested that the programme should be moved to the 5.35 p.m. spot because she and her friends were missing it due to being at school. He obliged and the show began running in the new slot in January 1988. The decision proved hugely popular and audiences rose greatly reaching over 21 million by 1990. The series introduced Jason Donovan and Kylie Minogue, who played Scott Robinson and Charlene Mitchell respectively, to Great Britain. The wedding of Scott and Charlene drew in an audience of 19.6 million viewers in the UK.

Popular American series included *Dynasty* (1981–89) with John Forsythe, Linda Evans and Joan Collins; *The A-Team* (1983–87) with George Peppard, Dirk Benedict, Dwight Schultz and Mr. T as four ex-members of a United States Army Special Forces Unit; *Cheers* (1982–93) a comedy set in a bar in Boston starring Ted Danson; *Fame* (1982–87) featuring students at the fictional New York City High School for the Performing Arts featuring Debbie Allen and Lori Singer; *ALF* (1986–90) a sitcom about a sarcastic extra-terrestrial who lives with the Tanner family; *LA Law* (1986–94); *The Wonder Years* (1988–93) a coming of age story featuring Fred Savage; *The Love Boat* (1976–90) the adventures of cruise liner passengers, and *Knight Rider* (1982–86) starring David Hasselhoff as Michael Knight who is aided in his fight against crime by an artificially intelligent car called KITT.

The Waltons was broadcast throughout the 1970s as well as at the beginning of the 1980s. It was a favourite with many people. It told the story of the lives of the Walton family in rural Virginia during the Great Depression and the Second World War. The pilot show, 'The Homecoming: A Christmas Story', first aired in 1971 and the series ran from September 1972 for nine seasons before it was cancelled in 1981. However, movie sequels were broadcast in the 1990s. The story revolved around John Walton Jr (John-Boy) and his family which included his six brothers and sisters, his parents John and Olivia Walton, and his grandparents Zebulon (Zeb) and Esther Walton. John-Boy was the oldest of the children and later becomes a journalist and novelist. The opening of each episode was narrated by a middle-aged John-Boy and was voiced by author Earl Hamner Jr.

In 1974, the Fonz was introduced to audiences in the ever-popular *Happy Days* (1974–84) starring Henry Winkler. It told the story of a 1950s family and their cool tenant, Arthur Fonzarelli. The series ran from 1974 until 1984 and was one of the decade's highest-rated series. It went on to spawn an equally popular half-hour comedy series, *Mork and Mindy*, which starred Pam Dawber and Robin Williams.

Soap (1977–81) featured the everyday chaotic lives of the Tates and the Campbells. Much of the comedy was whacky and hilarious and was a spoof

The Fonz (Henry Winkler) and Richie Cunningham (Ron Howard) in the popular American television series *Happy Days*.

of the many serious soaps that appeared on American TV at the time. One of the funniest characters was Burt (played by Richard Mulligan) who in later episodes was kidnapped by aliens and replaced with 'Alien Burt'. Memorable characters include Jessica Tate (Katherine Helmond) and her husband, Chester (Robert Mandan), Benson (Robert Guillaume) the sarcastic butler, Jodie (Billy Crystal) the gay son, Chuck (Jay Johnson) a ventriloquist, and Mary Campbell (Cathryn Damon) the sister of Jessica Tate. Apart from alien abduction, the show included demonic possession, murder, insanity, a faked death, a cult and blackmail. Each show began with a recap of the previous episode and the words, 'Confused? You won't be, after this week's episode of ... *Soap*.'

Taxi (1978–82) followed the lives of the employees of the fictional Sunshine Cab Company based in Manhattan. It featured the disillusioned Alex Reiger (Judd Hirsch), single mother Elaine Nardo (Marilu Henner), boxer Tony Banta (Tony Danza), struggling actor Bobby Wheeler (Jeff Conaway), aging hippie Reverend Jim Ignatowski (Christopher Lloyd), Latka Gravas (Andy Kaufman) and despotic dispatcher Louie De Palma (Danny DeVito). The show went on to win eighteen Emmy Awards and is fondly remembered. It made stars of many of its cast particularly Danny DeVito and Andy Kaufman.

The American TV series *M*A*S*H* ran between 1972 and 1983 and was based on the movie of the same name. The TV show starred Alan Alda and Wayne Rogers as Captain Hawkeye Pierce and Trapper John McIntyre, two army surgeons based at a Mobile Army Surgical Hospital during the Korean War. The show was a comedy and played with a laughter track in the US but this was removed in the UK. With its often dark humour and poignant story lines, very popular and a record breaking 125 million people watched the final show. Also appearing in the first series were Loretta Swit (Margaret 'Hot Lips' Houlihan), Jamie Farr (Max Klinger), William Christopher (Father Mulcahy), McLean Stevenson (Henry Blake), Larry Linville (Frank Burns) and Gary Burghoff (Radar O'Reilly). The cast changed over the years introducing new characters and actors.

The Dukes of Hazzard (1979–85) was easy viewing for Saturday nights and featured the adventures of the Duke Boys, who were cousins Bo Duke (John Schneider) and Luke Duke (Tom Wopat). The show also featured their attractive female cousin, Daisy (Catherine Bach). The show had a star car, The General Lee, and a host of memorable characters such as Boss Hogg and Sheriff Rosco P. Coltrane. The show drew a lot from the popular Burt Reynolds movies of the time.

One of the most popular, not-to-be-missed, shows on television during the late 1970s and the 1980s was *Dallas* which told the story of an American oil-rich family and all the dramas that went with their day-to-day lives. The series started with the marriage of Bobby Ewing and Pamela Barnes. Their families were sworn enemies in the oil business. Bobby's brother, J.R., threw a spanner in the works at every turn with his various schemes and dirty deals. The cliffhanger at the end of the 1970s involved the shooting of J.R. and a huge campaign was launched with the slogan 'Who Shot JR?'. Storylines at the time were kept secret and the episodes arrived in the UK by plane under guard so no one knew what was going to happen until the episode was broadcast. Other popular characters in the show included Jock Ewing (Jim Davis), the head of the family; Miss Ellie (Barbara Bel Geddes), his wife; Sue Ellen (Linda Gray), J.R.'s alcoholic wife; Lucy (Charlene Tilton), Jock's granddaughter; and Pam's brother Cliff (Ken Kercheval). People were hooked by the twists and turns of the Ewing family but it started to lose its appeal after the death of Bobby Ewing. He later returned to the show and it was explained that the whole previous series had been 'a dream'. This was too much for even the most ardent viewers, but still it continued. In 1979, Dallas spawned an off-shoot, *Knot's Landing*.

US detective and crime series included *Cagney and Lacey* (1982–88) starring Sharon Gless and Tyne Daly as New York City police detectives;

Magnum PI (1980–88) starring Tom Selleck as an Hawaii-based private investigator; *Moonlighting* (1985–89) starring Cybill Shepherd and Bruce Willis as private detectives; *Miami Vice* (1984–89) starring Don Johnson and Philip Michael Thomas as two undercover Metro-Dade Police Department detectives working in Miami; *Hill Street Blues* (1981–87) featuring members of the fictional police station, Hill Street, and starring Daniel J. Travanti, Veronica Hamel and James B. Sikking; *CHiPs* (1977–83), the story of two California Highway Patrol motorcycle cops starring Erik Estrada and Larry Wilcox; *Charlie's Angels* (1976–81) a female detective agency originally starring Jaclyn Smith, Kate Jackson and Farrah Fawcett; *Remington Steele* (1982–87) featuring a private detective agency and starring Stephanie Zimbalist and Pierce Brosnan, *Police Squad!* (1982) a spoof police show starring Leslie Nielsen, Alan North and Peter Lupus; *Murder She Wrote* (1984–96) with Angela Lansbury as mystery writer and amateur detective Jessica Fletcher; *Columbo* (1968–2003) with Peter Falk as the hapless detective; *The Rockford Files* (1974–80) with James Garner; *Hawaii Five-O* (1968–80) starring Jack Lord; *Quincy ME* (1976–83) with Jack Klugman as a police pathologist; and *TJ Hooker* (1982–85) the story of a veteran police sergeant, starring William Shatner.

There were also many sci-fi shows on TV during the 1980s. As well as *Doctor Who*, the BBC also produced *Blake's 7* (1978–81). The show featured seven renegades and their adventures in a stolen spaceship. Gareth Thomas played Blake, Paul Darrow played Avon and Michael Keating played Vila. Despite wobbly sets, it was incredibly popular and was watched by 10 million people in the UK. Clive James described it as 'classically awful'. The show was created by Terry Nation, who also wrote scripts for *Doctor Who* and invented the main character's most deadly enemy, the Daleks.

Battlestar Galactica (1978–80) cashed in on the success of the movie, *Star Wars* and most of the action took place on a spaceship. The show starred Lorne Greene and Richard Hatch and involved the characters' war with a race of robots called the Cylons. The show returned in 1980 but, to save money, found itself earthbound. The show returned for a new series in 2003 but never regained its original popularity.

Buck Rogers in the 25th Century (1979–81) starred Gil Gerard as the title character and also featured Erin Gray and Wilfrid Hyde-White. Many of the props and costumes were recycled from *Battlestar Galactica*, which was still being made at the time. The story tells of an astronaut, Buck Rogers, who after being launched in his spacecraft in May 1987 finds himself frozen for 504 years before his spacecraft is discovered in the year 2491.

The Incredible Hulk (1978–82) starred Bill Bixby as Dr David Banner, a scientist who, after being hit by gamma rays turns into the Incredible Hulk whenever he becomes upset. His catch line each week was 'Don't make me angry, you wouldn't like me when I'm angry!' The Hulk was played by Lou Ferrigno who looked huge at the time but today, with so many bodybuilders around, doesn't look quite as big as he once did.

Other popular American shows included *The Golden Girls* (1985–92) a comedy about four older women who shared a home in Miami, starring Beatrice Arthur, Betty White, Rue McClanahan and Estelle Getty; *Diff'rent Strokes* (1978–86) starring Gary Coleman and Todd Bridges as Arnold and Willis Jackson, two boys from Harlem who are cared for by a well-off Park Avenue businessman and widower, Phillip Drummond; *Fantasy Island* (1978–84) about an island where all your dreams come true, starring Ricardo Montalbán and Hervé Villechaize; *Mork and Mindy* (1978–82) a comedy about a manic alien featuring Robin Williams and Pam Dawber; *Quantum Leap* (1989–93) starring Scott Bakula as a time-hopping scientist; *Little House on the Prairie* (1974–83) the story of Laura Ingalls and her family; *Knots Landing* (1979–93) a spin-off of *Dallas* set in a fictitious coastal suburb of Los Angeles; *Falcon Crest* a story of the Californian wine industry starring Jane Wyman and Robert Foxworth (1981–90); *The Twilight Zone* (1985–89) a remake of Rod Serling's 1950s science fiction series; *MacGyver* (1985–92) an adventure series starring Richard Dean Anderson as a secret agent; *Roseanne* (1988–97) a comedy featuring the Conner family and starring Roseanne Barr and John Goodman; *St Elsewhere* (1982–88); *Star Trek : The Next Generation* (1987–94) featuring Patrick Stewart; *Airwolf* 1984–87); *Baywatch* (1989–99); *Blue Thunder* (1984) starring James Farentino and Dana Carvey featuring an advanced police helicopter used to battle crime; *Doogie Howser MD* (1989–93) starring Neil Patrick Harris as a teenage physician; *Hardcastle and McCormick* (1983–86) featuring Brian Keith as Judge Milton C. Hardcastle and Daniel Hugh Kelly as ex-convict and race car driver Mark 'Skid' McCormick; *LA Law* (1986–94) a legal drama series starring Harry Hamlin, Jimmy Smits and Susan Dey; *Manimal* (1983) featuring Simon MacCorkindale as Dr Jonathan Chase who had the ability to change into various animals; *Married with Children* (1987–97) a sitcom starring Ed O'Neill and Katey Sagal, following the life of ex-high school football player Al Bundy and his wife Peggy; *My Two Dads* (1987–90) a sitcom starring Paul Reiser, Greg Evigan, and Staci Keanan; *Saved by the Bell* (1989–93) about a group of high school friends and their principal, starring Mark-Paul Gosselaar, Dustin Diamond, Lark Voorhies; and *Street Hawk* (1985) the story of ex-motorcycle cop Jesse Mach (Rex Smith) and his battle against crime.

There were many fondly remembered television adverts from the decade. The advert for Scotch VHS video tapes featured a skeleton and the voice of Brian Wilde, better known for his role as Mr Barrowclough in *Porridge* and as Foggy in *Last of the Summer Wine*. Featuring Archie the skeleton, the slogan for the advert was 'Re-record not fade away'. It stated that Scotch tapes would last forever and offered a lifetime guarantee. The advert was directed by Bill Mather at Aardman Animations who also used another *Last of the Summer Wine* actor, Peter Sallis (Clegg) in its later production of *Wallace and Gromit*.

Other memorable adverts included one for Hamlet featuring Gregor Fisher as 'Baldy Man'; the dancing Hofmeister bear; the Levi jeans ad; and the Nescafé coffee advert featuring Sharon Maughan.

Memorable quotes from television of the decade:

'This time next year, we'll be millionaires!' – Del Boy, *Only Fools and Horses*.
'I have a cunning plan.' – Baldrick, *Blackadder*.
'What 'chu talkin' 'bout, Willis?' – *Diff'rent Strokes*.
'Don't make me angry, you wouldn't like me when I'm angry.' – David Banner, *The Incredible Hulk*.
'Whoa!' – The Fonz, *Happy Days*.
'Nanu Nanu.' – Mork, *Mork and Mindy*.
'Boss, boss. It's the plane.' – *Fantasy Island*.
'You get nothing for two in a bed.' – Jim Bowen, *Bullseye*.
'Come on down.' – Leslie Crowther, *The Price is Right*.
'I'm free!' – Mr Humphries, *Are You Being Served*.

10

Movies

'Nobody calls me chicken' is a phrase that every 1980s movie-goer will know off by heart. The decade included many classic and fondly remembered movies and one of the most popular was *Back to the Future* which was directed by Steven Spielberg and spawned two equally successful sequels. Today, the movies are shown regularly on television particularly during holiday times.

In the film, Marty McFly accidentally travels back to 1955 in Doc Emmett Brown's DeLorean time machine, meeting his parents and becoming his mother's love interest. With the aid of a younger Doc in the year 1955, Marty successfully returns back to the future in the memorable final scene featuring Doc Brown hanging from the town's clock with a lightning conductor, the only way to repower the Delorean.

Michael J. Fox, star of the hugely successful *Back to the Future* movies which also starred Christopher Lloyd as Doc Emmett Brown, arrives at an award ceremony. The movies were directed by Steven Spielberg.

The film starred Michael J. Fox as Marty and Christopher Lloyd as Emmett Brown. Prior to the movie, Lloyd was best known for his role as Jim Ignatowski in the hit comedy series *Taxi* and Fox for his role as Alex P. Keaton in *Family Ties*. The movie became the highest-grossing film of 1985 and is also remembered for featuring *The Power of Love* by Huey Lewis and the News. Michael J. Fox also starred in the less successful *Teen Wolf* during the same year. *Back to the Future II* was released several years later in 1989 and *Back to the Future III* was released the following year in 1990. The trilogy proved highly popular.

The Empire Strikes Back (1980) was the second movie released in the Star Wars franchise and was followed by *Return of the Jedi* in 1983. The huge success of the original film made a sequel inevitable and once more reunited Luke Skywalker, Han Solo, Princess Leia, Chewbacca, C–3PO and R2D2. *The Empire Strikes Back* is set three years after the original story. The Galactic Empire, headed by the Emperor and Darth Vader, pursue Luke Skywalker and the Rebel Alliance. Vader tracks Han Solo, Princess Leia Organa, and others across the galaxy while Luke, under the instruction of Jedi Master Yoda studies The Force. When Vader traps Luke's friends, Luke has to decide whether to continue with his training to become a full Jedi Knight or to face Vader and save them. During a final fight sequence, Darth Vader reveals that he is actually Luke's father.

The action continued in *Return of the Jedi* released in 1983. The movie starred Mark Hamill, Harrison Ford, Carrie Fisher, Billy Dee Williams, Anthony Daniels, David Prowse, Kenny Baker, Peter Mayhew and Frank Oz. The tale continues with the Galactic Empire, under the command of its Emperor, building a second Death Star with the aim to destroy the Rebel Alliance. With the Emperor planning to personally supervise the last stage of its construction, the Rebel Fleet launches a full-scale attack on the Death Star with the aim of preventing its completion and killing the Emperor in the process thus bringing to an end the Empire's dominance over the galaxy. Meanwhile, Luke strives to return his father, Darth Vader, back to the light side of The Force. All three movies were highly successful and brought in huge revenues, however, a new *Star Wars* movie wasn't released until 1999 when *A Phantom Menace* hit the screens. By then, the use of computers, CGI, and more advanced technology and special effects greatly enhanced the movie and its sequels but, to many, the first three films, made in the 1970s and 1980s, were always the best.

James Bond had several outings during the decade and movies included *For Your Eyes Only* (1981), *Never Say Never Again* (1983), *Octopussy* (1983), *A View to a Kill* (1985), *The Living Daylights* (1987) and *Licence to Kill* (1989).

For Your Eyes Only, Octopussy and *A View to a Kill* all starred Roger Moore as the enigmatic secret agent. Sean Connery returned to the role of 007 for one final movie, *Never Say Never Again*. Roger Moore retired from the part after *A View to a Kill* and Timothy Dalton replaced him as James Bond in two further movies, *The Living Daylights* and *Licence to Kill*. All were hugely successful. Timothy Dalton resigned from the role after *Licence to Kill* but it wasn't until 1995 that a new Bond film hit the screens, this time starring Pierce Brosnan.

Indiana Jones was first introduced to the movie-going public in 1981 with *Raiders of the Lost Ark* with the film later followed by *Indiana Jones and the Temple of Doom* in 1984. Harrison Ford starred in the lead role. Sean Connery joined Ford in the final Indiana Jones movie of the 1980s, *Indiana Jones and the Last Crusade* in 1989.

Sequels to highly successful films appeared regularly at the cinema over the decade and these included *Smokey and the Bandit Ride Again* (1980) starring Burt Reynolds; *Any Which Way You Can* (1980) starring Clint Eastwood and his orangutan, Clyde; *Mad Max 2* (1981) starring Mel Gibson; *Halloween II* (1981) featuring Jamie Lee Curtis; *Rocky III* (1982) starring Sylvester Stallone; *Star Trek II : The Wrath of Khan* (1982) with William Shatner, Leonard Nimoy and DeForest Kelley; *Conan the Destroyer* (1984) starring Arnold Schwarzenegger; *Mad Max Beyond Thunderdrome* (1985) with Mel Gibson; *Rocky IV* (1985); *Rambo : First Blood Part II* (1985) both starring

Sylvester Stallone starred in the ever-popular *Rocky* and *Rambo* movies during the decade as well as appearing in the wartime escape movie *Victory*.

Sylvester Stallone; *Jaws : The Revenge* (1987) with Michael Caine; *Rambo III* (1988) again starring Sylvester Stallone; *Lethal Weapon 2* (1989) featuring Mel Gibson as well as Patsy Kensit; and *Ghostbusters II* (1989) starring Bill Murray, Dan Aykroyd, Harold Ramis, Sigourney Weaver and Rick Moranis.

Many of the follow-up movies were almost as good as the original but some, notably *Jaws: The Revenge* (1987), failed to hit the mark. After police chief Brody, played by Roy Scheider in previous films, dies of a heart attack, his wife becomes convinced that a great white shark is seeking revenge on her family. It follows them on holiday to the Bahamas. The movie starred Michael Caine as Hoagie Newcombe, a carefree airline pilot.

Michael Caine also appeared in some of the biggest hits of the decade including *Victory* (1981); *Educating Rita* (1983) with Julie Walters; *The Jigsaw Man* (1983); *Hannah and Her Sisters* (1986); and *Dirty Rotten Scoundrels* (1988) with Steve Martin.

Victory brought together a host of stars including Sylvester Stallone, Max von Sydow, Daniel Massey and Michael Caine as well as footballers Bobby Moore, Osvaldo Ardiles, Hallvar Thoresen, Werner Roth, Pelé and many others. The film's plot involves Allied Prisoners of War preparing for a soccer game against the German National Team to be played in Nazi-occupied Paris, while the French Resistance and British officers are making plans for the team's escape. The movie isn't entirely historically accurate and is remembered for its crowd scenes at the end where the extras can be seen wearing platform shoes, tank tops, flares, parka coats and other fashions that did not belong in the Second World War era.

Sylvester Stallone was a huge box office draw in the 1980s and as well as appearing in *Victory*, he also starred in *First Blood* (1982) and its many sequels as well as in the *Rocky* movies.

Arnold Schwarzenegger also proved to be a huge cinema attraction during the decade and his movies included *Conan the Barbarian* (1982), *Conan the Destroyer* (1984), *The Terminator* (1984), *Red Sonja* (1985), *Commando* (1985), *Raw Deal* (1986), *Predator* (1987), *The Running Man* (1987), *Red Heat* (1988) and *Twins* (1988). His biggest hit film during the decade was *The Terminator* in which Schwarzenegger played a cyborg killer sent from the future to 1984 to assassinate Sarah Connor, played by Linda Hamilton. Connor's son will one day save the human race from machines in a post-apocalyptic future. Michael Biehn plays Kyle Reese, a soldier from 2029, who is also sent back to protect Connor. The movie was directed by James Cameron and became a huge hit at the box office. There were several sequels including *Terminator 2: Judgment Day*, *Terminator 3: Rise of the Machines*, *Terminator Salvation* and *Terminator Genisys*. In a departure from his serious roles, Schwarzenegger turned to comedy in 1988 when he played Julius Benedict starring opposite Danny DeVito in *Twins*.

Popular comedians who had screen success during the decade included Steve Martin, Eddie Murphy and Robin Williams.

Steve Martin was a huge star during the decade and appeared in many hit movies during the 1980s including *Pennies from Heaven* (1981) a musical drama written by Dennis Potter and also starring Bernadette Peters, Christopher Walken, and Jessica Harper; *Dead Men Don't Wear Plaid* (1982) a comedy mystery film co-starring Rachel Ward; *The Man with Two Brains* (1983) a comedy directed by Carl Reiner and also starring Kathleen Turner; *The Lonely Guy* (1984) about greetings card writer and his bad luck with women; *Three Amigos* (1986) also starring Chevy Chase and Martin Short as three silent film stars; *Little Shop of Horrors* (1986) a musical rock comedy directed by Frank Oz that included special appearances by Jim Belushi, John Candy, Christopher Guest and Bill Murray; *Roxanne* (1986) a romantic comedy based on the play *Cyrano de Bergerac* and also starring Daryl Hannah; *Planes, Trains and Automobiles* (1987) also starring John Candy, about a marketing executive trying desperately to get home to Chicago in time for Thanksgiving with his family; and *Dirty Rotten Scoundrels* (1988) a story about two con men, co-starring Michael Caine; and *Parenthood* (1989) also starring Tom Hulce, Rick Moranis, Martha Plimpton, Joaquin Phoenix, Keanu Reeves, Jason Robards and Mary Steenburgen.

Eddie Murphy was one of the biggest box office draws in the 1980s. His hit movies during the decade included *48 Hrs* (1982) with Nick Nolte, they play a cop and a criminal working together to catch two cop killers; *Trading Places* (1983) with Dan Aykroyd about two men, an upper-class broker and a homeless street hustler, who exchange lives when they become part of an elaborate bet, also starring Don Ameche and Ralph Bellamy; *Beverly Hills Cop* (1984) in which Murphy played Axel Foley, a street-smart Detroit cop; *Best Defense* (1984) a forgettable military-type comedy which also starred Dudley Moore; *The Golden Child* (1986) in which Murphy is told he is The Chosen One and is destined to save the saviour of all mankind, a movie which also starred Charles Dance and Charlotte Lewis; *Beverly Hills Cop II* (1987) a sequel featuring Detroit police detective Axel Foley; and *Coming to America* (1988) about the crown prince of Zamunda who travels to the United States in the hope of finding a bride, which also starred Arsenio Hall, James Earl Jones, Shari Headley, and John Amos.

One of the biggest stars of the 1980s was Robin Williams who was still appearing in the highly popular TV series *Mork and Mindy* at the beginning of the 1980s. His success in the role led to a long film career and he appeared in many successful movies during the decade including *Popeye* (1980) a musical which also starred Shelley Duvall as Olive Oyl; *Good Morning, Vietnam* (1987) a comedy in which Williams plays a radio DJ on Armed Forces Radio Service in Vietnam; *The Adventures of Baron Munchausen* (1988) a Terry Gilliam fantasy also starring Eric Idle, Jonathan Pryce, Oliver Reed, and Uma Thurman; and the coming-of-age movie, *Dead Poets Society* (1989). In *Dead Poets Society*, Williams played teacher, John Keating, who became an inspiration to his pupils through his love of poetry. The movie also starred Ethan Hawke. It was a huge success in the cinema and won the BAFTA Award for Best Film as well as an Academy Award for Best Original Screenplay.

Harrison Ford was a huge star in the 1980s. As well as appearing in the hugely successful *Star Wars* movies as Han Solo, he also appeared in *Blade Runner* (1982) playing Rick Deckard whose job it was to track rogue replicants, co-staring with Rutger Hauer and Sean Young; *Witness* (1985) about a detective protecting a young Amish boy, which also starred Kelly McGillis; *The Mosquito Coast* (1986) about a family who leave their home to live a simpler life in the jungles of Central America, which co-starred Helen Mirren and River Phoenix; and *Frantic* (1988) an American-French mystery thriller film directed by Roman Polanski.

Horror movies were popular during the decade and these included *The Shining* (1980) directed by Stanley Kubrick starring Jack Nicholson and Shelley Duvall; *Friday 13th* (1980) a slasher movie starring Adrienne King, Betsy Palmer, Harry Crosby, Laurie Bartram and Kevin Bacon; *The Fog* (1980) directed by John Carpenter and starring Adrienne Barbeau, Jamie Lee Curtis, Janet Leigh and Hal Holbrook; *An American Werewolf in London* (1981) directed by John Landis and starring David Naughton and Jenny Agutter; *The Evil Dead* (1981) a Sam Raimi film starring Bruce Campbell, Ellen Sandweiss and Betsy Baker; *Poltergeist* (1982) written by Steven Spielberg and starring JoBeth Williams, Craig T. Nelson, Heather O'Rourke, and Beatrice Straight; *Christine* (1983) about a possessed car, starring Keith Gordon, John Stockwell and Harry Dean Stanton; *Gremlins* (1984) with Zach Galligan, Phoebe Cates, Hoyt Axton, Frances Lee McCain and Corey Feldman; *A Nightmare on Elm Street* (1984) starring Robert Englund as Freddy Kruger; *Fright Night* (1985) with William Ragsdale, Chris Sarandon and Roddy McDowall; *The Fly* (1986) starring Jeff Goldblum; *Hellraiser* (1987) a Clive Barker movie starring Sean Chapman; and *The Lost Boys* (1987) a vampire comedy starring Jason Patric, Corey Haim, Kiefer Sutherland, Jami Gertz and Corey Feldman.

The Shining tells the story of an aspiring writer and recovering alcoholic, Jack Torrance (Jack Nicholson), who accepts a job as an off-season caretaker at an isolated hotel in the Colorado Rockies. He's joined in the winter months by his wife Wendy (Shelley Duvall) and their young son Danny (Danny Lloyd) who possesses 'the shining', a psychic gift that enables him to see into the hotel's gruesome past. The chef at the hotel, Dick Hallorann (Scatman Crothers), also has the same gift and can telepathically communicate with Danny. The family learn that the previous caretaker at the hotel went mad and killed his family and himself. With the influence of supernatural forces, Jack's feels that his sanity is deteriorating and starts to act the same way as his predecessor.

Friday the 13th told the story of a group of teenage camp counsellors who are murdered one by one by an unseen killer while trying to re-open a deserted summer camp. A box office success, the movie spawned seven sequels and a television series in the 1980s alone, followed by a further three films, and a remake in 2009.

An American Werewolf in London was directed by John Landis. Two American students, David Kessler (David Naughton) and Jack Goodman (Griffin Dunne), are attacked on the Yorkshire moors by a werewolf while backpacking in England. Jack is killed but David survives and is taken to hospital. All is fine until the appearance of a full moon when he finds himself transforming into a werewolf. The movie also starred Jenny Agutter as a nurse who falls in love with David. The film has since gained cult status and a sequel *An American Werewolf in Paris* was released in 1997.

Poltergeist told the story of Steven and Diane Freeling who live in an estate called Cuesta Verde in Orange County, California. Steven is a thriving real estate developer while his wife takes care of their children Dana, Robbie, and Carol Anne. One night, Carol Anne wanders downstairs and starts talking to the family's television set, which is showing static following the station's close-down. The next night, while the Freelings are fast asleep, Carol Anne again stares at the static on the television when suddenly, a ghostly white hand reaches out, which is then followed by a violent earthquake. When the shaking stops, Carol Anne announces 'They're here'. The movie was written and produced by Steven Spielberg and led to two sequels, *Poltergeist II: The Other Side* (1986) and *Poltergeist III* (1988). A remake starring Sam Rockwell, Jared Harris, and Rosemarie DeWitt was released in 2015 but never gained the popularity of the original movie.

A Nightmare on Elm Street introduced the fire-ravaged Freddy Kruger to the world, a character with a razor-blade sharp glove that haunted the dreams of susceptible teenagers. The movie was directed by Wes Craven and starred Heather Langenkamp, John Saxon, Ronee Blakley, Amanda Wyss, Jsu Garcia, Robert Englund and Johnny Depp. It proved to be highly successful at the box office and produced seven sequels. The film was remade in 2010 with a different cast but failed to reach the popularity of the 1984 version.

The Fly was a remake of a classic 1950s film which originally starred David Hedison. In the later version, Jeff Goldblum plays scientist, Seth Brundle, who invents a machine for teleportation. Using the machine, his DNA becomes combined with that of a fly which has got into the machine, and he is slowly taken over by the insect leading to his death at the end of the movie. The movie also starred Geena Davis.

Many popular movies of the 1980s were based on well-known novels. Stephen King's books were behind many successful movies of the decade and these included *The Shining* (1980); *Creepshow* (1982); *The Dead Zone* (1983); *Christine* (1983); *Cujo* (1983); *Children of the Corn* (1984); *Firestarter* (1984); *Silver Bullet* (1985); *Cat's Eye* (1985); *Stand By Me* (1986); *Maximum Overdrive* (1986); *The Running Man* (1987); *Creepshow 2* (1987) and *Pet Sematary* (1989).

Science fiction movies of the 1980s included *Escape from New York* (1981) about a federal prisoner, Snake Plissken (Kurt Russell), who has 24 hours to rescue the President of the United States; *ET The Extra-Terrestrial* (1982) about a lost alien trying to return home to his own planet; *Tron* (1982) starring Jeff Bridges as a software programmer who is transported inside a mainframe computer; *War Games* (1983) a film starring Matthew Broderick, Dabney Coleman, and Ally Sheedy about a hacker who unwittingly accesses WOPR (War Operation Plan Response), a United States military supercomputer; *Ghostbusters* (1984) an organisation of ghost hunters, starring Dan Aykroyd and Harold Ramis; *Dune* (1984) starring Kyle MacLachlan and set in the distant future, telling the story of the conflict between rival noble families; *Runaway* (1984) with Tom Selleck and Cynthia Rhodes about a police officer assigned to track down dangerous robots; *Weird Science* (1985) about boys who create a virtual girl using their computer, starring Anthony Michael Hall, Ilan Mitchell-Smith and Kelly LeBrock; *Brazil* (1985) a Terry Gilliam movie reminiscent of George Orwell's *Nineteen Eighty-Four* and starring Jonathan Pryce, Robert De Niro and Katherine Helmond; *Aliens* (1986) a sequel again starring Sigourney Weaver as Ellen Ripley returning to the moon where her crew encountered a hostile alien creature; *RoboCop* (1987) starring Peter Weller as a law enforcing half-man/half-machine; *Honey, I Shrunk the Kids* (1989) starring Rick Moranis as an inventor who accidentally shrinks his children; and *The Abyss* (1989) with Ed Harris, Mary Elizabeth Mastrantonio and Michael Biehn about a SEAL team who discover underwater alien life.

Steven Spielberg's *E.T. the Extra-Terrestrial* (1982) was a huge box office success in 1982. The movie starred Henry Thomas, Dee Wallace, Peter Coyote,

Robert MacNaughton, Drew Barrymore and Pat Welsh and told the story of Elliott who makes friends with an alien (ET), who is stuck on Earth and trying to get back to his own planet. Elliott and his siblings hide ET from the government while trying to help the extra-terrestrial to return home. When released, the film became an instant blockbuster, surpassing *Star Wars* to become the highest-grossing film. The movie is timeless and is regularly shown on the television and enjoyed by new generations of children and their families.

Fantasy movies of the decade included *Excalibur* (1981) starring Nicol Williamson, Nicholas Clay, Cherie Lunghi, Helen Mirren and Liam Neeson; *The Dark Crystal* (1982) featuring the voices of Stephen Garlick, Lisa Maxwell, Billie Whitelaw, Percy Edwards, and Barry Dennen; *The NeverEnding Story* (1984) with Noah Hathaway, Barret Oliver, Tami Stronach and Patricia Hayes; *Legend* (1985) directed by Ridley Scott and starring Tom Cruise, Mia Sara and Tim Curry; *Return to Oz* (1985) starring Nicol Williamson, Jean Marsh, Piper Laurie and Fairuza Balk; *Highlander* (1986) the story of an immortal warrior, starring Christopher Lambert, Sean Connery, Clancy Brown, and Roxanne Hart; *Labyrinth* (1986) a musical fantasy directed by Jim Henson and starring David Bowie and Jennifer Connolly; and *The Princess Bride* (1987) a romantic comedy fantasy adventure featuring Cary Elwes, Robin Wright, Mandy Patinkin and Chris Sarandon.

Highlander became a cult movie and spawned a series of sequels as well as a TV series. In the film, Christopher Lambert played a Scottish swordsman, Connor MacLeod, one of several immortal warriors who could only be killed by decapitation. MacLeod is originally trained by another immortal swordsman, Ramirez, played by Sean Connery, and lives on for several centuries before being confronted in the present time by Kurgan (Clancy Brown), his greatest enemy, who wishes to kill him. The movie wasn't a huge success when it was first released but has gained popularity over the years and is fondly remembered today.

Superhero films included *Flash Gordon* (1980), *Superman II* (1980), *Superman III* (1983), *Supergirl* (1984), *Red Sonja* (1985), *Superman IV: The Quest for Peace* (1987) and *Batman* (1989).

All three Superman movies released in the decade featured Christopher Reeve in the title role with Gene Hackman as Lex Luthor and Margot Kidder as Lois Lane. In *Superman II*, Terence Stamp played the evil General Zod, the ruthless leader of three Kryptonian prisoners previously banished to the Phantom Zone who are unwittingly set free by Superman.

Flash Gordon starred Sam J. Jones as the title character and also featured Melody Anderson, Topol, Max von Sydow, Timothy Dalton, Brian Blessed and Ornella Muti. The movie was similar in many ways to the original

Buster Crabbe serial of the 1930s and since its release has gained a cult following. Perhaps its best remembered for Brian Blessed (Prince Vultan) bellowing 'Gordon's alive!'

Musicals of the decade included *The Blues Brothers* (1980) starring John Belushi and Dan Aykroyd; *Annie* (1982) with Albert Finney as Daddy Warbucks; *Grease 2* (1982) a follow-up to the original hit musical and starring Michelle Pfeiffer and Maxwell Caulfield; *Flash Dance* (1983) featuring Jennifer Beals and Michael Nouri; *Footloose* (1984) with Kevin Bacon and John Lithgow; *Dirty Dancing* (1987) with Patrick Swayze and Jennifer Grey; and *La Bamba* (1987) with Lou Diamond Phillips.

Dirty Dancing was primarily a dance movie but also featured music from Bill Medley and Jennifer Warnes; Otis Redding; The Blow Monkeys; Frankie Valli and The Four Seasons; The Drifters; and many others. In the film, Patrick Swayze plays a dance instructor called Johnny Castle who falls in love with Frances 'Baby' Houseman while working at her family's resort. The film was hugely successful at the box office and, later, was the first film to sell more than a million copies on home video. The movie is remembered for the phrase '*Nobody puts Baby in the corner.*'

The Blues Brothers has gained cult status over the years. The 1980 movie starred John Belushi and Dan Aykroyd as 'Joliet' Jake and Elwood Blues, who were originally characters featured on the American NBC variety series *Saturday Night Live.* The movie is a musical comedy and features the brothers trying to recreate their rhythm and blues band so that they can raise enough money to save the Catholic orphanage they were brought up in. The memorable soundtrack not only featured The Blues Brothers but also included Ray Charles, James Brown, Aretha Franklin and Cab Calloway.

War films included *Merry Christmas, Mr Lawrence* (1983) with David Bowie; *Red Dawn* (1984), *Platoon* (1986), *Full Metal Jacket* (1987) and *Empire of the Sun* (1987).

Clint Eastwood continued to be a huge box office star in the 1980s and starred in many hit movies during the decade. These included *Bronco Billy* (1980); *Any Which Way You Can* (1980); *Honkytonk Man* (1982); *Firefox* (1982); *Sudden Impact* (1983); *Tightrope* (1984); *City Heat* (1984); *Pale Rider* (1985); *Heartbreak Ridge* (1986); *The Deal Pool* (1988); and *Pink Cadillac* (1989). *Sudden Impact* and *Dead Pool* continued the Harry Callahan series of movies with Eastwood once again playing the hardened, laconic, San Francisco-based cop. *Dead Pool* was the fifth and final Dirty Harry movie.

There were many other blockbusters released during the decade and the best of these during 1980 included *Raging Bull,* starring Robert De Niro and directed by Martin Scorsese; *Airplane!,* a spoof disaster movie starring Leslie Nielsen, Robert Stack, Lloyd Bridges and Peter Graves; *Caddyshack,* featuring Chevy Chase, Rodney Dangerfield and Bill Murray; *The Blue Lagoon,* a story of two shipwrecked children, starring Brooke Shields and Christopher Atkins; *Dressed to Kill,* a thriller with Michael Caine, Angie Dickinson and Nancy Allen; and *9 to 5,* starring Jane Fonda, Lily Tomlin, and Dolly Parton.

Raging Bull starred Robert De Niro as middleweight boxer Jake LaMotta. The movie was based on LaMotta's memoir *Raging Bull: My Story.* The film also featured Joe Pesci as Joey, LaMotta's brother and manager. Cathy Moriarty played LaMotta's wife with supporting roles from Nicholas Colasanto, Theresa Saldana, and Frank Vincent. The film received mixed reviews when it was released but went on to be nominated for eight Academy Awards and won De Niro his second Oscar for Best Actor. The movie was made after De Niro first read LaMotta's memoir while filming *The Godfather II.* He approached Martin Scorsese who initially wasn't interested in the project but eventually agreed to make the movie. It was filmed in black and white and De Niro famously put on 60 pounds to play the later LaMotta. Today, the movie is regarded as a modern classic.

Airplane! was a satirical disaster film, a send up of the movie *Airport,* which starred Burt Lancaster, and was written and directed by David and Jerry Zucker and Jim Abrahams. The spoof movie starred Robert Hays and Julie Hagerty and featured Leslie Nielsen, Robert Stack, Lloyd Bridges, Peter Graves, Kareem Abdul-Jabbar, and Lorna Patterson. The movie was a parody of the many disaster films that were being made at the time and featured surreal humour and fast-paced slapstick comedy, spawning a sequel and also influencing the similar style TV show *Naked Gun*, which also starred Leslie Nielsen. The movie was the fourth highest-grossing film of 1980.

9 to 5 starred Jane Fonda, Lily Tomlin and Dolly Parton as three women working in an office who do their best to get even with their company's sexist bigot of a boss, played by Dabney Coleman. The three eventually kidnap their boss and, in his absence, make various changes around the office including flexible working hours, same pay for male and female employees, a job-sharing programme as well as a day-care centre for workers with children. The movie featured Parton's first film acting role and was a huge box office success. A spin-off television sitcom was broadcast between 1982 and 1983 and then again between 1986 and 1988. In the first series, Dolly Parton's younger sister, Rachel Dennison, played her role alongside Rita Moreno and Valerie Curtin.

Box office hits of 1981 included *The Cannonball Run,* starring Burt Reynolds, Roger Moore, Dom DeLuise and Farrah Fawcett taking part in a cross-country road race; *Body Heat,* with William Hurt and Kathleen Turner; *Stripes,* starring Bill Murray and Harold Ramis; *On Golden Pond,* with strong portrayals by Henry Fonda, Katherine Hepburn and Jane Fonda; and *Chariots of Fire,* starring Nigel Havers, Ben Cross and Ian Charleson.

Body Heat starred William Hurt as Ned Racine, an inept lawyer, who embarks on an affair with Matty Tyler Walker (Kathleen Turner), the wife of rich businessman, Edmund Walker. Racine suggests murdering Edmund Walker so that his wife can inherit his wealth. The murder is carried out by the couple and later, Matty fakes her own death and Ned ends up in jail trying to convince the authorities of the deception. The atmospheric movie was set against a backdrop of a Florida heatwave. The film was responsible for launching Kathleen Turner's movie career and also starred Richard Crenna, Ted Danson, J. A. Preston and Mickey Rourke.

On Golden Pond starred father and daughter team, Henry and Jane Fonda, as well as all-time great, Katherine Hepburn in a story about an elderly couple – the cantankerous retiree Norman Thayer (Henry Fonda) and his wife Ethel (Katherine Hepburn) – who holiday each year at their vacation home in New England on the shores of Golden Pond. The couple are visited by their daughter, Chelsea (Jane Fonda), who brings with her, her new fiancé together with his teenage son, Billy. Billy is left behind and bonds with Norman. When Chelsea returns, she tries to repair her relationship with her father before it is too late. The movie proved hugely successful and became the second-highest grossing film of 1981. The film was nominated for ten Academy Awards winning Best Actor (Henry Fonda), Best Actress (Katherine Hepburn) and Best Adapted Screenplay (Ernest Thompson).

Chariots of Fire told the based-on-truth story of two athletes who took part in the 1924 Olympics. The runners, Eric Liddell, a Scottish Christian, and Harold Abrahams, an English Jew, with the British team, compete and return home triumphant with a gold medal. The movie starred Ben Cross (Abrahams) and Ian Charleson (Liddell) and was directed by David Puttnam. The film also featured Nigel Havers, Ian Holm, Lindsay Anderson, John Gielgud, Cheryl Campbell and Alice Krige in supporting roles. The movie was nominated for seven Academy Awards and won four. The memorable soundtrack, written and performed by Vangelis, won the Academy Award for Best Original Score.

Major movies of 1982 included *Sophie's Choice,* with Meryl Streep, Kevin Kline and Peter MacNicol; *An Officer and a Gentleman,* starring Richard Gere, Debra Winger and Louis Gossett Jr; and *Tootsie,* starring Dustin Hoffman.

Sophie's Choice starred Meryl Streep as a Polish immigrant, Sophie, who shares a boarding house with her partner, Nathan, played by Kevin Kline, as well as a young writer, Stingo (Peter MacNicol). Sophie informs Stingo that before arriving in America, her husband and father were murdered in a German work camp, and that she was interned at Auschwitz. Stingo later discovers that Sophie's father was a Nazi sympathizer and confronts her and she admits the truth. Meryl Streep won the Academy Award for Best Actress and the movie was also nominated for Best Cinematography (Néstor Almendros), Best Costume Design (Albert Wolsky), Best Music (Marvin Hamlisch) and Best Adapted Screenplay (Alan J. Pakula).

An Officer and a Gentleman starred Richard Gere as Aviation Officer Candidate Zack Mayo and movie featured Debra Winger, Robert Loggia, Lisa Blount, Louis Gossett Jr and David Caruso. The movie told the story of Zack Mayo and his struggle to complete a thirteen-week training programme as a Navy pilot under the strict supervision of Gunnery Sergeant Emil Foley (Louis Gossett Jr). Debra Winger played Paula Pokrifki, Mayo's love interest in the film. The movie went on to become the third-highest-grossing film of 1982, after *E.T.: The Extra Terrestrial* and *Tootsie*. The movie won the Academy Award for Best Supporting Actor (Louis Gossett Jr) as well as Best Music, Original Song for *Up Where We Belong*.

Tootsie starred Dustin Hoffman as a jobbing actor who no one wants to work with because he's a perfectionist. He hears of an acting vacancy in the daytime soap opera *Southwest General* for a female character and decides to adopt a female persona, Dorothy Michaels. The movie also starred Jessica Lange, Terri Garr, Dabney Colman, Bill Murray, Sydney Pollack and Geena Davis.

Oliver Stone wrote the 1983 hit movie *Scarface*, which was directed by Brian De Palma and starred Al Pacino as the gangster Tony Montana.

The blockbusters of 1983 included *Scarface*, starring Al Pacino as powerful drug kingpin, Tony Montana; *Risky Business*, a coming-of-age comedy starring Tom Cruise and Rebecca De Mornay; *Trading Places*, a comedy starring Eddie Murphy and Dan Aykroyd; *Twilight Zone* based on the popular 1950s television series and starring Vic Morrow; *Silkwood*, a drama about a nuclear whistle-blower and a union activist, starring Meryl Streep, Cher and Kurt Russell; *Superman III, a* superhero action film starring Christopher Reeve, Richard Pryor, Margot Kidder and Robert Vaughn; and *Terms of Endearment*, a comedy drama featuring Shirley MacLaine, Debra Winger, Jack Nicholson, Danny DeVito, Jeff Daniels, and John Lithgow.

Scarface was directed by Brian De Palma and written by Oliver Stone, based on the original 1932 movie of the same name. The story follows a refugee from Cuba, Tony Montana (Al Pacino), who first arrives in Miami in the 1980s with few possessions and little money who, through criminal activity, eventually becomes a powerful drug kingpin. The movie also starred Michelle Pfeiffer, Steven Bauer, Robert Loggia, F. Murray Abraham and Mary Elizabeth Mastrantonio. Al Pacino was nominated for a Golden Globe as Best Actor – Motion Picture Drama.

Twilight Zone was produced by Steven Spielberg and John Landis and was based on the popular Rod Serling science fiction TV show which was originally broadcast between 1959 and 1964. The movie starred Vic Morrow, Scatman Crothers, Kathleen Quinlan and John Lithgow with Dan Aykroyd and Albert Brooks featured in the prologue segment. The movie featured four different stories including *Time Out; Kick the Can*; *It's a Good Life*; and *Nightmare at 20,000 Feet*. Vic Morrow and two children were killed during a helicopter during the making of the film leading to civil and criminal action against the filmmakers.

Terms of Endearment was a comedy-drama movie, taken from Larry McMurtry's 1975 novel and was directed, written and produced by James L. Brooks. The movie starred Shirley MacLaine, Debra Winger, Jack Nicholson, Danny DeVito, Jeff Daniels and John Lithgow and covered a thirty-year period showing the relationship between Aurora Greenway (Shirley MacLaine) and her daughter Emma (Debra Winger). The movie was well received and was nominated for eleven Academy Awards.

Top movies of 1984 included *The Karate Kid*, a martial arts drama film with Ralph Macchio, Pat Morita, Elisabeth Shue, and William Zabka; *Police Academy*, comedy mayhem starring Steve Guttenberg, Kim Cattrall, and G.W. Bailey; *Once Upon a Time in America*, a crime drama co-written and directed by Italian film maker Sergio Leone and featuring Robert De Niro and James Woods; *1984*, a dystopian science fiction film based on George Orwell's book of the same name and starring John Hurt, Richard Burton, Suzanna Hamilton, and Cyril Cusack; *Amadeus,* a fictionalised biography of Wolfgang Amadeus Mozart featuring F. Murray Abraham, Tom Hulce, Elizabeth Berridge and Simon Callow; *This is Spinal Tap,* a spoof mockumentary about the fictional British heavy metal band Spinal Tap, starring Christopher Guest, Michael McKean, and Harry Shearer; *Splash,* a love story about a man and a mermaid with Tom Hanks and Daryl Hannah;

Romancing the Stone, an adventure movie starring Michael Douglas, Kathleen Turner and Danny DeVito; and *Paris, Texas,* a road movie directed by Wim Wenders and starring Harry Dean Stanton, Dean Stockwell, Nastassja Kinski and Hunter Carson.

Once Upon a Time in America was an epic crime drama directed by Sergio Leone. It starred Robert De Niro, James Woods, Elizabeth McGovern, Joe Pesci, Tuesday Weld and Treat Williams and told the story of best friends David 'Noodles' Aaronson (De Niro) and Maximilian 'Max' Bercovicz (Woods) who lead a group of youths from the ghetto who get involved in the world of organised crime and eventually become major gangsters in New York City. The movie explored the theme of childhood friendship as well as greed and betrayal. The film's memorable soundtrack was composed by Ennio Morricone.

Splash was directed by *Happy Days'* Ron Howard for Touchstone Pictures and starred Tom Hanks, Daryl Hannah, John Candy and Eugene Levy. The movie followed a young man, Allen Bauer (Hanks), who falls in love with a woman (Hannah) who unknown to him is a mermaid. The movie was

Michael Douglas, star of the hit movies *Romancing the Stone* (1984) and *The Jewel of the Nile* (1985) which also starred Kathleen Turner and Danny DeVito. He also starred in *Fatal Attraction* and *Wall Street* during the decade.

a huge success when it was released and was nominated for an Academy Award for Best Writing, Original Screenplay. A follow-up TV movie called *Splash, Too* was released in 1988 and featured a different cast.

Romancing the Stone starred Michael Douglas as an exotic bird smuggler, Jack Colton, who is enlisted by novelist Joan Wilder (Kathleen Turner), whose sister Elaine has been kidnapped by illegal antiquities dealers, cousins Ira and Ralph (Danny DeVito). After receiving a map, she is instructed by the kidnappers to travel to Columbia, where Wilder meets Colton after being deliberately stranded in the jungle and offers to pay him $375 to help her. The clues contained in the map eventually lead to the discovery of an emerald but their journey to locate it and free Wilder's sister is fraught with danger as others try to get their hands on the map to locate the emerald for themselves. The movie launched Kathleen Turner's film career and spawned a sequel, *The Jewel of the Nile* (1985).

Major movies of 1985 included *The Goonies,* an adventure comedy movie directed by Richard Donner starring Josh Brolin, Corey Feldman and Martha Plimpton; *The Breakfast Club,* a comedy drama starring Emilio Estevez, Anthony Michael Hall, Judd Nelson, Molly Ringwald and Ally Sheedy; *St Elmo's Fire,* a coming-of-age movie starring Emilio Estevez, Rob Lowe, Andrew McCarthy, Demi Moore, Judd Nelson, Ally Sheedy and Mare Winningham; *A Room With a View,* a romance based on E. M. Forster's novel of the same name and starring Helena Bonham Carter, Julian Sands, Maggie Smith, Denholm Elliott, Daniel Day-Lewis, Judi Dench and Simon Callow; *Out of Africa,* a romantic drama, directed and produced by Sydney Pollack, and starring Robert Redford and Meryl Streep; *Silverado,* a Western featuring Kevin Kline, Scott Glenn, Danny Glover and Kevin Costner; and *The Color Purple,* a period drama directed by Steven Spielberg and starring Whoopi Goldberg, Danny Glover, Desreta Jackson, Margaret Avery and Oprah Winfrey (in her first movie role).

The Goonies was directed by Richard Donner with a screenplay written by Chris Columbus based on a story by Steven Spielberg. The action adventure comedy told the story of a group of kids who resided in the 'Goon Docks' area of Astoria in Oregon. In an effort to save their homes from demolition, they find an old Spanish map that takes them on an adventure to uncover the long-lost treasure of One-Eyed Willy, an infamous seventeenth-century pirate. While trying to locate the fortune, they are pursued by a family of vagabonds, desperate to find the treasure for themselves. The movie starred Sean Astin as Michael 'Mikey' Walsh, Josh Brolin as Brandon 'Brand' Walsh, Jeff Cohen as Lawrence 'Chunk' Cohen, Corey Feldman as Clark 'Mouth' Devereaux, Kerri Green as Andrea 'Andy' Carmichael, Martha Plimpton as Stephanie 'Stef' Steinbrenner and Jonathan Ke Huy Quan as Richard 'Data' Wang. The movie was nominated for best adventure motion picture.

The Breakfast Club was comedy-drama movie which was written, produced, and directed by John Hughes. Its cast included Emilio Estevez, Anthony Michael Hall, Judd Nelson, Molly Ringwald and Ally Sheedy, all playing teenagers who spend one Saturday in school detention with their strict and grumpy teacher played by Paul Gleason. On release of the movie, the main cast members became known in the press as 'The Brat Pack'. The movie is said to sum up the 1980s and has been described as one of the best films of the decade.

The Color Purple was a coming-of-age period drama movie which was directed by Steven Spielberg. It was based on the Pulitzer Prize-winning 1982 novel written by Alice Walker. The movie starred Whoopi Goldberg, Danny Glover, Desreta Jackson, Margaret Avery, Oprah Winfrey, Rae Dawn Chong, Willard Pugh and Adolph Caesar. The film told the story of Celie Harris, a young black woman living in Georgia in the early 20th century, who rises up against a background of domestic violence, poverty, racism, and sexism. The movie featured Oprah Winfrey in her first film role and proved hugely successful, being nominated for eleven Academy Awards.

Box office successes of 1986 included *Ferris Bueller's Day Off*, a teen comedy starring Matthew Broderick; *Stand By Me,* a coming-of-age movie starring Wil Wheaton, River Phoenix, Corey Feldman, and Jerry O'Connell; *Top Gun,* the story of a young naval aviator with Tom Cruise, Kelly McGillis, Val Kilmer, Anthony Edwards, and Tom Skerritt; *Crocodile Dundee,* an Australian outback comedy starring Paul Hogan; and *Pretty in Pink,* a romantic comedy starring Molly Ringwald, Harry Dean Stanton and Andrew McCarthy.

Stand By Me was based on a novella (*The Body*) written by Stephen King. Four boys who live in a small town in Oregon follow a trail looking for the dead body of a missing boy. The movie had memorable performances from Wil Wheaton (Gordon 'Gordie' Lachance), River Phoenix (Christopher 'Chris' Chamber), Corey Feldman (Theodore 'Teddy' Duchamp) and Jerry O'Connell (Vernon 'Vern' Tessio). The movie also featured Kiefer Sutherland as John 'Ace' Merrill and John Cusack as Denny Lachance. Richard Dreyfuss played an older Gordon Lachance and narrated the story, which also featured the memorable track 'Stand By Me' by Ben E King.

Top Gun starred Tom Cruise and Kelly McGillis alongside Val Kilmer, Anthony Edwards and Tom Skerritt. In the movie, Cruise played Lieutenant Pete 'Maverick' Mitchell, a pilot based aboard the aircraft carrier USS *Enterprise*. With his Radar Intercept Officer, Nick 'Goose' Bradshaw (Anthony Edwards), the two are offered places to train at the US Navy's Fighter Weapons School at Naval Air Station Miramar in San Diego, California. The movie won an Academy Award for Best Original Song for 'Take My Breath Away' by Giorgio Moroder and Tom Whitlock. The movie was said to have increased the sales of bomber jackets, and Ray-Ban Aviator sunglasses by 40 per cent, after being worn by the main characters in the film.

Crocodile Dundee made a star of Australian Paul Hogan all around the world after his portrayal as the outback-weathered Mick Dundee. The movie idea was suggested by Paul Hogan (also one of the writers) and was inspired by the true-life exploits of the real-life Rod Ansell, an Australian cattle grazier and buffalo hunter who became stranded in the outback for fifty-six days. The movie also starred Hogan's future wife, Linda Kozlowski, as newspaper reporter Sue Charlton who travels to Australia to interview Dundee. The movie became a huge success becoming the second-highest-grossing film in the United States in 1986. It spawned two sequels, *Crocodile Dundee II* (1988) and *Crocodile Dundee in Los Angeles* (2001).

Popular movies of 1987 included *Lethal Weapon,* a police drama featuring Mel Gibson and Danny Glover; *Raising Arizona,* a crime comedy starring Nicolas Cage and Holly Hunter; *The Untouchables,* a gangster film directed by Brian De Palma and starring Kevin Costner and Robert De Niro; *Masters of the Universe,* a fantasy action movie starring Dolph Lundgren, Frank Langella, Courteney Cox and Meg Foster; *Spaceballs,* a comedy sci-fi film, co-written and produced and directed by Mel Brooks, and starring Bill Pullman, John Candy and Rick Moranis; *Fatal Attraction,* a psychological thriller starring Michael Douglas and Glenn Close; *Moonstruck,* a love story starring Cher and Nicolas Cage; *Wall Street,* a story of a stockbroker, starring Michael Douglas, Charlie Sheen, and Daryl Hannah; *Bigfoot and the Hendersons,* a fantasy comedy starring John Lithgow, Melinda Dillon, Don Ameche and David Suchet and *Mannequin,* a romantic comedy about a man who falls in love with a shop window dummy, starring Andrew McCarthy and Kim Cattrall.

Lethal Weapon was the first in a series of movies which introduced mismatched Los Angeles Police Department detectives, Martin Riggs (Mel Gibson) and Roger Murtaugh (Danny Glover). The movie begins with LAPD Homicide Sergeant Roger Murtaugh being partnered with Sergeant Martin Riggs, on transfer from the narcotic division. Murtaugh hears from Michael Hunsaker, a Vietnam War friend and now banker, who wishes to meet up. Before they can meet, Hunsaker's daughter, Amanda, apparently commits suicide by leaping from her apartment balcony. However, the detectives discover that autopsy reports reveal that Amanda was poisoned with drain cleaner, making the case a possible homicide. Hunsaker informs Murtaugh of his concerns about his daughter's involvement in drugs, prostitution and pornography. Riggs and Murtaugh investigate uncovering a web of crime. The film spawned three sequels as well as a television series featuring a complete new cast.

The Untouchables starred Kevin Costner as Bureau of Prohibition agent, Eliot Ness, in his bid to apprehend Al Capone played by Robert De Niro. The movie was directed by Brian De Palma and also starred Sean Connery, Charles Martin Smith and Andy Garcia. The film was set in the world of gangsters who make their living plying an illegal liquor trade. It was nominated for four Academy Awards, of which Sean Connery won the award for Best Supporting Actor.

Fatal Attraction was a psychological thriller directed by Adrian Lyne which starred Michael Douglas as Dan Gallagher, a successful, happily married Manhattan lawyer. In the course of his work, he meets meet Alexandra 'Alex' Forrest, an editor for a publishing company, with whom who he has an affair. He ends it but is stalked by Forrest forcing him to move away. However, he soon finds that he's been followed and in an infamous scene, Forrest kills the family's pet rabbit. The movie also starred Glenn Close as Forrest and Anne Archer as Beth Rogerson Gallagher. The movie is one of the most memorable of the decade and was nominated for six Academy Awards.

The big movies of 1988 included *Who Framed Roger Rabbit,* a live-action/animated comedy film with Bob Hoskins, Christopher Lloyd and Joanna Cassidy; *Mississippi Burning,* showing racial tension in the deep south of America and featuring Gene Hackman and Willem Dafoe; *Rain Man,* about a man and his autistic brother starring Tom Cruise and Dustin Hoffman; *Beetlejuice,* a Gothic comedy with Michael Keating; *Young Guns,* a Western featuring Emilio Estevez, Kiefer Sutherland, Lou Diamond Phillips, Charlie Sheen, Terence Stamp and Jack Palance; *Big,* a fantasy comedy starring Tom Hanks; *Mystic Pizza,* a coming-of-age movie starring Annabeth Gish, Julia Roberts and Lili Taylor; *Willow,* a fantasy directed by Ron Howard and starring Warwick Davis, Val Kilmer and Joanne Whalley; *A Fish Called Wanda,* a comedy starring John Cleese, Kevin Kline, Michael Palin and Jamie Lee Curtis; and *The Land Before Time,* an animated adventure drama film.

Rain Man was a comedy-drama road movie directed by Barry Levinson. It starred Tom Cruise as Charlie Babbitt, who discover after his rich father's death that all his estate has been left to his other son, Raymond, played by Dustin Hoffman. Charlie Babbitt kidnaps his autistic brother and they embark on a journey, bonding along the way, and ending up in a casino in Las Vegas where Raymond counts cards resulting in him winning enough money to clear Charlie's debts. *Rain Man* was the highest-grossing movie of the year and won four Oscars at the sixty-first Academy Awards including Best Picture, Best Original Screenplay, Best Director, and Best Actor in a Leading Role for Hoffman.

Big was a fantasy comedy film which was directed by Penny Marshall. It starred Tom Hanks as Josh Baskin, a twelve-year-old boy who makes a wish by putting a coin in an unusual arcade fortune teller machine called Zoltar. His wish is to be big and he soon finds that he's turned into an adult overnight. The machine disappears but, as a grown-up he finds himself a job at MacMillan Toys after impressing its owner with his insights into the games and toys that children really want to play with. Baskin eventually tracks the Zoltar machine down to Sea Point Park and making another wish, he becomes a child again.

A Fish Called Wanda was written by, and starred, John Cleese who played a barrister, Archie Leach, who is enlisted by a criminal gang to represent George Thomason, played by Tom Georgeson. Thomason is the leader of a gang of diamond thieves but is betrayed by gang members Wanda and Otto who hope to recover the collection of recently stolen gems for themselves. However, the diamonds have been moved and Wanda seduces Leach, hoping that he can get Thomason to plead guilty and reveal the location of the missing diamonds. The gang consisted of Wanda Gershwitz (Jamie Lee Curtis), Otto West (Kevin Kline) and Ken Pile (Michael Palin). The movie was nominated for three Academy Awards: Best Director, Best Original Screenplay and Best Supporting Actor, which was won by Kevin Kline.

The hit movies of 1989 included *Bill and Ted's Excellent Adventure,* a teen comedy starring Keanu Reeves and Alex Winter; *When Harry Met Sally,* a romantic comedy starring Billy Crystal and Meg Ryan; *National Lampoon's Christmas Vacation,* a mayhem comedy featuring Chevy Chase, Beverly D'Angelo, Randy Quaid and Juliette Lewis; *The Little Mermaid,* an animated musical fantasy romance featuring the voices of Jodi Benson, Christopher Daniel Barnes, Pat Carroll and Samuel E. Wright; *Field of Dreams,* a fantasy-drama sports film with Kevin Costner, James Earl Jones, Ray Liotta and Burt Lancaster; *Uncle Buck,* a comedy starring John Candy, Amy Madigan, Gaby Hoffmann and Macaulay Culkin; *The Burbs,* a comedy horror thriller starring Tom Hanks, Bruce Dern, Carrie Fisher, Rick Ducommun and Corey Feldman; *Look Who's Talking,* a romantic comedy starring John Travolta and Kirstie Alley; and *Shirley Valentine,* a romantic comedy-drama starring Pauline Collins and Tom Conti.

Bill & Ted's Excellent Adventure was a science fiction comedy movie directed by Stephen Herek. It starred Alex Winter (Bill S. Preston), Keanu Reeves (Ted 'Theodore' Logan), and George Carlin and is the story of two high school slackers who, by travelling through time, manage to collect together various figures from history which they produce at their end of the year history presentation. A sequel, *Bill & Ted's Bogus Journey* was released in 1991.

Field of Dreams told the story of Ray Kinsella (Kevin Costner) and his family, corn farmers in Iowa. At the opening of the movie, Kinsella discusses his turbulent relationship with his deceased father, a devout baseball fan. One evening, while in his cornfield, Kinsella hears a voice which says, 'If you build it, he will come'. He sees an apparition of a baseball diamond in the field. His wife doubts what he thinks he heard and saw, but agrees to him building a baseball field in part of the corn field. One night, Kinsella sees a man on the newly built field and recognises him as Shoeless Joe Jackson, a long-dead baseball player who was idolised by his father. Excited to play baseball again, Joe asks Kinsella if other members of his team can play there and later returns with seven additional players. The movie also starred Ray Liotta (Shoeless Joe Jackson), James Earl Jones (Terence Mann) and Burt Lancaster (Archibald 'Moonlight' Graham).

Shirley Valentine was based on Willy Russell's one-character stage play and followed middle aged housewife Shirley Valentine, played by Pauline Collins, who has become bored with her life. When her best friend wins a holiday to Greece, she travels with her embarking on a holiday romance with a Greek tavern owner, Costas Dimitriades, played by Tom Conti. The movie featured an array of British stars including Alison Steadman, Julia McKenzie, Joanna Lumley, Sylvia Sims and Bernard Hill. The movie was nominated for two Academy Awards and Pauline Collins won the BAFTA award that year for Best Actress in a Leading Role.

Memorable quotes from movies of the decade:

'Gordon's alive!' – Prince Vultan, *Flash Gordon* (1980).

'I am your father' – Darth Vader, *The Empire Strikes Back* (1980).

'He-e-e-e-re's Johnnie!' *The Shining* (1980).

'ET phone home' – ET, *ET the Extra-terrestrial* (1982).

'They're here!' – Carol Anne Freeling, *Poltergeist* (1982).

'Wax on, wax off.' – Mr Miyagi, *The Karate Kid* (1984).

'I'll be back!' – *The Terminator* (1984).

'We came. We saw. We kicked its ass.' – Ghostbusters (1984).

'Nobody calls me chicken!' – Marty McFly, *Back to the Future* (1985).

'Alright, alright, Mickey's a mouse, Donald's a duck, Pluto's a dog. What's Goofy?' – Gordie, *Stand By Me* (1986).

'Be afraid. Be very afraid.' – The Fly (1986).

'There can be only one.' – Highlander (1986).

'Feed me! Feed me!' – Little Shop of Horrors (1986).

'Nobody puts Baby in a corner.' – Johnny Castle, *Dirty Dancing* (1987).

11

Comics and Books

Paperboys were still seen on the streets during the 1980s. They would get up early to deliver the household's newspaper or, better still, if you were a kid, your favourite weekly comic. There was a vast selection of popular comics produced during the decade. Some of the best and most fondly remembered publications are listed below.

2000 AD (1977–present) was originally produced by IPC before being sold to Fleetway Comics. During the 1980s, and since, it has been popular for its Judge Dread strips. In 1980, a new character was introduced to the Judge Dread stories. Judge Death, an undead judge from another dimension, became Dread's new nemesis in stories drawn originally by Brian Bolland. Other strips included Mean Arena, which revolved around a violent high-tech street football game; Meltdown Man, whose hero finds himself transported by a nuclear explosion to a genetically engineered far future; the return of Strontium Dog, which included a mutant bounty hunter; and Dash Decent, a parody of the popular *Flash Gordon* movies. Other strips during the decade included Rogue Trooper, a genetic infantryman; Ace Trucking Co, cashing in on the CB radio craze; D. R. & Quinch; and The Ballad of Halo Jones, created and drawn by Alan Davis and Ian Gibson. *2000 AD* continues to be sold today and since 2007 has been available online.

The Beano (1938–present). *The Beano* had been a favourite comic since the 1930s. By the 1980s, it was still as popular as ever and featured Dennis the Menace and Gnasher on the cover as the main strip. Other popular strips of the 1980s included Lord Snooty, Biffo the Bear, Minnie the Minx, Smudge, Rasher, Ivy the Terrible, Simply Smiffy, Roger the Dodger, Calamity James, Karate Sid, The Germs, Fatty Fudge, Little Plum, Baby Face Finlayson and The McTickles, and a new character, Little Monkey. The comic had a major revamp in 1988 which marked *The Beano's* 50th anniversary. More pages were added and there was more colour added throughout. The comic has been read and enjoyed by generations of children and, today, is still much loved.

The Beezer (1956–93) was a well-loved comic that entertained children for almost 40 years. It originally came in A3 size (like its sister comic, *Topper*), which made it twice as big as other comics. The comic was reduced to A4 size in 1981. Popular strips in *The Beezer* during the 1980s included Ginger; Pop, Dick and Harry; The Hillys and the Billies; The Banana Bunch; Baby Crockett; Colonel Blink; The Numskulls; The Jellymen; Little Mo; Young Sid the Copper's Kid; My Pal Ropey; Smiffy; Scrapper; Plug; and many more.

The Black Hole (1980) was published by IPC Magazines and was issued to tie in with the movie of the same name. The comic which featured characters from the movie was only published for one month at the beginning of 1980.

Blue Jeans (1980–91) was a weekly comic for girls published by D. C. Thomson & Co. Ltd. It contained photo strips as well as pop news, interviews and articles on fashion as well as readers' true confessions. It was similar to the ever-popular *Jackie* and sometimes came with a free gift; the first issue's gift being a pot of glitter.

Buddy (1981–83) was a weekly comic for boys and concentrated on adventure strips. The first issue, published on 14 February 1981, came free with a 'Pop Pistol and Two Bullets.' Issue 2 came free with a 'Banshee Wailer' and Issue 3 came free with a 'Super Zoomer.' *Buddy* often used strips which had originally appeared previously in other D. C. Thomson titles including Limp Along Leslie, a strip from *Wizard*; The Wolf of Kabul, first published in *Hotspur*; Deep Sea Danny's Iron Fish, similar to the *Beano*'s Iron Fish; Jonah – The Biggest Jinx on the Seven Seas; and Billy the Cat, another former *Beano* character. Original strips in the comic included Tuffy – A Boy All Alone, a story about an orphan; Hammer, about a ninth century Briton battling Vikings); and Boy on the Run about a young boy escaping from the mysterious Man in Black.

Bunty (1958–2001) was aimed at girls and featured short comic strip stories as well as a letters page, puzzles and competitions. The back page originally featured a cut-out doll with paper clothes and later a poster. Regular strips included The Four Marys, about four teenage girls living at a boarding school; Bunty – 'a girl like you,' about a blonde girl and her friends Haya and Payal; Penny's Place about a girl whose parents owned a cafe; Moira Kent and Lorna Drake, who both started life as aspiring ballet dancers; Lona the Wonder Girl; and Princess of the Pops.

Buster (1960–2000) was a favourite comic of many youngsters for several decades. When the comic was first released in 1960, an advert in the *Daily Mirror* announced that Buster was the son of their own comic strip character, *Andy Capp*. The first issue, published on 23 May 1960, had an all-important free gift – a 'Balloon Bleeper!' The free gift with Issue 2 was a 'Zoomer Jet' which you whizzed around your head on a piece of string. Issue 3 gave away a 'Fool 'Em All Dodger Kit,' which consisted of a false nose, moustache and glasses. By the 1980s, the comic cost 30p and came out every Monday. Popular characters featured during the decade included Vampire Brats; Tom Thug's Skooldayz; Pete and his Pimple; Ricky Rainbo; Chalky; Melvyn's Mirror; and Mighty Mouth.

Champ (1984–85) was football-based comic for boys which lasted for just one year before becoming amalgamated with *Spike* and then *Victor*. Issue 1 came out on Saturday 25 February 1984 and featured a free 'Super Soccer Slide Guide.' There were ten pages of football every week as well as creepy tales, comic capers and school shocks. Strips included Charlie 'Iron' Barr; Limp-Along' Leslie; and Dennis the Menace's Fun Section.

Cheeky Weekly (1977–80) was published every Monday by IPC Magazines Ltd and ran for 117 issues. It merged with *Whoopee!*, originally as a sixteen-page pull-out section. The debut issue came with a free 'Red Jet Rattler' (a self-build model aeroplane). Regular characters and strips included Cheeky's Week, drawn by Frank McDiarmid; Lily Pop; Posh Claude; Walter Wurx; Jogging Jeremy; Baby Burpo; Baker's Boy; Sid the Street Sweeper; Ursula the Usherette; and Six Million Dollar Gran.

Commando Comics (1961–present). Featuring stories from the First and Second World War, the pocket-sized comic became one of the most popular British war comics. It was launched by D. C. Thomson & Co. Ltd (who also published *The Beano* and *The Dandy*) in 1961 and featured tales of loyalty, courage, cowardice and patriotism.

Crisis (1988–91) was a fortnightly comic which was a spin-off of *2000 AD* starting with two main stories Third World War and New Statesmen, a superhero strip by John Smith and Jim Baikie. The comic was published by Fleetway in response to the popularity of the rival comic *Deadline*.

The Crunch (1979–80) was published for a year before merging with *The Hotspur*. It ran for a total of fifty-four issues. Popular strips included The Kyser Experiment, Clancy and the Man, Arena, The Mantracker, Hitler Lives, The Walking Bombs, Who Killed Cassidy?, Crag, Starhawk, Kill the Hit Man, The Mill Street Mob, Space Wars and Ebony.

The Dandy (1937–2012). *The Dandy* came out in 1937 with *The Beano* following it in 1938. They were published on alternate weeks during the Second World War because of paper and ink rationing. By 1949, normal weekly publishing continued and during the 1960s, the comic was read all over the country. Popular characters in *The Dandy* included Korky the Cat and Desperate Dan, which became the comic's longest running strips.

The first issue of *The Dandy* was published on 4 December 1937. It was then known as *The Dandy Comic*. It was different from other comics of the day because it used speech balloons instead of captions. The first *Dandy Annual* was released in 1938 and was originally called *The Dandy Monster Comic*. An annual has been published every year ever since. The annuals always came out at Christmas time and in the 1980s were much appreciated presents. In 1954, the first *Desperate Dan Book* was published. It mostly consisted of strips that had appeared in the comic throughout the year. *The Dandy* eventually consisted of all comic strips, but the earlier issues had also included text strips with few illustrations. Some of these text strips included Jimmy's Pocket Grandpa, British Boys and Girls Go West. Sales eventually slumped from 2 million a week in the 1950s to just 8,000 a week sixty years later, leading to the comic closing in December 2012.

Deadline (1988–95) was created by *2000 AD* artists Brett Ewins and Steve Dillon and featured a combination of comic strips and written articles aimed at older readers. Strips featured in the comic included Tank Girl; Wired World; Planet Swerve; Hugo Tate; Cheeky Wee Budgie Boy; Timulo; A-Men; Space Boss; Exit; Johnny Nemo; Box City and Ruby Chan.

Debbie (1973–83) was a comic for girls published by D. C. Thomson. It featured comic strips as well as photo stories covering a range of subjects including romance, science fiction, horror and suspense, period drama, humour and superhero. It was one of the most successful girls' comics and ran for 518 issues before being absorbed into *Spellbound*. Sister titles included *Bunty*, *Judy* and *Mandy*.

Doctor Who Magazine (1979–present) featured weekly strips featuring the Doctor and his enemies. From 1980s onwards, it was published monthly. As well as strips, the magazine also featured general articles about the television show as well as a news section and a letters page. Comic strips featuring the Daleks had appeared previously in *TV Century 21* as well as *TV Comic* during the 1960s and later, in the 1970s, appeared in *Countdown* and *TV Action*.

The Eagle (1982–94) made a return in the 1980s as a weekly comic published by IPC. It absorbed many other titles including *Scream!* (1984), *Tiger* (1985), *Battle* (1988), *Mask* (1988) and *Wildcat* (1989) before it was cancelled in January 1994. The main strip in the comic, as in the 1950s version, was Dan Dare although the character was the great-great-grandson of the original. Much of the comic, to start off with, featured photo-stories, but drawn stories returned with Issue 79 published in 1983. Popular strips included Ant Wars, reprinted from *2000 AD*; The Avenger by Tom Tully and Mike Western; Billy's Boots, originally in *Tiger*; Bloodfang;

The Brothers; Charley's War, reprinted from *Battle*; The Collector, a photo story; Computer Warrior; and Comrade Bronski.

Fast Forward (1989–95) was a weekly children's magazine published to compete with the hugely popular *Look-in*. The magazine featured a pull-out poster in its centre, mainly of television celebrities, as well as containing cartoon strips of celebrities and presenters who appeared on *Children's BBC,* including Andi Peters. Also featured were Edd the Duck and Gordon the Gopher as well as an *EastEnders* comic strip.

Girl (1981–90) was published by IPC and took its name from a previous title first produced in 1951. In 1982, the comic absorbed the publication *Dreamer*. Popular strips in the 1980s version of *Girl* included Nine to Four; Patty's World; The Haunting of Uncle Gideon; The Pink Flamingo; Slaves of the Nightmare Factory; The Evil Mirror; Wish of a Witch; The Runaway Bridesmaid; The Perfect Pest; To Catch a Thief; and No Mother for Marty.

Grange Hill Magazine (1980) was published to tie in with the popular TV show. It featured photos and stories of the cast as well as comic strips. The magazine, which cost 50p, lasted for only two issues.

Hoot (1985–86) was published by D. C. Thomson. Its main cover story featured Cuddles, a mischievous schoolboy, a strip which originally appeared in the comic *Nutty*. Regular strips included The Bash Street Kids; Colonel Blink; Dogsbody; Jay R; Lord Snooty; Piggles; Polar Blair; Sam's Secret Diary; Snackula; The Three Bears; and Wanta Job Bob. Many of the strips had previously appeared in other D. C. Thomson & Co. Ltd titles. After a year, the comic merged into *The Dandy*.

Hot-Shot (1988–89) was a football comic published by Fleetway. It was endorsed by Gary Lineker but only lasted a year before it was merged with *Roy of the Rovers*. Popular strips included Family Fortune; The Louts of Liberty Hall; and Striker.

The Hotspur (1933–81). *The Hotspur* was originally a story paper for boys, which was first published in 1933 but it was re-launched as a comic in 1959 and was renamed *The New Hotspur*. Its name returned to just being *The Hotspur* in 1963. In the 1970s, *The Hotspur* merged with *Hornet* and then *The Crunch*. Popular strips included Coral Island, Jonny Jett, King Cobra, Spring Heeled Jack, Union Jack Jackson and X-Bow. It was eventually incorporated into *The Victor* in 1981 although *The Hotspur* appeared as an annual until 1991.

Hwyl (1949–89) was the first comic to be published in the Welsh language and lasted for forty years before closing in 1989. The word 'Hwyl' translated to English as 'fun'.

It's Wicked! (1989) was a short-lived comic produced by Marvel. It featured many supernatural comic strips. The character 'Slimer' from the

American cartoon The Real Ghostbusters featured on the cover. Regular strips included Clare Voyant; Ghosthunters; Ghostman Bat and His Black and White Rat; Gordon Gremlin; Inspector Spectre: Private Eye; Slimer; Toad in the Hole; and Winnie the Witch Doctor.

Jack and Jill (1954–85) featured Jack and Jill of Buttercup Farm who regularly appeared on the front page of the comic and was based on the well-loved nursery rhyme. The stories were told in rhyming couplets and regular characters within the comic included Harold Hare, Teddy and Cuddly, Flipper the Skipper, Chalky the Blackboard Boy and Douglas Dachshund.

Jackie (1964–93) was a favourite girls' magazine for many years. It was the best-selling teen magazine in the UK for ten years and included pop pin-ups, fashion and beauty tips, gossip, comic strips and short stories.

Jackpot (1979–82) was published by IPC and ran for three years before being merged into *Buster*. Strips included Angel's (Proper) Charlies; Class Wars; It's a Nice Life; Jack Pott; Little Adam and Eva; Milly O'Naire and Penny Less; Richie Wraggs; Sherlock Jnr: The Clued-Up Kid; The Teeny Sweeny; and The Winners.

Jinty (1974–81) was a popular girls' comic published weekly by IPC which ran for seven years. It had previously merged with the earlier comics *Lindy* and *Penny* before itself merging with *Tammy* in 1981. Strips included Angela's Angels; Clancy on Trial; Concrete Surfer; Dora Dogsbody; A Dream for Yvonne; Fran of the Floods; Friends of the Forest; Girl in a Bubble; The Haunting of Hazel; Make-Believe Mandy; Miss No-Name; The Robot Who Cried; The Slave of Form 3B; The Snobs and the Scruffs; and A Spell of Trouble.

Judy (1960–91). The success of D. C. Thomson's first comic for girls, *Bunty*, led to the company publishing *Judy*. Between them, the comics had a readership of over one million. Judy included within its pages a mix of romance, school- and girl-next-door stories. In 1991, the comic merged with *Mandy*.

Look Alive (1982–87) was issued by IPC as a replacement for *Look and Learn* which the publishers felt had become old-fashioned and it was thought that children would prefer something more modern.

Look and Learn (1962–82) was popular with teachers and parents because, although it was a comic, it was also educational. Piles of the comics could be found in classrooms of the 1980s and were read when it was too wet to play outside during break times. It contained a variety of interesting articles, featuring information on topics from volcanoes to the Loch Ness

Monster. There was also a long-running science fiction strip called The Trigan Empire. Its worldwide pen pal pages proved to be very popular. The first issue sold 700,000 copies and this settled down to about 300,000 for later issues. Early features included stories about Charles I, Vincent van Gogh, *The Arabian Nights* and *Three Men in a Boat*.

Look-in (1971–91) was a hugely successful magazine for twenty years. It featured popular celebrities, photos and articles of TV and pop stars, competitions and a centre page colour pull-out but its main feature was the many comic strips of the favourite children's television programmes, all of which were being shown on the ITV network at the time. It was first published by Independent Television Publications but later by IPC. It was seen as a successor to the earlier *TV21* as well as being a junior version of the *TV Times*. The memorable covers were painted painted by Arnaldo Putzu and Ivan Rose. Popular comic strips featured during the 1980s included Airwolf; ALF; The A-Team; Battlestar Galactica; Buck Rogers in the 25th Century; Bucks Fizz; Charlie's Angels; CHiPs; Dogtanian; Elvis : The Story; Gilbert the Alien; Haircut One Hundred; It's Madness; Magnum PI; and Mork and Mindy.

Mandy (1967–91). *Mandy* was a British comic for girls which was first issued in January 1967, with a 'free Rainbow Ring'. Popular strips included Glenda the Guide; Skeleton Corner; Very Important Pupil; and The Girls at Knock-Out Academy. Most stories were serialised and lasted between eight and twelve issues.

Masters of the Universe (1986–90) was published as a comic, fortnightly, for seventy-two issues. There was also a monthly comic which ran for twenty-eight issues. It featured all the characters from the television show in a range of action adventures.

Mates Magazine (1975–80) was produced for girls and featured articles and photos relating to celebrities and pop stars, with a colour poster pull-out, with articles about fashion, true life stories and competitions. In 1980, the magazine merged with *Pink*.

Misty (1978–80) was a girls' magazine published by Fleetway and featured a selection of comic strips, usually relating to supernatural and horror stories. It also included complete stories, text stories, and serials. When it ended in 1980, it was merged with another Fleetway publication *Tammy*. Strips included Moonchild, about a girl who uses her power of telekinesis on a bully; Raggsy Doll, about a cursed doll; Miss T, a comic strip about a witch; Cilla the Chiller, about a schoolgirl ghost; School of the Lost, the story of a girls' boarding school; Whistle and I'll Come featuring the ghost of a dog; The Cats of Carey Street, in which cats fight off a council development; *The Black Widow,* about a widow who avenges her husband's death; and When The Lights Go Out, about a schoolgirl who gets turned into a shop room dummy.

My Guy Magazine (1978–2000) was a magazine for teenage girls and featured photo love stories, features and competitions. Long before they were famous, Hugh Grant, George Michael, Tony Hadley, Alex Kingston and Tracey Ullman appeared in photo strips within its pages. The magazine lasted for twenty-two years before ceasing in 2000.

Nikki (1985–89) was published for girls by D.C. Thomson and lasted for 237 issues. Its most notable strip was The Comp which afterwards continued in *Bunty* when *Nikki* ceased to be published.

Nipper (1987) was a short-lived comic that only lasted for sixteen issues before it merged with *Buster*. Strips included Blaster and Bignoise; Brad Break, about an accident prone character who is always in hospital with a broken limb; Double Trouble, a story about twins Jon and Suzy, always trying to outdo each other; Felix The Pussycat; First-Time Fred; Frankie's Flashlight; James Pond; and Magic Trainers.

Nutty (1980–85) was published by D. C. Thomson and ran for 292 issues before merging with *The Dandy*. Its main strip, and the most popular, was Bananaman which was drawn by John Geering. Other strips included Big 'n Bud; Blubba and the Bear; Cannonball Kid; Dick Turban, Desert Highwayman; Ethel Red; General Dumbo; and Horace Cope.

Oh Boy (1978–84) was a magazine for teenage girls featuring photos and articles about male television and pop stars. It was eventually merged with *My Guy* and became a romantic fiction magazine,

Oink! (1986–88) was a weekly comic published by Fleetway. Although aimed at children, it was influenced by the adult magazine *Viz* as well as the satirical *Mad* magazine. Its run was controversial leading to some newsagent chains branding it unsuitable for children. In 1987, the comic also became a computer game. Notable strips included Uncle Pigg; The Street-Hogs; Harry the Head; Billy's Brain; Horace 'Ugly Face' Watkins; and Weedy Willy.

Penny (1979–80) was a short-lived comic for girls published by IPC which featured stories of Enid Blyton's *Secret Seven* as well as an adaptation of the classic *Little Women*. Other features included Tansy of Jubilee Street; Sad Sal and Smiley Sue; Ginny and Shep; The Village Clock; Waifs of the Waterfall; and Tales of Katy-Jane. It later merged with *Jinty*.

Photo-Love Magazine (1979–86) featured photos, pin-ups and articles about current television and pop stars as well as photo strips (one featured a young Fiona Bruce) and competitions.

Pink (1973–80) was a comic for girls which ran for 377 issues. It was a mixture of comic strips with features on music and fashion. Romance-based strips included including Don't Let Him Fool You, Faye!; The Haunting of Jilly Johnson; Remember, Rosanna, Remember!; Shadow of Fear; Memories of Mike; The Island of Stones; Rich Girl, Poor Girl; Looking for Eddie; Sugar Jones; and Patty's World.

Pippin (1966–86) was published by Polystyle Publications Ltd and featured characters from pre-school television shows. Regular strips included The Pogles, Bizzy Lizzy, Joe, The Woodentops, Andy Pandy, Bill and Ben, Camberwick Green, Trumpton and Chigley as well as many others. The comic also featured a puzzle page, readers' letters and a story from the Bible.

Playhour (1954–87). *Playhour* was a companion comic to *Jack and Jill* but aimed at slightly older children. The comic contained tales of television favourites such as *Pinky & Perky, Bill and Ben the two Flower Pot Men, The Magic Roundabout* and *Sooty*. Other stories included Billy Brock's Schooldays, The Wonderful Tales of Willow Wood, Little Red Squirrel and Norman Gnome.

Poot! (1985–90) was a comic for adults which was often read by children. Its tagline was 'silly cartoons and smart-arse satire for grown ups'. Its first issue sold only 500 copies but the readership grew to 50,000 before it closed. Strips included Sven the Saxophone, Desmond Hoo, Young Fred Crombie the Undead Zombie, Short Fat Ugly Bald Stupid Man, about a middle-aged superhero; Winston the Cuddly Christmas Pudding, and Plopper Jenkins.

Roy of the Rovers (1976–95) was an extremely popular comic and featured a football strip of Melchester Rovers soccer hero, Roy Race. The character originally appeared in *Tiger* in 1954. Roy's final strip in the magazine was in 1993 when he lost his foot in a helicopter crash, which ended his career. The subsequent strips featured his son, Rocky. In 1988, a *Roy of the Rovers* computer game was produced for the Commodore 64, the Amstrad CPC and the ZX Spectrum. There was also a Melchester Rovers Subbuteo team manufactured as well as a board game.

School Fun (1983–84) was a short-lived comic whose first issue came with 'a free slippy, sticky snake'. Its tagline was 'The happiest read of your life!' It lasted for thirty-three issues before being merged with *Buster*.

Scream! (1984) was a weekly horror comic published by IPC Magazines. It lasted for just fifteen issues. Strips included The Dracula File, the leading story; Fiends and Neighbours, a re-print from the popular comic *Cor!*; A Ghastly Tale; Library of Death; Monster; and Tales from the Grave.

Shoot! (1969–2008) was a popular football magazine which included news stories and articles, as well as a colour pull-out and photos of top players. It also featured a regular comic strip, Paul Trevillion's You Are The Ref. Probably the most popular football magazine ever, it sold 120,000 copies a week at its height.

Star Wars Weekly (1978–80) was published by Marvel and reprinted comic strips from the American version of the comic. The publication cost 10p. After Issue 117, the comic was renamed *The Empire Strikes Back Weekly* to tie-in with the release of the new movie. The first issue came with a free gift, a cut-out cardboard X-Fighter.

Tammy (1971–84) was a weekly comic for girls published by Fleetway. Strips and stories included Alison all Alone; Betina at Ballet School; Dawn and Kerry, Double for Trouble; Derry the Dowser; and The Four Friends at Spartan School. The comic had previously merged with several other popular girls' comics including *Sally, Sandie, June, Jinty,* and *Misty.* In 1984, the title disappeared after being merged with *Girl.*

Teddy Bear's Playtime (1981) was a short-lived comic for nursery age children. The comic became part of the *Jack and Jill* publication on October 1981.

ThunderCats (1987–91) featured stories and characters from the popular television series and was published by Marvel UK. The comic started off being issued weekly and then fortnightly before becoming a monthly. Marvel UK also issued seasonal specials, paperbacks, and annuals connected with the comic.

Tiger (1954–85) was originally launched in 1954 under the title *Tiger – The Sport and Adventure Picture Story Weekly.* Its most popular strip was Roy of the Rovers which told the story of fictional footballer Roy Race and his team, Melchester Rovers. The strip became so popular that eventually Roy of the Rovers had his own comic. *Tiger* merged with several comics over the following years becoming *Tiger and Hurricane, Tiger and Jag, Tiger and Scorcher* before finally merging with *The Eagle.*

The Topper (1953–90). *The Topper's* most popular strip was Mickey the Monkey, who appeared on the front page of the comic for many years. He was very similar to Biffo the Bear in the *Beano.* Other well-loved characters included Beryl the Peril, Desert Island Dick, Keyhole Kate, Send for Kelly and Sir Laughalot. In 1990, the comic was merged with another long-running D. C. Thomson title, *The Beezer.*

Transformers (1984–92) was published by Marvel UK and lasted 332 issues. The comic featured reprinted stories from the American version of the publication as well as new strips written and drawn by British artists, the main writer being Simon Furman.

TV Comic (1951–84) was published weekly by Beaverbrook and, from 1960, by Polystyle Publications and featured stories based on popular TV shows.

Early strips included Sooty; Coco the Clown; Noddy and Lenny the Lion and later *Treasure Island*, *The Lone Ranger* and *Black Beauty*. Between 1964 and 1979, it produced stories from *Doctor Who* as well as strip cartoons relating to popular Gerry Anderson serials. By the 1980s, it was featuring strips based on *The Pink Panther*, *Popeye*, *The A-Team*, *Tales of the Gold Monkey*, *Tom and Jerry*, *Scooby-Doo* and Laurel and Hardy. Battle of the Planets, which was drawn by former Dan Dare artist Keith Watson, appeared in the comic between 1981 and 1983. Its demise came in 1984 due to falling sales.

Twinkle (1968–99) was published weekly by D. C. Thomson & Co. and was aimed at young girls. The comics featured comic strips, dress-up dolls, as well as a Twinkle Club letters page, together with puzzles. Popular strips featured in the comic included Nurse Nancy (illustrated by Sabine Price); Jenny Wren; Witch Winkle; Polly's Magic Paintbox; Goldilocks and her Three Bears; My Baby Brother; The Three Pennys; Patsy Panda; Patty Pickle; Sally Sweet; Molly and her Dollies; and Dandy Lion.

Victor (1961–92) was an action comic for boys featuring stories of war and bravery. Notable strips featured in the comic included Alf Tupper; I Flew With Braddock; Sergeant Bob Millar of the Coldstream Guards, tales of a front line soldier in the First World War; Morgyn the Mighty – Master of Black Island, which had previously appeared in *The Rover* and *The Beano*; Gorgeous Gus; Joe Bones the Human Fly; Figaro, about an overweight, incompetent Mexican outlaw, who previously featured in *The Topper*; The Hammer Man – Chell Puddock, about a medieval knight who wielded a hammer instead of a sword; Gerald Cadman, about a cowardly British officer; and Send for Saxon.

War Picture Library (1958–84) was a sixty-four-page pocket library war comic, which was published by Amalgamated Press/Fleetway and continued for 2,103 issues. Each issue included a full story, starting with Fight Back to Dunkirk on 1 September 1958 and ending with Wings of the Fleet on 3 December 1984.

Warlord (1974–86) was originally published by D. C. Thomson and featured wartime adventures. The success of the comic led to IPC releasing its own similar title *Battle Picture Weekly* (1975–88). By 1978, *Warlord* absorbed a similar comic called *Bullet*. In 1986, *Warlord* was absorbed into the more popular war-based comic *The Victor*. Notable strips in *Warlord* included Lord Peter Flint (Codename: Warlord); Union Jack Jackson; Spider Wells; Bomber Braddock; and Wingless Wonder.

Whizzer and Chips (1969–90) was a children's favourite for twenty-one years and featured two comics *Whizzer* and *Chips* with their own individual characters and puzzles. Its slogan was 'Two comics in one, double the fun!'. Several comics were merged with *Whizzer and Chips* over the years including *Knockout* in 1973, *Krazy* in 1978, *Whoopee!* in 1985 and *Scouse Mouse* in 1989. Memorable characters and strips included Sid's Snake; Champ; Joker; Lazy Bones; Strange Hill; Sweeny Toddler; and Oddball.

Whoopee! (1974–85) was merged with the comic *Shiver and Shake* soon after it was first published. The first issue came with 'a free squirter ring'. The comic later absorbed the comics *Cheeky* and *Wow!* before, as already mentioned, it merged with *Whizzer and Chips*. Popular characters included Ad Lad; Blinketty Blink; Blunder Puss; Calculator Kid; Daisy Jones' Locket; Evil Eye; Frankie Stein; Mustapha Million; The Bumpkin Billionaires; and Willy Worry.

Wildcat (1988–89) was a short-lived comic featuring science fiction stories about colonists who escape the Earth in a spacecraft called Wildcat just prior to the planet being destroyed in the year 2500. The comic ran for just twelve issues before in was merged with *Eagle* in 1989.

Wow! (1982–83) ran for a year before being merged with *Whoopee!* in 1983. Popular strips included Adam and his Ants, a strip originally featured in *Cor!*; Barney's Badges; Bill and Coo, about a boy and his pet pigeon; The Goodies and the Baddies; Gulliver's Troubles; Ossie, the story of an ostrich; Penny Dreadful; Shipwreck Kids; and Hi De Hi Hi De Hooooo, a tale of a haunted holiday camp.

All British comics produced their own annuals which were a must for Christmas presents and were eagerly looked forward to.

American comics featured more glossy covers and full colour strips. Adverts within their pages featured X-Ray Specs, Sea Monkeys and Charles Atlas's bodybuilding course. X-Ray specs allowed you to apparently see through your hand and people's clothing. They consisted of a pair of cardboard glasses with two eye holes cut out which contained feathers. Looking through the feathers gave the illusion of being able to see through things. The advert for Sea Monkeys showed a family of creatures in a fish bowl smiling and doing tricks. Even in the advert, they looked nothing like monkeys (more like aliens) and there was more disappointment to come. Once the kit arrived (a sealed packet of powder), the 'monkeys' turned out to be nothing more than tiny shrimps when added to water. Charles Atlas's bodybuilding course featured an advert showing a thin teenager, at the beach, having sand kicked in his face by other youths. After taking the bodybuilding course, he was able to sort out the bullies and soon had a wonderful girlfriend. Other adverts included writing and art courses as well as many other strange and peculiar products that only could be found in American comics.

Some of the best American comics of the time included *Archie Comics, Batman, Casper the Friendly Ghost, The Flintstones,* as well as various Marvel and DC comics featuring *The Hulk, Spiderman* and *Superman.* There was something weird and wonderful, at the time, about anything that came from America and their comics and sense of humour differed greatly from the humour that was found in British comics such as *The Beano* and *The Dandy.*

Comics were well read and much loved by children during the 1980s and many are still very fondly remembered today.

There were also many pop magazines produced during the decade and these included *Beatbox* (1984); *Fabulous 208* (1964–80); *The Face* (1980–2004); *Jackie* (1964–93); *Just Seventeen* (1984–2004); *No 1* (1983–87); *Record Collector* (1980–present); *Right On!* (1972–2011); *Sassy* (1988–94); *Smash Hits* (1978–2006) and *Tiger Beat* (1965–present).

Pop newspapers included *Melody Maker* (1926–2000); *New Musical Express (NME)* (1952– present); and *Sounds* (1970–91).

Memorable books published during the decade included *The NeverEnding Story* by Michael Ende; *The Snowman* by Raymond Briggs; *Peepo!* by Janet and Allan Ahlberg; *Goodnight Mister Tom* by Michelle Magorian; *Dear Zoo* by Rod Campbell; *Alfie Gets In First* by Shirley Hughes; *The BFG* by Roald Dahl; *Peace At Last* by Jill Murphy.

Before the 1980s, many children learned to read at school by using Janet and John books as well as a huge range of titles published by Ladybird. Originally Janet and John books had been published in America but in 1949, publishers James Nisbet & Co. licensed the books to the United Kingdom and they became immensely popular as school reading books in the 1950s and 1960s. The books featured children living a middle-class life. The books were illustrated by Florence and Margaret Hoopes. However, by the 1970s, the books became outdated and became less popular as teaching aids.

Ladybird books first appeared in 1915 and were published by Wills & Hepworth. All carried the distinctive Ladybird logo. In 1964, the company started producing their Key Words Reading Scheme series, which was used extensively. The series contained thirty-six small-format hardback books. In the 1960s, the Learnabout series was published. Ladybird books covered a whole range of subjects including fairy tales, fiction, science, history, geography, wildlife, sport, transport, royalty and classic tales. Their books were much loved and fondly remembered today.

Enid Blyton's books have been read by generations and sum up many people's childhoods. Her popular books included Noddy and the Three Golliwogs, a term that is no longer acceptable, but the most fondly remembered featured the Famous Five and the Secret Seven. The first Famous Five book, *Five on a*

Treasure Island, was published in 1942. It featured a group of young children, Julian, Dick, Anne and Georgina, more commonly known as George. They were accompanied on their adventures by Timmy the dog. All the stories took place in the summer holidays when the children met up after returning from the respective boarding schools. Enid Blyton wrote twenty-one books featuring the Famous Five, the last one being *Five Are Together Again,* which was published in 1963. The books were hugely successful and sold millions as did the books in her similar series, The *Secret Seven. The Secret Seven* included Peter, Janet (Peter's sister), Jack, Barbara, George, Pam and Colin. These series were still being read in the 1980s as parents who remembered them from their own childhoods introduced their children to the adventure stories.

Another well-read series of Enid Blyton books was the *Five Find-Outers*. Characters featured included Frederick Algernon 'Fatty' Trotteville, who was the leader of the group, Laurence 'Larry' Daykin, Margaret 'Daisy' Daykin, Philip 'Pip' Hilton and Elizabeth 'Bets' Hilton. They were joined by Fatty's Scottish terrier, Buster. The series of mystery books were published between 1943 and 1969 and included fifteen stories including *The Mystery of the Burnt Cottage, The Mystery of the Disappearing Cat* and *The Mystery of the Secret Room.*

Popular fiction for children included *The Lion, the Witch and the Wardrobe,* which was published in 1950 and was written by C. S. Lewis. David Geoffrey Bles, who published the book, feared that tales of fantasy might not be well received but children loved the book and soon after several other works in the Narnia saga were published including *Prince Caspian: The Return to Narnia* (1951), *The Voyage of the Dawn Treader* (1952), *The Silver Chair* (1953), *The Horse and His Boy* (1954), *The Magician's Nephew* (1955) and *The Last Battle* (1956). The series is still popular today.

Warne's Observer books were published between 1937 and 2003 and were also very popular with children. The small hardback books could fit in your pocket and featured subjects including birds, trees, astronomy, cars, aircraft, animals, butterflies, spaceflight and dogs. They were ideal for any inquisitive mind and were ideal to discover information about the world around you.

I-Spy books were equally popular. Originally, when the books were first released, an article appeared in the *Daily Mail,* featuring 'Big Chief I-Spy' (the head of the Redskins) which recorded his I-Spy triumphs in tracking and spotting. Messages and passwords were printed for members of the I-Spy club who were known as the Great Tribe. Booklets could be bought for 6*d* and covered subjects such as I-Spy insects, wild fruits, fungi, wild flowers, history, the unusual, dogs, trees and on the road, etc. The books contained many illustrations and the I-Spyer had to spot the objects and write down when and where the object was spotted. For each one seen, points were awarded. When the book was full, it could be sent to Big Chief I-Spy and an Order of Merit would be sent together with booklet. The books had to be signed by a teacher or parents as well as the name of the entrant's school. The craze proved incredibly popular and continues today. Charles Warrell produced the first I-Spy booklet in 1948 and by 1956, Arnold Cawthrow became the second Big Chief I-Spy. By the 1980s, David Bellamy was Big Chief I-Spy continuing the books' interest in both nature and the outdoor life.

Books featuring Rupert Bear were also immensely popular. Rupert had first appeared in the *Daily Express* on 8 November 1920 to boost sales and to compete with their rivals, the *Daily Mail* and the *Daily Mirror*. By 1935, the stories were being told and illustrated by Arthur Bestall who had previously illustrated *Punch*. He continued to illustrate the Rupert comic strips until he was well into his 90s. From 1936, a Rupert annual was published and thousands of children were given them for Christmas presents. The white bear was as familiar to children in the '80s as he had been to their parents and grandparents.

Christmas annuals were loved by all and featured collections of strips from well-loved comics as well as the latest TV characters and cartoons. Most children would receive several annuals for Christmas and these often included the *Beano* and the *Dandy* which were favourites for many years.

Classic stories such as *Treasure Island, Robinson Crusoe, The Swiss Family Robinson, Robin Hood* and *William Tell* continued in popularity throughout the 1980s although they had been around for many years. All featured adventurous tales which appealed to children who enjoyed re-enacting scenes while playing outdoors.

Treasure Island was first published in 1883 and was written by Scottish author, Robert Louis Stevenson and featured a story of pirates and buried treasure. It had originally been serialised in the children's magazine *Young Folks* between 1881 and 1882. It famously featured Long John Silver in a story narrated by Jim Hawkins.

A thirteen-part serial, *The Adventures of Robinson Crusoe*, was first aired on the BBC in 1965 and is fondly remembered and was repeated often, especially in school summer holidays. The television show was originally made in France and dubbed into English. At the same time, its memorable musical soundtrack was added. The original book was written by Daniel Defoe and was first published in 1719. It told the tale of a castaway stranded on a desert island near Trinidad. While there, he encountered cannibals and mutineers before being finally rescued. The book was thought to be based on the story of Alexander Selkirk who was a Scottish castaway who had been stranded on an island in the Pacific called Más a Tierra. The island was renamed Robinson Crusoe Island in 1966. The book hasn't lost any of its charm over the several hundred years since it was first written and, with the TV series, fuelled the imaginations of children in the 1980s.

Gulliver's Travels was a novel originally published in 1726, Written by an Irish author and clergyman Jonathan Swift. At the time, it was universally read and has remained in print ever since. During the 1960s, two television shows were made based on the book. The first, *The Three Worlds of Gulliver* was first broadcast in 1960. It starred Kerwin Mathews and featured special effects by Ray Harryhausen. In 1968, Hanna-Barbera produced a cartoon called *The Adventures of Gulliver*. The book tells of Lemuel Gulliver's voyages around the globe. In his first adventure, he finds himself washed ashore after a shipwreck and becomes the prisoner of little people on the island of Lilliput. The same idea was also later used in the successful television show, *Land of the Giants*. At first, Gulliver is seen as an enemy of the Lilliputians but later becomes their hero before displeasing the king and his court. He makes his escape and his second adventure takes him to the land of Brobdingnag, which is inhabited by giants. There are many more voyages and adventures featured in the book although his visit to Lilliput is the most retold and well-known story.

The *Swiss Family Robinson* told an all-action adventure story about a family shipwrecked in the East Indies while en route to Port Jackson in Australia. The book was first published in 1812 and was written by Johann David Wyss, a Swiss pastor. The story featured the family's struggle to survive on an island and their numerous adventures before finally being rescued. In 1960, Walt Disney made a film of the book, which starred John Mills, which was hugely successful. The 1960s television series, *Lost in Space* was loosely based on the book and featured the story of a futuristic family, also called Robinson, who found themselves stranded in space. Re-runs ensured that children in the 1980s still found the story to be exciting.

The Bible was also well-read by children in the 1980s. All schools had religious teachings at the time and many children were given bibles by their schools to read and learn. To many, the stories were just as interesting and exciting as stories by Enid Blyton, especially when read out loud by a teacher in class.

There were many other wonderful books read throughout the 1980s. Most featured adventures that appealed to the imaginations of young children, many of whom spent most of their leisure time, when not reading, outdoors.

12

Music

The high street during the 1980s featured far more record stores than it does today and these included Virgin, HMV and Our Price. Other retailers such as W. H. Smith, Woolworths and Boots also sold records and cassettes. Vinyl long playing albums and singles proved more popular than cassettes but both were soon to be superseded by a new technology, the CD (compact disc). CDs were developed by Philips and Sony and were first introduced in 1982. The first public demonstration of a CD took place on the BBC's *Tomorrow's World* in 1981 when Kieran Prendiville showed that even by spreading jam on the disc, it still played perfectly. This seemed to far outweigh the quality of vinyl, which was easily scratched, and regularly played with various pops and crackles. The CD chosen for the demonstration was the *Living Eyes* album by the Bee Gees. It was a whole year before the first commercial album was released on 17 August 1982 ABBA's 'The Visitors'.

In 1980, chart toppers included Pink Floyd with 'Another Brick in the Wall', Blondie with 'Atomic', The Jam with 'Going Underground', Dexy's Midnight Runners with 'Geno', Abba with 'The Winner Takes it All' and David Bowie with 'Ashes to Ashes'.

Meanwhile, in Japan, fifty titles were released on CD 1 October 1982, the first being Billy Joel's *52nd Street* which had previously been released on vinyl. In March 1983, after the Japanese launch, CD players and discs were released in the UK, Europe and America. Not everybody embraced the new technology. At first, CD players were expensive and some felt the compact discs might be a fad and would never entirely replace the good old fashioned vinyl long playing record. CD players soon came down in price and many people began to replace their old scratchy records with digitally enhanced, almost indestructibly, compact discs. Many records which had once been treasured were simply discarded or thrown away. For years, however, the three formats (vinyl, cassette and CDs) continued to be sold side by side. Vinyl and cassettes sold well into the 1990s before finally succumbing to the new technology. However, there were a few purists who held onto their LPs, claiming they preferred their sound.

Brothers in Arms (1985) by Dire Straits became the first album to sell a million copies on CD. The first artist to have his entire back catalogue transferred to the new medium was David Bowie, all released by RCA records in 1985. Mono versions of the first four albums issued by The Beatles were released on CD on 26 February 1987. By 1988, 400 million CDs were manufactured worldwide.

Music varied greatly throughout the decade and featured various styles including Post Punk, New Romantic, Rock, Goth, Reggae, Mod, Ska, Indie, House, Garage, Electronic, Hip-Hop, Soul and Synthpop.

The New Romantic era grew out of London nightclubs, particularly Billy's and The Blitz Club nearing the close of the 1970s. New Romantics were influenced by the likes of David Bowie and Roxy Music, developing glam rock fashions including white frilly shirts which led to their name linking them to the original Romanticists of the nineteenth century. The style of music made much use of synthesisers and early bands associated with the sound included Visage and Ultravox as well as Adam and the Ants, Culture Club, Spandau Ballet, Human League and Duran Duran.

A New Romantic shirt worn by bands such as Spandau Ballet and Adam and the Ants.

Visage were a synthpop band who originally formed in 1978. They are mainly remembered for their hit 'Fade to Grey', which was released towards the end of 1980. They had two Top 20 albums, *Visage* and *The Anvil*, as well as five singles that appeared in the top 30. Their third album, *Beat Boy*, wasn't so successful and the group split up in 1985. The band members included Steve Strange, Midge Ure, Rusty Egan, Billy Currie, John McGeoch, Barry Adamson and Dave Formula.

The decade produced the very first *Now That's What I Call Music* compilation in 1983, a double album, produced in both vinyl and cassette. It featured thirty UK hit singles including 'You Can't Hurry Love' by Phil Collins, 'Is There Something I Should Know?' by Duran Duran, 'Red, Red Wine' by UB40, 'Temptation' by Heaven 17, 'Double Dutch' by Malcolm McLaren, 'Total Eclipse of the Heart' by Bonnie Tyler, 'Karma Chameleon' by Culture Club, 'Too Shy' by Kajagoogoo, 'Down Under' by Men at Work, 'Baby Jane' by Rod Stewart, 'Wherever I Lay My Hat (That's My Home)' by Paul Young and '(Keep Feeling) Fascination' by The Human League as well as many others.

Many music programmes were featured on the television during the decade including *Top of the Pops*, Channel 4's *The Tube* (1982–87) with Jools Holland and Paula Yates, ITV's *The Chart Show* (1986–89) which aired on Saturday mornings, *Network 7* (1987–88) presented by Magenta Devine, Sankha Guha and Tracey MacLeod; *No Limits* (1985–87) with Jeremy Legg, Lisa Maxwell, Tony Baker and Jenny Powell; *Cheggers Plays Pop* (1978–86) hosted by Keith Chegwin; *Something Else* (1978–82) a BBC2 youth show featuring live music from the latest bands; *The Old Grey Whistle Test* (1971–88) presented by Bob Harris, Annie Nightingale, Andy Kershaw, Mark Ellen, Richard Skinner and others; *Rapido* (1988–92); broadcast on BBC2 and presented by Antoine de Caunes; *Pop Quiz* (1981–84) hosted by Mike Read; *Razzmatazz* (1981–87) a Tyne Tees show presented by Alastair Pirrie, Lyn Spencer, Brendan Healy, Suzanne Dando and Lisa Stansfield; *Get It Together* (1977–81) hosted by Roy North, Linda Fletcher and Megg Nicol; *The Hit Man and Her* (1988–92) a dance show hosted by Pete Waterman and Michaela Strachan; and a reworking of the 1950s show *Juke Box Jury* which was hosted by Jools Holland in 1989 and featured a panel of celebrity guests.

Top of the Pops included music from the charts and featured many of the top DJs of the day including Gary Davies, Paul Gambaccini, Peter Powell, Richard Skinner, Simon Bates, Tommy Vance, Steve Wright, John Peel and Janice Long. There were many more as well as endless guest presenters including Elton John, B. A. Robertson, Debbie Harry, Roger Daltrey and Cliff Richard. The show ran from 1 January 1964 until its final show on 30 July 2006. The resident dancers on the show during the decade included

Legs & Co (1976–81) and Zoo (1981–83). Regular members of Legs & Co included Lulu Cartwright, Patti Hammond, Sue Menhenick, Rosemary Hetherington, Pauline Peters and Gill Clark.

Top of the Pops is still greatly missed by many who remember their childhood sitting in front of the television waiting for their favourite band or artist to come on. By the 1980s, more videos were played on the show including memorable ones by Ultravox ('Vienna'), Adam and the Ants ('Stand and Deliver'), The Human League ('Don't You Want Me') and Michael Jackson's 'Thriller'.

With the introduction of Channel 4 on 2 November 1982, a new music show hit the screens. *The Tube* was hosted by Jools Holland and Paula Yates and featured live music and interviews. The show ran for five series between 5 November 1982 and 26 April 1987. It was made by Tyne Tees Television and also featured Leslie Ash and Muriel Gray. The Jam performed on the first edition giving their last live performance before breaking up later that year. The show promoted the careers of many artists including U2, The Proclaimers and Frankie Goes to Hollywood. The programme also introduced the comedy duo, French and Saunders.

The Chart Show was first shown on Channel 4 between April 1986 and 2 January 1989 before moving to ITV on 7 January 1989. The ITV show was

Michael Hutchence, lead singer with INXS. The first video broadcast on *The Chart Show* in 1986 was the song 'What You Need' by INXS.

broadcast on Saturday mornings until 22 August 1998 when it was replaced by *CD: UK*. The show consisted totally of videos of the artists involved with no live music. The first video to be shown on the show was 'What You Need' by INXS.

Network 7 was screened on Channel 4 in 1987 and 1988 between noon and 2 p.m. on Sunday afternoons. The show was created by Jane Hewland and Janet Street-Porter. Presenters on the show included Jaswinder Bancil, Murray Boland, Magenta Devine, Sankha Guha, Eric Harwood, Tracey MacLeod, Sebastian Scott, and Trevor Ward.

No Limits aired on BBC2 between 1985 and 1987 and ran for four series. The show was originally developed by Jonathan King for Channel 4. An advert for new presenters appeared in *The Sun* newspaper and the show eventually went out on BBC2 on Tuesdays at 6pm. The original presenters were Jeremy Legg and Lisa Maxwell who fronted the first series before Tony Baker and Jenny Powell presented the final three series. The show was based in a different town every week and featured pop videos as well as videos about the area they were filming in. The show also included the British and US pop charts.

MTV was launched in the United States on 1 August 1981 and the first music video shown on the new channel was 'Video Killed the Radio Star' by The Buggles. Other hits of the day were 'Run Like Hell' and 'Don't Leave Me Now'.

The first number one of the decade came from Pink Floyd with 'Another Brick in the Wall'. The song came from the group's rock opera of 1979, *The Wall* and was written by the band's bassist Roger Walters. The song became the group's only number one in the UK while also topping the charts in America and Germany. The song also reached number fifty-seven in the disco chart in the US. The track was seen as a protest against the strict schooling of the time and was Pink Floyd's first single since they released 'Point Me At the Sky' in 1968, which proved to be their last number one hit in the 1970s. The group were nominated for a Grammy for 'Another Brick in the Wall' but lost to 'Against the Wind' by Bob Seger. Rolling Stone later placed the track at number 375 on their list of the 500 greatest songs of all time. The video was shown on Top of the Pops during January and is remembered for including a nightmarish cartoon drawn by Gerald Scarfe which featured large goose-stepping hammers. It also showed the occupants of the school being fed through a large mincemeat machine as well as depicting a hideous marauding marionette of a headmaster bearing down on his pupils. The single, as well as the album *The Wall*, were banned in South Africa during 1980; the song, which included the lyrics 'we don't need no thought control' was used as a rallying cry by those opposed to the policies of the apartheid regime.

Number Ones throughout the decade included:

1980

'Another Brick in the Wall' (Part II) by Pink Floyd

'Brass in Pocket' by The Pretenders

'The Special AKA Live' by The Special AKA featuring Rico

'Coward of the County' by Kenny Rogers

'Atomic' by Blondie

'Together We Are Beautiful' by Fern Kinney

'Going Underground' by The Jam

'Working My Way Back to You' by The Detroit Spinners

'Call Me' by Blondie

'Geno' by Dexy's Midnight Runners

'What's Another Year' by Johnny Logan

'Theme from MASH' by The Mash

'Crying' by Don McLean

'Xanadu' by Olivia Newton-John and the Electric Light Orchestra

'Use It Up and Wear It Out' by Odyssey

'The Winner Takes It All' by ABBA

'Ashes to Ashes' by David Bowie

'Start!' by The Jam

'Woman in Love' by Barbra Streisand

'The Tide Is High' by Blondie

'Super Trouper' by ABBA

'(Just Like) Starting Over' by John Lennon

'There's No One Quite Like Grandma' by St Winifred's School Choir

The biggest hit of the year came from Pink Floyd with 'Another Brick in the Wall (Part II)' which stayed at the top of the charts for five weeks. 'Brass in Pocket' by The Pretenders knocked it off the top spot and remained there for two weeks until The Special A.K.A. featuring Rico with 'The Special A.K.A. Live!' replaced them, again for two weeks.

Country music entered the chart with Kenny Rogers reaching number one with 'Coward of the County'. The Jam had their second UK number one with 'Going Underground' which they followed up later in the year with 'Start!'

Dexy's Midnight Runners had their first chart topper with 'Geno', a tribute to soul singer Geno Washington, and The Detroit Spinners hit number one with 'Working My Way Back to You'.

With the popularity of *M*A*S*H* on television, the theme tune, together with the words used in the movie, hit the top spot. 'Theme from MASH

(Suicide is Painless)' by The Mash stayed at the number one spot for three weeks.

Don McLean also topped the chart for three weeks with 'Crying', a song written by Roy Orbison.

Olivia Newton-John and the Electric Light Orchestra reached number one with 'Xanadu' which was the theme tune from the 1980s movie of the same name. It stayed at the top for two weeks.

David Bowie had his second number one with 'Ashes to Ashes', which revisited the character Major Tom from his previous hit, 'Space Oddity'. The Police had their third number one with 'Don't Stand So Close to Me', which stayed at the top for four weeks.

Other hits included 'Use It Up and Wear It Out' by Odyssey; 'Feels Like I'm in Love' by Kelly Marie, a song originally written for Elvis Presley by Ray Dorset of Mungo Jerry; and 'Woman in Love' by Barbra Streisand, written by Barry and Robin Gibb of the Bee Gees.

ABBA had two number one hits during the year with 'The Winner Takes It All' and 'Super Trouper', the latter being the group's last UK number one

Blondie topped the chart three times with 'Atomic', 'Call Me' and 'The Tide is High', the last being a cover of a song originally recorded by the Jamaican group, The Paragons.

Johnny Logan won the Eurovision song contest for Ireland sending 'What's Another Year' straight to the top of the chart for two weeks. The UK came third in the contest that year with 'Love Enough For Two' by Prima Donna.

After the tragic death of John Lennon at the beginning of December, '(Just Like) Starting Over' shot to the top of the charts but was unexpectedly knocked off the number one spot at the end of the year by 'There's No One Quite Like Grandma' by St Winifred's School Choir.

1981

'Imagine' by John Lennon
'Woman' by John Lennon
'Shaddap You Face' by Joe Dolce Music Theatre
'Jealous Guy' by Roxy Music
'This 'Ole House' by Shakin' Stevens
'Making Your Mind Up' by Bucks Fizz
'Stand and Deliver' by Adam and the Ants
'Being with You' by Smokey Robinson
'One Day In Your Life' by Michael Jackson
'Ghost Town' by The Specials

'Green Door' by Shakin' Stevens

'Japanese Boy' by Aneka

'Tainted Love' by Soft Cell

'Prince Charming' by Adam and the Ants

'It's My Party' by Dave Stewart and Barbara Gaskin

'Every Little Thing She Does Is Magic' by The Police

'Under Pressure' by Queen and David Bowie

'Begin The Beguine' by Julio Iglesias

'Don't You Want Me' by The Human League

The beginning of the year featured songs by John Lennon, the whole world being shocked by his death the month before. As well as 'Imagine' and 'Woman' reaching the top of the charts, Roxy Music also had a number one hit with the Lennon song, 'Jealous Guy'. 'Shaddap You Face' by Joe Dolce was a surprise hit, amazingly keeping Vienna by Ultravox off the top spot. The track was recorded soon after by Fawlty Tower's Andrew Sachs, in character as Manuel, but it only reached 138 in the UK chart. Shakin' Stevens had two hits during the year with 'This 'Ole House' and 'Green Door' as did Adam and the Ants, reaching the top of the charts with 'Stand and Deliver' and 'Prince Charming', both featuring memorable videos, the latter including a cameo from screen legend, Diana Dors.

Bucks Fizz went straight to number one after their record, 'Making Your Mind Up' won the 1981 Eurovision Song Contest in April that year. The band, featuring Bobby G., Mike Nolan, Jay Aston and Cheryl Baker went on to have several more hits during the decade.

The year introduced Marc Almond and Soft Cell with their hit 'Tainted Love' and it also featured number ones from Smokey Robinson, Michael Jackson, The Specials, The Police and Queen and David Bowie. Julio Iglesias made his first appearance in the charts with the classic, 'Begin The Beguine'. A surprising, but catchy, hit came from Aneka with 'Japanese Boy', which sold half-a-million copies making it one of the best-selling records of 1981. Dave Stewart and Barbara Gaskin released their own version of the classic 'It's My Party', which stayed at the number one spot for four weeks. Other hits included 'Being With You' by Smokey Robinson; 'One Day in Your Life' by Michael Jackson; and 'Ghost Town' by The Specials, a song reflecting the urban decay and unemployment in the UK at the time.

The biggest selling single of 1981 came from The Human League right at the end of the year. 'Don't You Want Me' stayed at the top of the charts for five weeks and was accompanied by a very memorable video directed by Steve Barron.

The best-selling LP of 1981 was *Kings of the Wild Frontier* by Adam and the Ants.

1982
'The Land of Make Believe' by Bucks Fizz
'Oh Julie' by Shakin' Stevens
'Computer Love /The Model' by Kraftwerk
'Town Called Malice' by The Jam
'The Lion Sleeps Tonight' by Tight Fit
'Seven Tears' by Goombay Dance Band
'My Camera Never Lies' by Bucks Fizz
'Ebony and Ivory' by Paul McCartney and Stevie Wonder
'A Little Peace' by Nicole
'House of Fun' by Madness
'Goody Two Shoes' by Adam and the Ants
'I've Never Been to Me' by Charlene
'Happy Talk' by Captain Sensible
'Fame' by Irene Cara
'Come On Eileen' by Dexy's Midnight Runners
'Eye of the Tige'r by Survivor
'Pass the Dutchie' by Musical Youth
'Do You Really Want to Hurt Me' by Culture Club
'I Don't Wanna Dance' by Eddy Grant
'Beat Surrender' by The Jam
'Save Your Love' by Renée and Renato

Bucks Fizz continued their Eurovision success with two further number ones during the year, firstly with 'The Land of Make Believe' and then with 'My Camera Never Lies'.

The Jam also had two number one hits during the year with 'Town Called Malice' and 'Beat Surrender', the latter being the band's final single.

Shakin' Stevens hit the top spot again with 'Oh Julie', his third number one hit.

Adam and the Ants split in early 1982 leading to Adam Ant launching a solo career. His first single 'Goody Two Shoes' went straight to number one.

German electronic band, Kraftwerk, hit the top with the double A side 'Computer Love/The Model'. 'The Model' was the song that was most played on UK radio stations.

'Fame', the theme from the popular television series, sung by Irene Cara, secured the top spot in July and stayed there for three weeks.

Another theme song which reached the top was 'Eye of the Tiger' by Survivor, which was featured in Sylvester Stallone's movie, *Rocky III*.

Paul McCartney had many number one hits over the years but his only one with Stevie Wonder; 'Ebony and Ivory', reached number one in April and stayed there for three weeks.

Dexy's Midnight Runners and the Emerald Express had their second hit with 'Come On Eileen', which stayed at the number four spot for four weeks. It came from their album *Too-Rye-Ay*.

Culture Club was featured on Top of the Pops performing 'Do You Really Want to Hurt Me' when they stood in for Shakin' Stevens who couldn't make it. Boy George's appearance was a topic of conversation and the song soon shot up the charts.

Musical Youth scored the number one spot all around the world with the catchy number, 'Pass the Dutchie'.

Madness had their first and only number one hit with 'House of Fun', which topped the charts for two weeks.

Novelty records included 'Happy Talk' by Captain Sensible; 'The Lion Sleeps Tonight' by Tight Fit; and 'Save Your Love' by Renée and Renato. Captain Sensible went on to have two more Top 30 hits during the decade: 'Wot!' reached number twenty-six in 1982 and 'Glad It's All Over' charted at number six in 1984. Tight Fit had two more chart singles after 'The Lion Sleeps Tonight': 'Fantasy Island', which reached number five, and 'Secret Heart' which only reached number forty-one. Renée and Renato's video for 'Save Your Love' took the record to the Christmas number one spot.

Other number ones of the year included 'Seven Tears' by The Goombay Dance Band, 'A Little Peace' by Nicole, 'I've Never Been to Me' by Charlene; and 'I Don't Want to Dance' by Eddy Grant.

The best-selling LP of 1982 was *Love Songs* by Barbra Streisand followed by *The Kids from Fame* and, in the number three spot, *Complete Madness* by Madness.

1983

'You Can't Hurry Love' by Phil Collins
'Down Under' by Men at Work
'Too Shy' by Kajagoogoo
'Billie Jean' by Michael Jackson
'Total Eclipse of the Heart' by Bonnie Tyler
'Is There Something I Should Know?' by Duran Duran
'Let's Dance' by David Bowie
'True' by Spandau Ballet

'Candy Girl' by New Edition
'Every Breath You Take' by The Police
'Baby Jane' by Rod Stewart
'Wherever I Lay My Hat (That's My Home)' by Paul Young
'Give It Up' by KC and the Sunshine Band
'Red Red Wine' by UB40
'Uptown Girl' by Billy Joel
'Only You' by The Flying Pickets

The first hit of the year was 'You Can't Hurry Love' by Phil Collins which knocked 'Save Your Love' by Renée and Renato's off the top spot and stayed there for two weeks.

The second number one of the year came from Australian rock band Men At Work with their catchy single 'Down Under'. The song had originally been released in 1980 as the B-side to their first single, 'Keypunch Operator'.

'Too Shy' by Kajagoogoo was the first single released from the band's debut album *White Feathers*. The band went on to have two more top ten hits in 1983 with 'Ooh to Be Ah' and 'Big Apple'.

'Billie Jean' was the second single released from Michael Jackson's album *Thriller*. It stayed at the top of the chart for one week before being replaced by 'Total Eclipse of the Heart' by Welsh singer Bonnie Tyler. 'Total Eclipse of the Heart' was written and produced by Jim Steinman and came from Tyler's fifth album *Faster Than the Speed of Night*.

'Is There Something I Should Know?' by Duran Duran was their eighth single and their first number one hit. By 1983, Duran Duran were incredibly popular and 'Union of the Snake' also hit the charts later that year peaking at number three.

'Let's Dance' by David Bowie stayed at the top of the charts for three weeks. The video was shot in Australia and featured an Aboriginal couple dancing to a song playing on the radio after finding a pair of red shoes. In the same year, Bowie appeared the movie in *Merry Christmas Mr Lawrence*. which also starred Tom Conti.

'True' by Spandau Ballet hit the top spot in April and stayed there for weeks. It was the sixth best-selling single of the year and became the band's biggest hit.

The Police shot to number one again with 'Every Breath You Take', which came from their album *Synchronicity*. It became the UK and US's top selling single of the year and stayed at the top of the British charts for four weeks. The record was the band's fifth number one.

'Baby Jane' by Rod Stewart became his sixth and final number one. It stayed at the top of the chart for three weeks in July and was knocked off the top spot by Paul Young with 'Wherever I Lay My Hat', which also topped the charts for three weeks.

Culture Club hit the top spot again in September with their record 'Karma Chameleon' which stayed at number one for six weeks and became the biggest selling single of the year. The well-remembered music video was set in Mississippi in 1870 but filmed at Desborough Island in Weybridge during the summer of 1983.

Towards the end of the year, Billy Joel stayed at the top spot for five weeks with 'Uptown Girl' which came from his album *An Innocent Man*. In the accompanying music video, Joel plays a mechanic who tries to impress a high-class uptown girl who arrives at his garage in her car looking for petrol. The video featured Christie Brinkley, who Joel married two years later.

Other hits of the year included 'Candy Girl' by New Edition, 'Give It Up' by KC and the Sunshine Band and 'Red Red Wine' by UB40.

The Christmas number one of 1983 was 'Only You' by The Flying Pickets. The song was written by Vince Clarke and was released by his band Yazoo, with vocals by Alison Moyet in 1982. On that occasion, the record reached number two.

Frankie Goes to Hollywood had three number one hits in 1984: 'Relax', 'Two Tribes' and 'The Power of Love'. Their first hit, 'Relax', was famously banned by the BBC.

The best-selling LP of 1983 was *Thriller* by Michael Jackson followed by Paul Young with *No Parlez* and, in the number three spot, *Colour By Numbers* by Culture Club.

1984
'Pipes of Peace' by Paul McCartney
'Relax' by Frankie Goes to Hollywood
'99 Red Balloons' by Nena
'Hello' by Lionel Richie
'The Reflex' by Duran Duran
'Wake Me Up Before You Go-Go' by Wham!
'Two Tribes' by Frankie Goes to Hollywood
'Careless Whisper' by George Michael
'I Just Called to Say I Love You' by Stevie Wonder
'Freedom' by Wham!
'I Feel for You' by Chaka Khan
'I Should Have Known Better' by Jim Diamond
'The Power of Love' by Frankie Goes to Hollywood
'Do They Know It's Christmas?' by Band Aid

The first number one of the year was 'Pipes of Peace' by Paul McCartney which stayed at the top for two weeks. The single had been released in December the previous year but was kept off the top spot by The Flying Pickets' 'Only You'. This was McCartney's only solo number one; his previous number ones being with The Beatles, Wings and Stevie Wonder. The video for 'Pipes of Peace' featured the story of the 1914 Christmas truce between British and German troops. It showed a British and a German soldier, who were both played by McCartney, who meet in No Man's Land and exchange photos of their loved ones while their comrades fraternise and play football. The video was filmed at Chobham Common in Surrey.

The record was knocked off the top spot in January by Frankie Goes to Hollywood with 'Relax', which topped the charts for five weeks. The single was the band's first release and had a sluggish response until the band appeared on *Top of the Pops* and the record shot up to number six in the charts overnight. After Mike Read refused to play the record because of its suggestive lyrics, the BBC banned the single and it rose up the charts to number two. By the time the record had reached number one, it had also been banned by *Top of the Pops* so only a photo appeared on the show when the number one record was announced. The ban stayed in place until 1984. Frankie Goes to Hollywood had two further number ones later in the year which were 'Two Tribes', which first hit the top spot in June, and stayed there for nine weeks, and 'The Power of Love', which topped the chart at the beginning of December and stayed there for one week.

After five weeks, 'Relax' was knocked off the top spot in March by German artist, Nena, with '99 Red Balloons'.

Lionel Richie hit the number one spot later in March with 'Hello' and stayed at the top of the charts for six weeks. The video is remembered for its story of a blind student who, having fallen in love with Richie, who plays an acting teacher, models clay into an image of her love – but the head was mocked by viewers for looking nothing like Richie.

Duran Duran's eleventh single 'The Reflex' went to number one in May and stayed there for four weeks. The song was taken from their third album *Seven and the Ragged Tiger* and was the band's most successful single. However, it became their last UK number one.

George Michael had three number one hits during the year. The first, with Andrew Ridgeley as the duo Wham!, was 'Wake Me Up Before You Go-Go' which topped the chart on 2 June and stayed there for two weeks. As a solo artist, Michael topped the chart for a second time in August with 'Careless Whisper' which stayed at number one for three weeks. Wham! again hit the top spot with 'Freedom' in October, which also stayed at number one for three weeks.

'Club Fantastic Megamix' was released in 1983 and reached number fifteen in the charts.

One of the biggest hits of the year was 'I Just Called to Say I Love You' by Stevie Wonder, which topped the chart in September and stayed there for six weeks. It became Wonder's best-selling single.

Other hits during the year included Chaka Khan with 'I Feel for You', a song written by Prince, and 'I Should Have Known Better' by Jim Diamond, which topped the chart for one week at the beginning of December.

The Christmas number one was 'Do They Know It's Christmas?' was written to aid the people who were suffering during the famine in Ethiopia. Band Aid consisted of an array of top artists including Bono, Sting, Boy George, Duran Duran, Bob Geldof and Midge Ure.

The best-selling LP of 1984 was *Count Slow Down* by Lionel Richie followed by Various Artists with *Hits 1* and, in the number three spot, *Legend* by Bob Marley and the Wailers.

1985

'I Want to Know What Love Is' by Foreigner

'I Know Him So Well' by Elaine Paige and Barbara Dickson

'You Spin Me Round (Like a Record)' by Dead or Alive

'Easy Lover' by Philip Bailey (duet with Phil Collins)
'We Are the World' by USA for Africa
'Move Closer' by Phyllis Nelson
'19' by Paul Hardcastle
'You'll Never Walk Alone' by The Crowd
'Frankie' by Sister Sledge
'There Must Be an Angel (Playing with My Heart)' by Eurythmics
'Into the Groove' by Madonna
'I Got You Babe' by UB40 and Chrissie Hynde
'Dancing in the Street' by David Bowie and Mick Jagger
'If I Was' by Midge Ure
'The Power of Love' by Jennifer Rush
'A Good Heart' by Feargal Sharkey
'I'm Your Man' by Wham!
'Saving All My Love for You' by Whitney Houston
'Merry Christmas Everyone' by Shakin' Stevens

The first number one of 1985 was 'I Want to Know What Love Is' by Foreigner, which remained at the top for three weeks. The single came from the group's fifth album, *Agent Provocateur* and remains their biggest hit to date.

Elaine Paige and Barbara Dickson went to number one in February with 'I Know Him So Well', a song from the musical *Chess,* which was written by ABBA's Benny Andersson and Björn Ulvaeus, together with Tim Rice. The track topped the charts for four weeks.

Pete Burns with Dead or Alive reached number one in March with 'You Spin Me Round (Like a Record)'. It held the top spot for two weeks before being replaced with 'Easy Lover' by Philip Bailey (of Earth, Wind and Fire) dueting with Phil Collins.

'We Are the World' recorded by USA for Africa went to number one in April and stayed there for two weeks. The song was written by Michael Jackson and Lionel Richie to raise money for the famine victims of Ethiopia. The super group contained America's top artists including Stevie Wonder, Paul Simon, Ray Charles, Billy Joel, Diana Ross, Cyndi Lauper, Bruce Springsteen, Smokey Robinson and many others.

Paul Hardcastle had a huge hit with '19' which topped the chart in May and stayed there for five weeks. The song's title referred to the average age of a soldier fighting during the Vietnam War.

'You'll Never Walk Alone' by The Crowd went to number one in June. This version of the song that has become a football anthem was released to raise money for the victims Bradford City stadium fire, in which fifty-six people died on 11 May 1985. The group who recorded it consisted of many celebrities including Gerry Marsden, Tony Christie, Rick Wakeman, John Conteh, The Kiki Dee, Colin Blunstone, The Nolans, John Entwistle of The Who, Motörhead, Phil Lynott and Smokie. The record stayed at the top for two weeks.

The catchy 'Frankie' by Sister Sledge hit the top spot in June and stayed there for four weeks before being replaced with 'There Must Be an Angel (Playing with My Heart)' by The Eurythmics which stayed at number one for one week. 'There Must Be an Angel' featured a harmonica solo by Stevie Wonder and became a worldwide hit.

'Into the Groove' by Madonna topped the chart in August and stayed there for four weeks. The track featured in the movie *Desperately Seeking Susan*, which starred Madonna alongside Rosanna Arquette.

A re-recording of Sonny and Cher's 'I Got You Babe', this time given a new sound by UB40 and Chrissie Hynde, reached number one for one week at the end of August before being replaced by 'Dancing in the Street' by David Bowie and Mick Jagger. That song was originally recorded by Martha and the Vandellas and had been a hit in 1964 before being covered by artists including the Mamas and the Papas in 1966 and Van Halen in 1982.

October saw Midge Ure at number one with 'If I Was' which was the first single released from his album, *The Gift*.

'The Power of Love' by Jennifer Rush topped the charts in October and stayed there for five weeks. The song went on to be covered by many artists including Air Supply, Dion and Laura Branigan.

The end of the year saw Feargal Sharkey with 'A Good Heart', Wham! with 'I'm Your Man' and Whitney Houston with Saving All My Love for You all topping the chart for two weeks each.

December saw Shakin' Stevens taking the top spot once again, this time with *Merry Christmas Everyone*, a song played every Christmas since.

The best-selling LP of 1985 was *Brothers in Arms* by Dire Straits followed by Phil Collins with *No Jacket Required* and, in the number three spot, *Like a Virgin* by Madonna.

1986

'West End Girls' by Pet Shop Boys

'The Sun Always Shines on TV' by A-ha

'When the Going Gets Tough, the Tough Get Going' by Billy Ocean

'Chain Reaction' by Diana Ross

'Living Doll' by Cliff Richard and The Young Ones

'A Different Corner' by George Michael

'Rock Me Amadeus' by Falco

'The Chicken Song' by Spitting Image

'Spirit in the Sky' by Doctor and the Medics

'The Edge of Heaven' by Wham!

'Papa Don't Preach' by Madonna

'The Lady in Red' by Chris de Burgh

'I Want to Wake Up' with You by Boris Gardiner

'Don't Leave Me This Way' by The Communards

'True Blue' by Madonna

'Every Loser Wins' by Nick Berry

'Take My Breath Away (Love Theme from Top Gun)' by Berlin

'The Final Countdown' by Europe

'Caravan of Love' by The Housemartins

'Reet Petite (The Sweetest Girl in Town)' by Jackie Wilson

The first number one of the year came from the Pet Shop Boys with 'West End Girls' which went on to win the Best Single at the Brit Awards of 1987.

The song was knocked off the top spot by 'The Sun Always Shines on TV' by A-ha which was the third single from their debut album *Hunting High and Low*.

When the 'Going Gets Tough, the Tough Get Going' by Billy Ocean took the top spot in February and stayed there for four weeks. The song came from the Michael Douglas movie *The Jewel of the Nile* and Douglas, with his co-stars Kathleen Turner and Danny DeVito, starred in the video that accompanied the track.

At the beginning of March, Diana Ross reached number one with 'Chain Reaction' followed by Cliff Richard and The Young Ones with 'Living Doll'. Both songs stayed at the top for three weeks. 'Living Doll', had been a hit for Cliff and The Drifters in 1959 as a movie theme, and was re-recorded for Comic Relief. The new hit featured members of the cast from TV's *The Young Ones* including Christopher Ryan, Nigel Planer, Rik Mayall and Adrian Edmondson.

George Michael had two number one hits during the year, first as a solo artist with 'A Different Corner' in April, and secondly as part of Wham! with 'The Edge of Heaven' which remained at number one for two weeks.

Madonna also had two hits with 'Papa Don't Preach' and 'True Blue'.

Falco topped the chart in May with 'Rock Me Amadeus' followed by 'The Chicken Song' by Spitting Image, which stayed at the top of the charts for three weeks.

In June, Doctor and the Medics went to number one with 'Spirit in the Sky', a song which had originally been a hit for Norman Greenbaum in 1970.

Chris De Burgh hit the top spot in August with 'The Lady in Red' which introduced audiences worldwide to his music. The song came from his album *Into the Light*.

The summer hit proved to be 'I Want to Wake Up with You' by Boris Gardiner, which was written by legendary Nashville songwriter Ben Peters.

'Don't Leave Me This Way' by The Communards reached number one in September and stayed there for four weeks. The song was originally a hit for Harold Melvin and the Blue Notes featuring Teddy Pendergrass in 1975. It was also a disco hit for Motown artist Thelma Houston in 1977.

Nick Berry appeared throughout 1986 as Simon Wicks in *EastEnders* and his record 'Every Loser Wins' went to the top of the charts in October and stayed there for three weeks. The song had also been heavily featured on the TV soap throughout the summer of 1986, which greatly helped its popularity.

The theme from Tom Cruise's hit movie *Top Gun* shot to the top of the charts in November; 'Take My Breath Away' by Berlin stayed at the number one spot for four weeks.

Swedish rock band Europe had the chart topper in November with 'The Final Countdown'. The track proved hugely popular worldwide and reached the number one spot in twenty-five countries.

The Housemartins released an acapella version of 'Caravan of Love' in November 1986, which reached number one in the UK singles chart on 16 December 1986. The song was only the second a cappella recording to top the charts, the former being 'Only You' by the Flying Pickets in 1983.

'Reet Petite (The Sweetest Girl in Town)' by Jackie Wilson knocked The Housemartins off the top spot and became the unseasonable number one of the year.

The best-selling album of 1986 was *True Blue* by Madonna followed by Dire Straits with *Brothers in Arm*' and, in the number three spot, *Now That's What I Call Music 8* a CD compilation by Various Artists.

1987

'Jack Your Body' by Steve 'Silk' Hurley

'I Knew You Were Waiting (For Me)' by Aretha Franklin and George Michael

'Stand by Me' by Ben E. King

'Everything I Own' by Boy George

'Respectable' by Mel and Kim

'Let It Be' by Ferry Aid

'La Isla Bonita' by Madonna
'Nothing's Gonna Stop Us Now' by Starship
'I Wanna Dance with Somebody (Who Loves Me)' by Whitney Houston
'Star Trekkin'' by The Firm
'It's a Sin' by Pet Shop Boys
'Who's That Girl' by Madonna
'La Bamba' by Los Lobos
'I Just Can't Stop Loving You' by Michael Jackson and Siedah Garrett
'Never Gonna Give You' Up by Rick Astley
'Pump Up the Volume' by MARRS
'You Win Again' by Bee Gees
'China in Your Hand' by T'Pau
'Always on My Mind' by Pet Shop Boys

The first number one of 1987, an instrumental, was 'Jack Your Body' by Steve 'Silk' Hurley. It was the UK's first house music number one, which paved the way for acid house music.

George Michael scored another number one hit in February, this time with the 'Queen of Soul' Aretha Franklin. Their duet 'I Knew You Were Waiting (For Me)' stayed at the top for two weeks. The song was Franklin's first and only number one hit in the UK.

'Stand By Me' by Ben E King hit the top of the chart towards the end of February after the track was used as the theme to the Stephen King movie of the same name. The song stayed at the top for three weeks.

'Everything I Own' by Boy George reached the top of the chart in March. The song was written by David Gates and was originally recorded by Bread in 1972. The hit was Boy George's first and only number one hit as a solo artist.

Towards the end of March, Mel and Kim hit the number one spot with the Stock, Aitken and Waterman catchy tune 'Respectable'. The song topped the chart for one week.

Ferry Aid released the Beatles' song 'Let It Be' in April. The single was recorded after the Zeebrugge Disaster on 6 March following the capsizing of the ferry MS *Herald of Free Enterprise*. The tragedy resulted in the deaths of 193 passengers and crew. All proceeds from sales of the record were donated to the charity set up after the disaster. The recording was organised by *The Sun* newspaper. Ferry Aid included Boy George, Kate Bush, Gary Moore, Mark Knopfler, Paul McCartney with others. The record stayed at the top for three weeks.

Madonna had two further number one hits with 'La Isla Bonita' in April and 'Who's That Girl' in July. 'Who's That Girl' came from the movie of the same name, which starred Madonna and Griffin Dunne.

'Nothing's Gonna Stop Us Now' by Starship hit the top spot in May and stayed there for four weeks before being replaced at number one by 'I Wanna Dance with Somebody (Who Loves Me)' by Whitney Houston.

'Star Trekkin' by The Firm hit the top of the chart in June. It parodied the TV show *Star Trek* and stayed at number one for two weeks. It was being replaced by The Pet Shop Boys with 'It's A Sin' in July, a song became the band's second UK number one single and was a huge hit all across Europe.

Los Lobos scored a hit with 'La Bamba' in August. The record had originally been a hit for Ritchie Valens in 1958. Los Lobos' version was used as the title track of the movie of the same name, which starred Lou Diamond Phillips. The record stayed at the top for two weeks.

Michael Jackson and Siedah Garrett reached the top on the 15 August with 'I Just Can't Stop Loving You'. The song was the first single released from Jackson's seventh album, *Bad*.

'Never Gonna Give You Up' by Rick Astley hit the top of the charts at the end of August. Another hit for Stockman, Aitken and Waterman, the track was the first single released from Astley's debut album, *Whenever You Need Somebody*. 'Never Gonna Give You Up' stayed at number one for five weeks and topped the charts in twenty-five countries worldwide.

'Pump up the Volume' by MARRS made number one on 3 October and stayed there for two weeks before being knocked off the top spot by the Bee Gees with 'You Win Again'. The song marked a comeback for the Bee Gees and topped the charts in many European countries.

'China in Your Hands' was a huge hit towards the end of 1987, staying at the top spot for five weeks. Sung by Carol Decker, the track came from T'Pau's album *Bridge of Spies*. It was the 600th single to top the UK charts and stopped George Harrison's 'Got My Mind Set on You' from reaching number one.

The Christmas number one of 1987 was 'Always on My Mind' by The Pet Shop Boys. The band and the song had originally been featured in an Elvis Presley tribute show and were so popular it led to the re-recording of the number that had also been a hit for Presley in 1972 and had also been recorded by Gwen McCray, Brenda Lee, John Wesley Ryles and Willie Nelson.

The best-selling LP of 1987 was *Bad* by Michael Jackson followed by U2 with *The Joshua Tree* and, in the number three spot, *Whitney* by Whitney Houston.

1988

'Heaven Is a Place on Earth' by Belinda Carlisle
'I Think We're Alone Now' by Tiffany
'I Should Be So Lucky' by Kylie Minogue

'Don't Turn Around' by Aswad
'Heart' by Pet Shop Boys
'Theme from S-Express' by S-Express
'Perfect' by Fairground Attraction
With a Little Help from My Friends' by Wet Wet Wet, Billy Bragg and Cara Tivey
'Doctorin' the Tardis' by The Timelords
'I Owe You Nothing' by Bros
'Nothing's Gonna Change My Love for You' by Glenn Medeiros
'The Only Way Is Up' by Yazz and the Plastic Population
'A Groovy Kind of Love' by Phil Collins
'He Ain't Heavy, He's My Brother' by The Hollies
'Desire' by U2
'One Moment in Time' by Whitney Houston
'Orinoco Flow' by Enya
'First Time' by Robin Beck
'Mistletoe and Wine' by Cliff Richard

The first number one of 1988 was 'Heaven Is a Place on Earth' by Belinda Carlisle which stayed at the top spot for two weeks. The track came from the former Go-Go's lead singer's second album, *Heaven on Earth*.

Tiffany reached number one at the end of January with 'I Think We're Alone Now', which had previously been a US hit for Tommy James and the Shondells in 1967. The single topped the charts for three weeks.

'I Should Be So Lucky' hit the number one spot in February and stayed at the top of the chart for five weeks. The track came from Minogue's debut album *Kylie* and was written and produced by Stock, Aitken and Waterman. The song was an international hit and reached number one in many countries including Australia, Hong Kong, Germany and Switzerland.

Aswad reached number one in March with 'Don't Turn Around', which was knocked off the top spot by The Pet Shop Boys with 'Heart'. The track became The Pet Shop Boys fourth and final chart-topper. The song came from their second album *Actually* and had originally been written for Madonna.

'Theme from S-Express' by S-Express hit the top spot at the end of April, staying there for two weeks. The dance track came from the band's debut album *Original Soundtrack*.

'Perfect' by Fairground Attraction went to number one during May followed by 'With a Little Help from My Friends' by Wet Wet Wet. The flipside of the record included another Beatles' song 'She's Leaving Home' sung by Billy Bragg and featuring Cara Tivey. Both tracks were recorded to aid the charity Childline.

The Timelords' hit the number one spot for one week in June with 'Doctorin' the Tardis'. The novelty song relied heavily on Gary Glitter's 'Rock and Roll', and 'Blockbuster!' by Sweet and the theme from *Doctor Who*.

'I Owe You Nothing' by Bros went to number one towards the end of June and stayed there for two weeks. Their first single 'When Will I Be Famous' had charted at number two the previous year.

The beginning of July saw Glenn Medeiros hit the top spot with 'Nothing's Gonna Change My Love for You' which topped the chart for four weeks.

One of the biggest hits of the year came from Yazz and the Plastic Population with 'The Only Way Is Up' which first reached number one on 6 August and stayed there for five weeks. The single had originally been released by soul singer Otis Clay in 1980.

Phil Collins topped the chart at the beginning of September with 'A Groovy Kind of Love' followed by The Hollies with 'He Ain't Heavy, He's My Brother'. Both records stayed at the top for two weeks each. The Hollies track topped the charts after being featured in a television advert for Miller Lite beer.

U2 had their first number one in the UK with 'Desire' during October which stayed at the top for one week. The track came from their album *Rattle and Hum*, the band's sixth album.

Whitney Houston took the top spot on 15 October with 'One Moment in Time'. The song was produced for the 1988 Summer Olympics in Seoul, South Korea. The track was Houston's third number one in the UK Singles Chart.

Enya reached number one in October with 'Orinoco Flow' which was followed in November by Robin Beck with 'First Time'. Both tracks stayed at the top for three weeks. 'First Time' gained popularity after it was used in a Coca-Cola commercial in 1987.

The seasonal number one came from Cliff Richard with 'Mistletoe and Wine', which remained at the top of the chart for four weeks. 'Mistletoe and Wine' was Richard's ninety-ninth single and his twelfth UK number one.

The best-selling LP of 1988 was *Kylie* by Kylie Minogue followed by Cliff Richard with *Private Collection: 1979–1988* and, in the number three spot, *Bad* by Michael Jackson.

1989

'Especially for You' by Kylie Minogue and Jason Donovan
'Something's Gotten Hold of My Hear't by Marc Almond featuring Gene Pitney
'Belfast Child' by Simple Minds

'Too Many Broken Hearts' by Jason Donovan

'Like a Prayer' by Madonna

'Eternal Flame' by The Bangles

'Hand on Your Heart' by Kylie Minogue

'Ferry Cross the Mersey' by The Christians, Holly Johnson, Paul McCartney, Gerry Marsden and Stock Aitken Waterman

'Sealed with a Kiss' by Jason Donovan

'Back to Life (However Do You Want Me)' by Soul II Soul featuring Caron Wheeler

'You'll Never Stop Me Loving You' by Sonia

'Swing the Mood' by Jive Bunny and the Mastermixers

'Ride On Time' by Black Box

'That's What I Like' by Jive Bunny and the Mastermixers

'All Around the World' by Lisa Stansfield

'You Got It (The Right Stuff)' by New Kids on the Block

'Let's Party' by Jive Bunny and the Mastermixers

'Do They Know It's Christmas?' by Band Aid II

The popularity of the Australian soap *Neighbours* in the UK had a great effect on the chart throughout the year. Kylie Minogue and Jason Donovan had the first number on of the year with the Stock, Aitken and Waterman song 'Especially for You'. The track came from Jason Donovan's debut album *Ten Good Reasons*. The pair repeated their success with chart toppers throughout the year. In March, Jason Donovan hit the top spot with 'Too Many Broken Hearts'; Kylie Minogue reached number one in April with 'Hand on Your Heart'; and Jason Donovan topped the chart again in June with 'Sealed with a Kiss', which had formerly been a hit for Brian Hyland in 1962 and again in 1975.

The second number one of the year was 'Something's Gotten Hold of My Heart' by Marc Almond featuring Gene Pitney. The record topped the charts for four weeks. The track had previously been a hit for Pitney in 1968. The video for the Marc Almond version was filmed in Las Vegas and featured both artists.

'Belfast Child' by Simple Minds reached the top of the chart on 25 February and stayed there for two weeks.

Madonna topped the chart again in March with 'Like a Prayer', which came from her album of the same name. The accompanying video featured Madonna as a witness to the murder of a white girl by white supremacists. The video caused an uproar from religious groups and others. The Vatican said that the video contained blasphemous use of Christian imagery. By this time, the track was already being used in a Pepsi advertising campaign and there was a call for people to boycott the company and its products. Pepsi ultimately gave in to the protests and cancelled the campaign but let Madonna keep her fee.

'Eternal Flame' by The Bangles hit the number one spot on 15 April. The song was a hit all around the world and stayed at the top of the chart for four weeks.

In May 1989, a charity re-recording of 'Ferry Cross the Mersey' was released to help those affected by the Hillsborough disaster, in which ninety-five Liverpool fans had lost their lives. The track was recorded by Liverpool artists The Christians, Holly Johnson, Paul McCartney, Gerry Marsden and Stock, Aitken and Waterman. The single stayed at number one in the UK for three weeks as well as topping the Irish chart.

'Back to Life (However Do You Want Me)' by Soul II Soul featuring Caron Wheeler reached number one in June and stayed there for four weeks before being replaced by Sonia's debut single 'You'll Never Stop Me Loving You', again written and produced by Stock, Aitken and Waterman. The track topped the chart for two weeks.

Jive Bunny and the Mastermixers had three number one hits in the charts during 1989. The first was 'Swing the Mood' which topped the chart for five weeks from 5 August. Their second hit was 'That's What I Like', which went to number one on 21 October and stayed there for three weeks. The third, 'Let's Party', topped the chart on 16 December and stayed there for one week. In chart history, they became the third act to reach the top spot with their first three singles. The others being Gerry and the Pacemakers in 1964 and Frankie Goes to Hollywood in 1984.

In between the first two Jive Bunny hits, 'Ride on Time' by Black Box topped the chart on 9 September. The song became a massive hit worldwide. The band was fronted by French model Katrin Quinol, who lip-synced during the video and at live performances. However, the voice heard actually belonged to the uncredited Loleatta Holloway who had had her 1980 disco hit 'Love Sensation' sampled by the band without her permission. Her lawyers succeeded in getting her a settlement of the complex matter for an undisclosed sum.

'All Around the World' by Lisa Stansfield hit the top spot on 11 November and stayed there for two weeks. The track came from her album *Affection* and became her biggest hit and was a Top 10 hit all over the world.

'You Got It (The Right Stuff)' by New Kids on the Block topped the charts on 25 November. The lead vocals were sung by Jordan Knight and Donnie Wahlberg and this number was the second single from the band's second album *Hangin' Tough*.

The Christmas number one was the charity record 'Do They Know It's Christmas?' by Band Aid II. The line-up for the super group included Bananarama, Big Fun, Bros, Cathy Dennis, D Mob, Jason Donovan, Kevin Godley, Glen Goldsmith, Kylie Minogue, The Pasadenas, Chris Rea, Cliff Richard, Jimmy Somerville, Sonia, Lisa Stansfield, Technotronic and Wet Wet Wet. The record was produced by Stock, Aitken and Waterman and topped the chart for three weeks.

The best-selling LP of 1989 was *Ten Good Reasons* by Jason Donovan followed by Simply Red with *A New Flame* and, in the number three spot, *...But Seriously* by Phil Collins.

During the decade, there had been a total of 191 singles that reached the number one spot. Of these, Madonna proved to be the most successful single act of the 1980s with 6 of her singles topping the chart. However, George Michael was involved with 8 number one singles; these included 2 chart-toppers as a solo artist, 4 as a member of Wham!, 1 dueting with Aretha Franklin and 1 as a member of Band Aid. The longest time a single spent at number one during the decade was nine weeks, that honour going to Frankie Goes to Hollywood's 'Two Tribes' in 1984.

Band Aid's 'Do They Know It's Christmas?' was the best-selling single of the 1980s and sold over 3.5 million copies, surpassing 'Mull of Kintyre' by Wings to become the best-selling single ever. 'Do They Know It's Christmas?' is the second best-selling song after Elton John's 'Candle in the Wind 1997'.

13
Technology

The 1980s was the decade of home computers, CDs, camcorders and many other inventions that became the forerunners for much of the technology that we have today.

Home Computers

Long before the internet, early home computers were used often for playing video games but were also used for word processing, homework and programming. Their capabilities were far less than today's modern computers but allowed their users to play simple arcade-style video games, usually laboriously uploaded up to the machine via a cassette tape.

Popular early home computers included the Sinclair ZX Spectrum, which was released in April 1982 and became the best-selling British home computer, however, the Commodore 64, released in August 1982, became the best-selling computer model of all time, selling over 17 million units. Other manufacturers of home computers during the time included Texas Instruments, BBC Micro, Amstrad, Apple, Atari and Acorn.

The ZX Spectrum home computer, first released in April 1982, became the best-selling British home computer. It was invented by Clive Sinclair and its popularity led to a host of software designers producing games and hardware for the system.

The BBC Micro was made by Acorn Computers of Cambridge and was initially released in 1981. It ran on a simple computer language known as BBC Basic.

The BBC Micro was made by Acorn Computers of Cambridge and was first released in 1981. It included a simple language known as BBC Basic, which even very young children could use. The BBC had introduced a literacy project and the computers were supplied to schools up and down the country; as a result, most children had access to one. Originally, the plan had been for the BBC to only produce 12,000 computers but the Micro became so popular that 24,000 were sold in 1982 and soon after, schools bought them thousands more. The Micro was expensive at the time costing £235 (approximately £700 at today's prices) and £335 (about £1,000 at today's prices) for the Model B, which went on to become the iconic version. The BBC Micro's appearance in classrooms, plus the government's initiative to teach computing skills in schools, revolutionised computing in Britain.

The Sinclair ZX Spectrum was manufactured by Sinclair Research and first appeared on the market in 1982. Its popularity led to a host of software designers producing games and hardware for the system. Some feel that it launched the IT market in the UK and Clive Sinclair, its inventor, was awarded a knighthood for his services to British industry.

During the early 1980s, the Spectrum's main competitors were the Commodore 64, the Dragon 32, the Oric-1, the Oric Atmos, BBC Micro and later the Amstrad CPC range. As with all home computers at the time, the Spectrum was made so that it could plug into a TV making it easy to play games, with sound output through a beeper on its side. Five million Spectrums were sold worldwide and its low price of £125 greatly appealed to British consumers. The home computer market grew steadily and there were many books and magazines to boost its popularity. In addition, many users designed their own games and programs, which were loaded, laboriously, onto the machine via an ordinary cassette player.

The Commodore C64 computer was released in August 1982 and became a best-selling model, selling in excess of 17 million units.

The Sony Walkman first appeared in the UK in 1980. It was originally built in Japan by engineer Nobutoshi Kihara for the Sony co-founder Masaru Ibuka.

Computers were used widely at home and by businesses throughout the 1980s but it wasn't until the late 1990s and the advent of the internet that it suddenly became essential for everyone to have their own personal computer.

The Sony Walkman

The Sony Walkman first appeared in the UK in 1980. Nowadays, iPods and MP3 players are commonplace, but the original personal music player appeared on the market in Japan in the late 1970s. The Sony Walkman allowed people, for the first time, to listen to music while on the move. In 1978, a prototype was built in Japan by engineer Nobutoshi Kihara for Sony's co-founder, Masaru Ibuka. Ibuka wanted to be able to listen to music while on long plane journeys so suggested the idea to Kihara. This eventually led to the first Walkmans being sold in Japan in 1979 and shortly afterwards, by the beginning of the 1980s, it was being made available all over the world. When the players first came out, anyone wearing one outdoors would have been a source of conversation, but they soon became commonplace. Other companies including Aiwa, Panasonic and Toshiba, produced similar machines and by 1983, cassettes were outselling vinyl for the first time. In 1986, the word Walkman entered the Oxford English Dictionary.

The Compact Disc

The Compact Disc (CD) was invented by Philips in 1981 and revolutionised the way we listened to music. Before the CD, most people listened to music either on vinyl records or on tape cassettes. The CD offered a better sound from a product that was advertised as scratch-proof and virtually indestructible. Gone were the 'clicks' and 'pops' found with vinyl records that were easily scratched or damaged. The market for vinyl remained fairly stable throughout the early 1980s but a gradual decline meant that by the end of the decade, sales of CDs had surpassed those of vinyl.

The first commercial CD to be produced, on 17 August 1982, was *The Visitors* by ABBA. Fifty titles were released in Japan on 1 October 1982 and the first of these was a re-release of the Billy Joel album *52nd Street*.

CD players really took off in the UK in the mid-1980s and led to many people replacing their old vinyl records with the new format. LPs were sold off, given away, or in many cases, thrown away. At the time, it seemed that vinyl had gone forever and the new technology was here to stay. Early players were very expensive but as they became mass produced, the machines dropped in price. Nowadays, the market in CDs has declined and there's a resurgence in sales of vinyl but most people today are happy to simply download their music onto their iPods or other devices.

The Camcorder

Early video filming involved using bulky, heavy equipment that either had to be connected to electricity or used a primitive form of battery with a very short life. But in 1982, both JVC and Sony announced the "CAMera/recorder", or camcorder, combinations. On June 1, 1982, JVC's camcorder used its new mini-VHS format, VHS-C. VHS stands for Video Home System. In Japan five months later, Sony announced its Betamovie Beta camcorder, which was promoted with the slogan 'Inside This Camera Is A VCR.' VCR is short Videocassette Recorder. The following year, Sony released the Betacam for home use. The first camcorder Sony sold for public use was the Betamovie BMC-100P. The camera used the same format tape as a Betamax video recorder. It had no form of playback and could only be used to film. In the same year, JVC released the first VHS-C camcorder, which worked with a smaller and more compact version of a VHS tape cassette. In 1984, Kodak introduced a new camcorder format incorporating 8 mm video tape.

Sony introduced its own compact 8 mm Video8 format in 1985. Panasonic, RCA and Hitachi began manufacturing camcorders in 1985 which took full-size VHS cassette with a capacity of 3 hours. The shoulder-mounted machines were more bulky and used by more serious users who sought better quality. Full-size Super-VHS (S-VHS) camcorders were produced in 1987, with Sony upgrading Video8 and releasing the Hi8 in competition with S-VHS. The smaller, compact video cameras gained popularity and remained the accepted format until, eventually, the digital camera took over. Goodbye to the risk of a tape becoming snagged and damaged.

The Mobile Phone

In 1983, the first commerically viable mobile phone was available. However, it wasn't until January 1985 that the first mobile phone call was made in UK. The event took place at London's St Katharine Docks using the Vodafone network. Amazingly, the first ever call was made by comedian Ernie Wise. A crowd formed close to the Dickens Inn to watch Wise call the Vodafone office in Newbury using a Transportable Vodafone VT1. The machine weighed 5 kilos and, at the time cost a whopping £2,000. The early phones, mainly used by businessmen, affectionately obtained the nickname, 'the brick'. Coverage, in the beginning, was limited to the London area. There were few users at first but as prices came down, phones became smaller, and coverage was more widespread, many people began purchasing their own mobile phones. Digital arrived in 1992 with two new networks, One2One and Orange, launching their first phones the following year, opening the market up to consumers. Today, mobile phones are widespread and it's uncommon for people not to own one. However, back in the 1980s they were only of use to well-off London dwellers.

Other tech advances

Other innovations during the decade included the Nintendo Entertainment System (1983), the Apple Macintosh (1983), DNA Fingerprinting (1985), Microsoft's Windows (1985), synthetic skin (1986), the disposable camera (1986), the first 3-D game (1987), disposable contact lenses (1987) and the Nintendo Gameboy (1989). In 1989, Tim Berners-Lee first proposed the idea of the World Wide Web.

Other 1980s based technology included microwaves and the cordless phone. Digital watches, first introduced in the 1970s, now evolved to include calculators. Digital radio alarm clocks took over from the shrill ringing of an analogue alarm clock. The ghetto blasters, also known as a boombox or jambox, became popular with their AF/FM radio plus one or two cassette tape recorder/players. And the piano in the parlour gave way to the home music keyboard, a smaller and more versatile option.

14

Christmas

There was much anticipation during the lead up to Christmas. In the 1980s, as in previous decades, many children had their own advent calendars which contained 25 doors. The child was allowed to open one door each day, beginning on 1 December to find pictures behind the doors of images such as candles, holly and religious themes. Most advent calendars at the time culminated in the nativity scene, featuring the baby Jesus, behind the door of the 25 December.

Younger children were, perhaps, more naive in the 1980s than today's youngsters with many more believing that there actually was a Santa Claus, who delivered all their presents. Every kid was thrilled at the thought of Santa visiting on the night of the 24th, sliding down the chimney, and leaving gifts. In the lead up to Christmas, many little ones would write letters to Santa listing him what they would like. Often young children were taken to large department stores to visit one of the various Santas there, who were all dressed up for the part with red robes and cotton wool beards. At home, on Christmas Eve, children would leave biscuits and milk for Santa's reindeer, led by Rudolph. Of course, much of this still goes on today but the length of time children believed that their gifts were made by elves and were delivered by Father Christmas seemed to be longer then than nowadays.

Television advertising aimed at children and popularising new toys appeared from 1 December onwards. Adverts featuring Action Men showed him having mock battles and getting up to all sorts of adventures. Scalextric tracks looked like something out of Le Mans. Manufacturers all made sure that they did their best to get children to pester their parents for their products and many campaigns were very successful. There seemed to be a craze for one particular toy every year. Fads of the decade included Cabbage Patch dolls, Rubik's Cubes, Masters of the Universe toys, Transformers, My Little Pony, Micro Machines and Boglins.

School life was more exciting leading up to Christmas. There was as much fun thinking about soon being off school as thinking about all the presents that were longed for. As the day got nearer, classrooms would be festooned with decorations, many home-made. Coloured paper rings would be put together in class and hung from the ceiling. Cards for relatives and other decorations were also made in class. Every class would have an end-of-term Christmas party, which often included food such as sausages on sticks with jelly and custard for afters. It was the one time of year that the school dinner ladies deviated from their usual school menu.

Children would be chosen to appear in the school nativity play and costumes would be made by their mums. Many costumes involved a sheet and a tea towel to cover their kids' heads but some could be quite inventive. Schools sold tickets for the nativity play which helped to raise funds and also probably paid for the party.

Traditional hymns would be sung including 'Little Town of Bethlehem', 'Away in a Manger', 'Oh Come All Ye Faithful'. 'Silent Night', 'Hark the Herald Angels Sing', and 'Once in Royal David's City'. Some schools had their own group of children who would knock on doors and sing Christmas carols. Some more enterprising children did it off their own bat and made themselves a few pennies. Popular Christmas carols included 'The First Noel', 'We Three Kings of Orient Are', 'While Shepherds Watched their Flock by Night', 'Ding Dong Merrily on High', God Rest Ye Merry Gentlemen', 'The Holly and the Ivy' and 'Good King Wenceslas' as well as songs such as 'We Wish You a Merry Christmas', 'Deck the Halls', 'Jingle Bells' and (I'm Dreaming of a) White Christmas'.

Christmas cards would be exchanged with school pals and other friends. Some schools would set up their own red post boxes, usually made out of a cardboard box and red crepe paper, and pupils would deposit their Christmas cards in there ready to be handed out in the final week of term.

At home, much fun would be had putting up decorations and decorating the Christmas tree. By the 1980s, most families had an artificial tree, which would be covered in tinsel as well as electric fairy lights although many people bought real trees to celebrate the occasion.

The Christmas editions of the *Radio Times* and the *TV Times* were looked forward to a great deal. They covered the two weeks over the Christmas season and were much read by children looking for their favourite programmes and cartoons. All the best programmes and films seemed to be shown at Christmas although many of the classic movies shown at that time of year such as *It's a Wonderful Life* or *Miracle on 34th Street* actually dated back to the 1940s. Every well-loved show had its own Christmas special and one of the most looked forward to, by both adults and children, was

The Morecambe and Wise Show. Children's shows such as *Blue Peter* showed children how to make nativity decorations such as angels and fairies for the top of the tree. Most involved a discarded cardboard loo roll insert!

Tucked up in bed on Christmas Eve, there was much excitement as the wait for Santa began. Imaginations ran wild and some children imagined that they could hear the sleigh bells of Santa's sleigh as they slowly fell asleep. When they awoke the next morning, usually very early, many would find a stocking and presents at the end of their bed, or under the tree, and would eagerly unwrap them before waking their parents, usually by jumping on them to show them what Santa had left (not realising they already knew!).

After playing with their toys, having breakfast and finally getting washed and dressed, all kids would be out on the streets on their new bikes, scooters or roller skates or flying their Action Men through the air. Other popular toys included the latest board games, as well as electronic and television games, which would be played by the whole family after dinner.

Christmas dinner was much looked forward to and anyone out playing would soon be called in. Dinner would involve roast turkey, or chicken, with roast vegetables, stuffing and gravy. After everyone was stuffed, the family would settle down to watch the television and enjoy the Christmas specials. By bedtime, it all seemed very sad that it was all now over. However, there was still Boxing Day and almost another ten days of school holidays to look forward to!

15

Notable Events

1980

On 29 January, the Rubik's Cube made its first appearance at the British Toy and Hobby Fair at Earl's Court in London. It became one of the decade's most popular toys.

On 2 April, the St Paul's riot began in Bristol after police raided the Black and White Café on Grosvenor Road. During the riot, 130 people were arrested, and 25 were taken to hospital and they included 19 police as well as members of the press.

On 30 April, the Iranian Embassy in London was seized by six armed men who took 26 people hostage. When their demands were not met, they killed a man and threw his body out of the embassy. The SAS forcibly retook the Embassy on 5 May, killing five of the terrorists.

On 21 May, the Star Wars movie The *Empire Strikes Back was* released in the United States. It was the second instalment in the original *Star Wars* trilogy.

Ronald Reagan was the 40th president of the United States between 1981 and 1989. He was succeeded by George H. W. Bush.

Above left: Margaret Thatcher with her husband Denis on the left. She served as Prime Minister of Great Britain between 1979 and 1990.

Above right: Michael Foot who succeeded James Callaghan as leader of the Labour Party after Callaghan announced his resignation on 15 October 1980.

On 23 June, Tim Berners-Lee started to work on ENQUIRE, a system that would eventually lead to the creation of the World Wide Web towards the end of the 1980s.

On 16 July, the former California Governor and actor, Ronald Reagan, was nominated for US President. He went on to defeat incumbent president, Jimmy Carter.

On 31 July, China's total population hit the one billion mark.

Between 7 and 31 of August, Lech Wałęsa led the first of many strikes at the Gdańsk Shipyard in Poland. The yard gained international fame when the trade union Solidarity was founded there in September 1980.

On 5 October, British Leyland launched its new Austin Metro, a three-door hatchback which was designed as a replacement for the popular Mini.

On 10 October, Prime Minister Margaret Thatcher gave her famous, 'The lady's not for turning' speech. The phrase was written by playwright Sir Ronald Millar, who had been responsible for writing Thatcher's speeches since 1973.

On 15 October, James Callaghan announced his resignation as leader of the Labour Party. He remained leader until November, when he was succeeded by Michael Foot.

On the evening of the 8 December, John Lennon was shot and killed by Mark Chapman in the archway of the Dakota Building, his home in New York City. Lennon was returning from the Record Plant Studio with his wife Yoko Ono when he was shot. Earlier that evening Lennon had autographed Chapman's copy of the just-released album *Double Fantasy*.

1981

On 12 April, the reusable space shuttle *Columbia* was first launched. It was the first space-rated orbiter used in NASA's Space Shuttle fleet and flew for twenty-eight missions before disintegrating during re-entry on 1 February 2003, resulting in the deaths of all seven on board.

On 2 January, police arrested serial killer Peter Sutcliffe, the 'Yorkshire Ripper', in Sheffield, South Yorkshire. It ended one of the largest investigations led by a British police force (*see* conviction details below).

On 16 January, Irish nationalist activist Bernadette Devlin McAliskey and her husband were shot and seriously wounded. She was shot nine times but survived the ordeal.

On 29 March, London held its first marathon. Almost 7,000 runners took part in the 26-mile run. The idea for the event came from former Olympic champion and journalist Chris Brasher together with athlete John Disley who were inspired by the New York marathon and the way it brought people together.

On 4 April, Bucks Fizz won the Eurovision Song Contest with 'Making Your Mind Up'. The event was held in Dublin. The song narrowly beat Germany's entry by four points.

Between 10 and 12 April there were riots in Brixton, with the main riot on 11 April. The whole of the UK was in the grip of a recession but this South

The *Columbia* Space Shuttle preparing for launch. On 12 April 1981, the reusable space shuttle *Columbia* was first launched. It was the first space-rated orbiter used in NASA's Space Shuttle fleet and flew for 28 missions.

Princess Di, the former Lady Diana Spencer, became one of the most-photographed women of the decade after she wed Prince Charles. Their wedding at St Paul's Cathedral on 29 July 1981 was watched by an estimated global TV audience of 750 million people.

London suburb had particularly high unemployment, poor housing, and a higher-than-average crime rate. Protesters threw petrol bombs, attacked police and looted shops. The police had 280 injuries and 45 members of the public were injured. Over 100 vehicles were set on fire and destroyed including 56 police vehicles. A total of 150 buildings were damaged, with 30 set alight. There were 82 arrests.

On 5 May, IRA volunteer, Bobby Sands, died in prison while on hunger strike. His death, with those of nine other hunger strikers, led to a new wave of Provisional IRA recruitment and activity.

On 22 May, Peter Sutcliffe was sentenced to life imprisonment after he was convicted of thirteen counts of murder and seven of attempted murder.

On 3 July, the Toxteth riots began after Merseyside police tried to arrest a youth and an angry crowd intervened. Soon after, the Chapeltown riots in Leeds started due to increased racial tension.

On 29 July, the wedding took place of Prince Charles and Lady Diana Spencer at St Paul's Cathedral. The marriage was a huge event watched by an estimated global TV audience of 750 million people. Street parties were held throughout the UK to celebrate the event.

On 8 September, the first episode of *Only Fools and Horses* was broadcast on BBC One. Starring David Jason as Del Boy, it went on to become the nation's favourite comedy. There were seven series: 1981–1983, 1985–1986, 1989 and 1990–1991. It also starred Nicholas Lyndhurst as Del's younger brother Rodney, and Lennard Pearce as their Grandad. After Pearce's death in 1984, his character was replaced by Del and Rodney's Great Uncle Albert, played by Buster Merryfield, who first appeared in February 1985.

On 16 September, the children's show *Postman Pat* was first aired on BBC One. The show was created by John Cunliffe with Ken Barrie providing the original voice for the character.

On 28 September, the popular children's cartoon *Danger Mouse* was first aired on ITV. It featured the voices of David Jason, Terry Scott and Edward Kelsey.

On 8 December, Arthur Scargill became President-elect of the National Union of Mineworkers.

On 19 December, the Penlee lifeboat disaster took place off the coast of South-West Cornwall. Sixteen people died including eight volunteer lifeboatmen.

1982

On 7 January, the Commodore 64, the 8-bit home computer was first introduced and became the best-selling computer sold selling over 17 million units.

On 11 January, Mark Thatcher, the son of British Prime Minister Margaret Thatcher, disappeared in the Sahara while taking part in the Dakar Rally. After a prolonged search, he was rescued three days later.

On 5 February, the London-based Laker Airways folded with debts of $270 million. Over 6,000 passengers were left stranded. The airline had been founded by Sir Freddie Laker in 1966 but struggled in later years due to the recession of the early 1980s.

On 19 February, the DeLorean Motor Company Car Factory in Belfast was put into receivership. The stainless steel DeLorean sports car with its gull-wing doors famously featured in the *Back to the Future* movies.

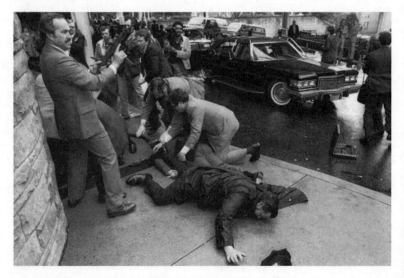

The scene after the attempted assassination of Ronald Reagan. The failed assassin was John Hinckley, a loner who was obsessed with Jodie Foster.

On 30 March, President Ronald Reagan and three other people were shot and wounded after he left a speaking engagement at the Washington Hilton Hotel. The failed assassin was John Hinckley, a loner who was obsessed with Jodie Foster after seeing her in the movie *Taxi Driver* who thought the assassination attempt would impress her.

On 2 April, the Falklands War began after Argentina invaded and occupied the Falkland Islands, a British dependency. Argentina claimed sovereignty of the islands.

On 2 May the British nuclear submarine HMS *Conqueror* sank the Argentine cruiser *General Belgrano*, killing 323 sailors on board.

On 13 May, the attempted assassination of John Paul II took place in St Peter's Square in Vatican City. The Pope was shot and wounded by Mehmet Ali Ağca, a Turkish national.

On 26 May, Aston Villa won the European Cup after beating Bayern Munich 1–0. The goal was scored by Peter Withe in the sixty-ninth minute of the game in Rotterdam.

On 9 June, the twenty pence coin went into circulation. The reverse of the coin was designed by William Gardner and featured a crowned Tudor rose.

On 14 June, the Falklands War ended when British troops reached the outskirts of Stanley after marching across East Falkland from San Carlos Bay. When they arrived, they found the Argentine forces waving flying white flags of surrender.

On 21 June, Prince William was born at St Mary's Hospital in Paddington, West London. He was christened William Arthur Philip Louis and his birth made him second in line to the throne after his father, Prince Charles.

On 20 July, the Provisional IRA detonated two bombs in central London. The Hyde Park and Regents Park bombings killed 8 soldiers, wounded 47 people and caused the deaths of 7 horses.

On 11 October, the *Mary Rose*, the flagship of Henry VIII, was raised from the Solent. It had sunk over 400 years earlier in 1545.

On 2 November, Channel 4 was launched. The first programme shown was the game show *Countdown*, hosted by Richard Whiteley. The Liverpool-based soap opera *Brookside* became another flagship programme of the new station.

1983

On 17 January, the wearing of front seatbelts in vehicles was made compulsory. Six years later, a law was passed that children younger than fourteen years of age were required to wear seatbelts in the rear of a car.

On 10 February, the dismembered remains of twelve men were found at a house in Muswell Hill, North London. Dennis Nilsen was arrested for their murder.

On 15 February, the Austin Metro became Britain's best-selling car. It easily outsold every other new car registered in the UK during January.

During March, the compact disc (CD) first went on sale in the United Kingdom. The revolutionary medium was predicted to replace vinyl records and audio cassettes.

On 26 March, Liverpool won the Football League Cup for the third year in succession. They beat Manchester United 2–1 in the final played at Wembley Stadium.

On 4 April, gunmen raided a Security Express van in London and escaped with a haul of £7 million, the biggest cash haul in British history.

On 21 April, the £1 coin was introduced in England and Wales replacing the paper £1 note.

On 9 June, Margaret Thatcher won a landslide victory to continue as Prime Minister with a majority of 144 seats over Michael Foot who led the Labour Party and earned just 28 per cent of the vote. Her popularity had been greatly boosted by the British victory in the Falklands War.

On 19 July, the Natural History Museum erected a new model of a flesh-eating dinosaur.

On 26 July, Victoria Gillick, a Catholic mother of ten, lost a case against the DHSS in the High Court of Justice. Her application sought to stop the distribution of contraceptives to children under the age of sixteen without parental consent.

On 10 October 1980, Prime Minister Margaret Thatcher gave her famous, 'The lady's not for turning' speech.

On 1 August, the new A-prefix car registration plates were launched, aiding the recovery of car sales following the slump at the start of the 1980s caused by the recession.

On 18 November, Janet Walton gave birth to six female babies after receiving fertility treatment.

On 26 November, approximately 6,800 gold bars worth almost £26 million were stolen from the Brink's-Mat vault at Heathrow Airport. Only a fraction of the gold was ever recovered.

On 6 December, the UK's first heart and lung transplant was carried out at Harefield Hospital.

On 17 December, an IRA car bomb exploded outside Harrods killing 6 people – 3 police and 3 members of the public. The bomb also injured a further 90 people.

1984

On 13 January, Britain was battered by hurricane-force winds resulting in the deaths of six people.

Between 7 February and 19 February, Great Britain and Northern Ireland took part in the Winter Olympics in Sarajevo, Yugoslavia, and won one gold medal, achieved by Torvill and Dean in the ice skating event.

On 12 March, Arthur Scargill instigated a national miners' strike in protest against proposed pit closures. Many miners joined the picket lines; the protests led to the death of a taxi driver when a block of concrete was dropped on his car as he drove a miner to work.

On 15 April, the comedian Tommy Cooper collapsed and died due to a heart attack while appearing on the live televised show, *Live from Her Majesty's*. He was sixty-three.

On 17 April, WPC Yvonne Fletcher was shot and killed by a gunman during a siege outside the Libyan Embassy in London. Another eleven other people were also shot but survived the ordeal.

On 8 May, The Queen opened the Thames Barrier, which was designed to protect London from floods.

On 19 May, Everton won the FA Cup, beating Watford 2–0. It was their first major trophy win for fourteen years. The two goals are scored by Andy Gray and Graham Sharp.

On 30 May, Liverpool won the European Cup for the fourth time. They won due to a penalty shoot-out victory after the final against AS Roma of Italy resulted in a 1–1 draw.

During June, unemployment in the UK reached a record high of approximately 3,260,000 people without jobs.

On 20 June, the education system received an exam shake-up in when it was announced that O-level and CSE exams were to be replaced by a new single exam, the GCSE. The first GCSE courses were forecast to begin in September 1986.

Between 28 July and 12 August, Great Britain and Northern Ireland took part in the Olympics in Los Angeles, California. They won a total of 5 gold, 11 silver and 21 bronze medals.

On 11 August, Zola Budd collided with Mary Decker while competing in the 3000 meters final at the Olympics. Neither contestant received medals. Budd, who had grown up in South Africa, had controversially been granted British citizenship earlier in the year so that she could compete for the UK. Decker was representing the USA.

On 15 September, the Princess of Wales gave birth to her second son, who was christened Henry Charles Albert David but known more commonly as Prince Harry. His birth made him sixth in line to the British throne.

On 23 October, BBC News newsreader Michael Buerk reported on the famine in Ethiopia, which had already resulted in the loss of thousands of lives. Various British charities including Oxfam and Save the Children started collections to aid the famine victims, many of whom were encamped close to the town of Korem. The news report shocked the world.

On 5 November, 800 miners ended their strike and returned to work.

On 20 November, British Telecom shares went on sale in the biggest share issue ever. Two million people (approximately 5 percent of the adult population) bought shares, which almost doubled the number of share owners in the UK.

On 11 December, 'Do They Know It's Christmas?' by the charity super group Band Aid shot to the top of the UK Singles Chart.

1985

On 1 January, the first mobile phone calls within the UK were made.

On 10 January, Sir Clive Sinclair's C5 battery powered vehicle was launched in the UK.

On 25 February, almost 4,000 further striking miners returned to their jobs leaving just over half of the miners in the UK on strike.

On 3 March, the Miners' Strike came to an end after one year. At its peak, it involved 142,000 mineworkers in the UK.

On 11 May, 56 people were killed and 265 were injured in the Bradford City stadium fire. The fire had been started by a discarded cigarette which ignited paper and other rubbish under the stand.

Also on 11 May, a fifteen-year-old boy was killed and a further twenty people were injured when Leeds United football fans rioted at the

Birmingham City stadium. The riot caused a wall to collapse which led to the death of teenager, Ian Hambridge.

On 13 August, the world's youngest heart-lung transplant patient underwent surgery at the Harefield Hospital in Middlesex. The patient was a three-year-old boy, Jamie Gavin.

On 22 August, fifty-five people were killed at Manchester International Airport after a British Airtours Boeing 737 caught alight soon after the pilot aborted the take-off.

On 1 September, a French-American joint expedition located the wreck of the RMS *Titanic*, lost since it sank in 1912.

On 4 September, divers took the first photographs and film of the wreckage of RMS *Titanic*, seventy-three years after its fatal voyage.

On 28 September, a violent riot took place in Brixton after a woman was accidentally shot by the police. One person was killed with 50 injured and more than 200 arrested.

On 6 October, PC Keith Blakelock was fatally stabbed during the Broadwater Farm Riot in Tottenham, London. The riot started after the death of Cynthia Jarrett during the previous day. Two of PC Blakelock's colleagues were taken to hospital with gunshot wounds, together with three journalists.

On 9 November, the Prince and Princess of Wales arrived in the United States where they met Ronald Reagan in Washington. Princess Diana famously danced with John Travolta during a gala dinner at the White House.

On 25 December, Comic Relief was launched. The charity was founded by Richard Curtis and comedian Lenny Henry in response to the famine in Ethiopia. The first Red Nose Day took place on Friday 5 February and raised over £15 million.

On 9 November 1985, the Prince and Princess of Wales arrived in the United States where they met Ronald Reagan in Washington. Princess Diana famously danced with John Travolta during a gala dinner at the White House.

1986

On 20 January, the United Kingdom and France announced plans to build a Channel Tunnel, which they hope to have up and running by the early 1990s.

On 28 January, the space shuttle *Challenger* exploded on take-off, resulting in the deaths of all seven crew members. The crew included five NASA astronauts as well as one payload specialist and a civilian school teacher, Christa McAuliffe.

During February, heavy snow and sub-zero temperatures hit much of the UK. It proved to be the coldest spell since January 1963.

On 7 April, Clive Sinclair sold the rights to the ZX Spectrum computer and his other inventions to Amstrad.

On 17 April, journalist John McCarthy was kidnapped by The Revolutionary Cells (RZ) in Beirut. In the same location, three further hostages were found dead. The Revolutionary Cells (RZ) claimed that the abductions were in revenge for the bombing of Libya by the US.

On 5 May, Liverpool won the Football League First Division title for a record sixteenth time after beating Chelsea 1–0. Liverpool's player-manager, Kenny Dalglish, scored the goal which won Liverpool the title.

On 10 May, Liverpool beat Everton 3–1 in the first ever all-Merseyside FA Cup final. Liverpool became the third team during the century to win the double.

On 10 June, Patrick Joseph Magee was sentenced to life imprisonment after being found guilty of the 1984 Brighton hotel bombing which targeted Prime Minister Margaret Thatcher and her cabinet.

On 29 June, Richard Branson broke the speed record for a transatlantic crossing by boat in *Virgin Atlantic Challenger II*. However, he was refused the Blue Riband award because its organisers said that the vessel wasn't a commercial passenger ship.

On 28 January 1986, the Challenger Space Shuttle exploded during take-off killing all seven crew members on board.

Also on 29 June, Argentina won the World Cup in Mexico beating West Germany. Gary Lineker won the Golden Boot in the contest being the leading scorer after achieving six goals.

On 1 July, Gary Lineker was transferred from Everton to FC Barcelona for a transfer fee of £2.75 million, making him the most expensive British footballer until then.

On 2 July, just a day after Gary Lineker's transfer, Ian Rush agreed to a £3.2 million move from Liverpool to Juventus of Italy, setting a new transfer record for a British footballer. However, he was loaned back to Liverpool for the season and his first game for Juventus didn't take place until the following year.

On 23 July, the marriage of Prince Andrew and Sarah Ferguson took place at Westminster Abbey. A total of 500 million viewers tuned in worldwide to watch the event on television, with a further 100,000 gathered to see their first public kiss as man and wife on the balcony of Buckingham Palace.

On 28 July, estate agent Suzy Lamplugh vanished after a meeting in London with a mysterious client known only a Mr Kipper. She was presumed murdered although her body has never been found.

On 29 August, May and Marjorie Chavasse, Britain's oldest surviving twins, celebrated their 100th birthday.

During August, seven years after the 'right to buy scheme' was created, the millionth council house was sold in the United Kingdom, purchased by its occupiers in Scotland.

On 6 November, forty-five people lost their lives when a Boeing 234LR Chinook helicopter, returning workers from the Brent oilfield, crashed while approaching Sumburgh Airport in the Shetland Islands.

On 6 November, Manchester United football club appointed Alex Ferguson as manager after their previous manager, Ron Atkinson, was dismissed after five years in the job. Manchester United had won two FA Cups under Atkinson's management but hadn't won a league title since 1967.

On 3 December, over 4 million people applied for shares in British Gas in anticipation of the company's flotation the following week.

1987

In January, large parts of the UK were affected by heavy snow and sub-zero temperatures.

On 13 January, Prince Edward resigned from the Royal Marines three months after enrolling. It was suggested that he planned to follow a career in the performing arts.

On 6 March, the ferry MS *Herald of Free Enterprise* capsized after departing from the harbour at Zeebrugge in Belgium. A total of 193 people on board were killed in the disaster.

On 30 March, Vincent van Gogh's painting *Vase with 15 Sunflowers* sold at Christie's auction house in London for a record £24,750,000.

On 3 April, jewellery belonging to the late Duchess of Windsor was sold at auction and fetched £31,000,000. The figure was six times the expected value.

On 5 April, the Football League Cup was won by Arsenal who beat Liverpool 2–1. It was their first win in the club's history and their first major trophy win since 1979. Charlie Nicholas scored both of the winning goals.

On 4 May, the Football League First Division title was won by Everton, the ninth time they'd won the title in the club's history.

On 8 May, members of the SAS killed eight members of the Provisional Irish Republican Army at Loughgall, County Antrim after a unit of the IRA launched an attack on the Royal Ulster Constabulary base in the village.

On 11 June, the general election saw Margaret Thatcher secure her third term in office. Her parliamentary majority, however, was decreased to 102 compared to the 144-seat majority she had gained previously during the election four years earlier.

On 30 June, the England striker, 26-year-old Peter Beardsley, became the most expensive player to transfer between British clubs, in a move from Newcastle United to Liverpool, costing a record £1,900,000.

On 12 July, a robbery at the Knightsbridge Safe Deposit Centre in Cheval Place netted £60,000,000. The robbery was led by Valerio Viccei, a lawyer's son from Italy.

On 19 August, a rogue gunman, Michael Ryan shot dead fourteen people in Hungerford. Ryan, an unemployed antique dealer and handyman, later ended his own life by shooting himself. Sixteen other people were also hurt in the incident.

On 11 October, Operation Deepscan, a project costing an estimated £1,000,000, failed to locate any trace of the legendary Loch Ness Monster.

Between 15 and 16 October, the UK was hit by hurricane-force winds, which battered much of south-east England. Twenty three people were killed and extensive damage was caused to property.

On 19 October, over £50,000,000,000 was wiped off the value of shares on the London stock exchange on Black Monday, the result of the Wall Street crash.

In December, Mikhail Gorbachev and Ronald Reagan signed the INF Treaty which agreed on the elimination of all nuclear and conventional missiles with ranges of 500–1,000 kilometres.

On 25 December, a record-breaking audience of 26,000,000 viewers tuned in to ITV's Christmas Day episode of *Coronation Street* to see Hilda Ogden (Jean Alexander) make her final appearance on the show after being a regular for twenty-three years.

In December 1987, Mikhail Gorbachev and Ronald Reagan signed the INF Treaty, which agreed on the elimination of all nuclear and conventional missiles with ranges of 500 to 1,000 kilometres.

1988

On 3 January, Margaret Thatcher became the longest-serving UK Prime Minister of the century. She had been in power for eight years and 244 days.

On 5 January, the new Comic Relief charity appeal was launched by *Blackadder* star Rowan Atkinson. After participation by people up and down the land, the first BBC Red Nose Day raised a total of £15,000,000 for charity.

Between 13 and 28 February, Great Britain and Northern Ireland competed at the Winter Olympics in Calgary in Canada but failed to win any medals.

On 6 March, Operation Flavius, which consisted of a Special Air Service team of the British Army, shot dead three unarmed members of a Provisional Irish Republican Army (IRA) Active Service Unit whilst in Gibraltar.

On 10 March, Prince Charles narrowly avoided death due to an avalanche while he was on a skiing holiday in Switzerland. The former equerry to the Queen, Major Hugh Lindsay, was killed in the accident.

On 11 March, the British £1 note ceased to be legal tender, having been replaced earlier by a coin.

On 2 June, US President Ronald Reagan and his wife Nancy visited the UK, meeting Prime Minister Margaret Thatcher and Queen Elizabeth II.

On 11 June, a concert was held at Wembley Stadium to celebrate the life of Nelson Mandela, the South African anti-apartheid icon whose seventieth birthday fell on that day. He had been imprisoned since 1964. Over 80,000 people attended the concert.

On 6 July, an explosion on the North Sea oil rig, *Piper Alpha*, resulted in the death of 167 workers.

Also on 6 July, a contractor's relief driver accidentally poisoned the water supply of Camelford in Cornwall by pouring twenty tonnes of aluminium sulphate into the wrong tank at a water treatment plan.

On 18 July, Paul Gascoigne became the first £2,000,000 footballer to be signed by a British club. The twenty-one-year-old midfielder joined Tottenham Hotspur after leaving Newcastle United.

On 8 August, the first child of the Duke and Duchess of York, later named Beatrice, was born at Portland Hospital in London. At the time, she was fifth in line to the throne but is currently ninth in line.

On 19 September, the actor Roy Kinnear was seriously injured after falling off his horse while filming *The Return of the Musketeers* in Spain. He died in hospital the following day.

On 12 December, a rail crash at Clapham Junction led to the deaths of thirty-five people.

On 21 December, Pan Am Flight 103 exploded, due to a terrorist bomb, over the Scottish town of Lockerbie. A total of 270 people were killed: 11 on the ground and all 259 people who were on board the plane.

1989

On 4 January, a memorial service took place to remember the 270 people who were killed in the Lockerbie air disaster two weeks previously. Prime Minister Margaret Thatcher and several other world leaders were among over 200 people who attended the church service at the village of Dryfesdale near Lockerbie.

On 8 January, the Kegworth air disaster took place when a British Midland Boeing 737 crashed onto the M1 motorway on the approach to East Midlands Airport. A total of 44 people were killed.

On 5 February, Sky Television started broadcasting the first satellite television service in the UK.

On 11 February, after the success of *Neighbours* on BBC One, ITV aired the first episode of the Australian soap *Home and Away*. The show had premiered in its own country the year before.

On 23 February, twenty-seven-year-old William Hague won the Richmond by-election in North Yorkshire for the Conservative Party after Leon Brittan left to join the European Commission.

Also on 23 February, *EastEnders* character Den Watts, portrayed by Leslie Grantham, left the series after his character was shot in an episode watched by over 20 million viewers.

On 26 March, the Brazilian Grand Prix was won by Britain's Nigel Mansell.

On 10 April, Nick Faldo won the golfing Masters Tournament making him the first English winner of the title.

On 15 April, the Hillsborough Disaster resulted in the deaths of 94 people. Over 300 people were taken to hospital. The incident occurred during the FA Cup semi-final at Hillsborough Stadium in Sheffield during the FA Cup semi-final, played between Nottingham Forest and Liverpool. The youngest victim was a ten-year-old boy and the oldest, sixty-seven-year-old Gerard Baron, who was the brother of the late former Liverpool player Kevin Baron.

On 20 May, Liverpool won the FA Cup final beating Everton 3–2.

On 20 August, a pleasure cruiser, the *Marchioness,* collided with a barge in the River Thames. Fifty-one people were killed.

On 31 August, it was announced by Buckingham Palace that Princess Anne and Captain Mark Phillips were to separate after being married for sixteen years.

In November the Berlin Wall was demolished, ending the Iron Curtain division of Europe.

On 6 December, the BBC decided to stop making any future episodes of *Doctor Who.* The programme had been regularly shown for twenty-six years, the final Doctor being Sylvester McCoy.

On 8 December, ITV's *Coronation Street* attracted an audience of almost 27 million viewers who tuned in to see the show's villain, Alan Bradley (Mark Eden) killed after being hit by a tram in Blackpool.

On 30 December, twenty-two people who were involved in the Lockerbie tragedy were recognised in the New Year's Honours list. There was also a knighthood for Liberal leader David Steel, the actress Maggie Smith became a Dame, and the boxer Frank Bruno and golfer Tony Jacklin were both made MBEs.

Above left: Protesters on the Berlin Wall in 1989. It was demolished during November of that year, ending the Iron Curtain division of Europe.

Above right: Sylvester McCoy and Sophie Aldred in their roles as Doctor Who and his assistant, Ace. Sylvester McCoy played Doctor Who between 1987 and 1989 before the series was cancelled by the BBC.

16

Memorable Personalities of the 1980s

Lysette Anthony (1963–) was born Lysette Anne Chodzko on 26 September 1963. She is remembered for her role as Christa in *Auf Wiedersehen, Pet* during 1984 and as Angie in the popular sitcom *Three Up Two Down* (1985–89), which also starred Michael Elphick. She appeared in many popular comedies and dramas during the 1980s including *Lovejoy, The Gentle Touch, Home to Roost, Jack the Ripper* and *Oliver Twist*. Photographer David Bailey described her as 'The Face of the Eighties'.

Michael Barrymore (1952–), a former Butlin's redcoat, appeared in many hit shows during the decade including *Get Set Go!* (1984), *Strike It Lucky* (1986–94) and *Michael Barrymore's Saturday Night Out* (1988–89). He was born Michael Ciaran Parker on 4 May 1952 and found fame after appearing on *New Faces* in 1979, which he won, before becoming a regular panellist on *Blankety Blank*.

Jeremy Beadle (1948–2008) was a television presenter, radio presenter, writer and producer. He was a regular face on television during the 1980s appearing on *Eureka* (1981), *Game for a Laugh* (1981–85), *The Saturday Show* (1983), *TV-am* (1984), *Definition* (1984–86), *People Do the Funniest Things* (1987), *Beadle's About* (1986–96), *Chain Letters* (1987) and *Born Lucky* (1989). He started his career in 1973 hosting a live show on BBC Radio London before writing comedy material for Terry Wogan, Michael Aspel, Noel Edmonds and Kenny Everett.

Jim Bowen (1937–2018) was well-known throughout the 1980s as the host of the darts-based game show *Bullseye*. He was born Peter Williams on 20 August 1937 and first appeared on television in the hit 1970s show *The Comedians*. In 1975, he presented Thames Television's *You Must Be Joking*, which started the careers of Ray Burdis, John Blundell, Pauline Quirke and

Jim Bowen, the host of ITV's incredibly popular darts-based game show *Bullseye*.

the pop group Flintlock. He also appeared in *Last of the Summer Wine* as well as on *The Wheeltappers and Shunters Social Club*. In 1982, he played a crooked accountant in ITV's drama *Muck and Brass* and later appeared in *Jonathan Creek* and Peter Kay's *Phoenix Nights*.

Judith Chalmers (1935–) is best known for presenting ITV's holiday show Wish *You Were Here?*, which was broadcast between 1974 and 2003. She was born on 10 October 1935 and began her broadcasting career aged thirteen when she was selected for BBC Northern Children's Hour by producer Trevor Hill. In the 1960s, she presented *Family Favourites* and *Woman's Hour* on BBC radio and also played Susan in *The Clitheroe Kid*. In the 1980s, she was also the host of the Miss World contest on ITV.

Annabel Croft (1966–) was born on 12 July 1966 and was a professional tennis player during the 1980s before starting a career in television, appearing in *Treasure Hunt* (1989), *The Best of Magic* (1989) and *Interceptor* (1989–90).

Annabel Croft was a professional tennis player during the 1980s before embarking on a career in television, appearing in *Treasure Hunt* (1989), *The Best of Magic* (1989) and *Interceptor* (1989–90).

Leslie Crowther (1933–96) was well known in the 1980s for hosting the popular game show *The Price is Right*. He was born on 6 February 1933 and his first broadcasting appearance was on Radio Luxembourg as a member of the Ovaltineys Concert Party. During the 1950s, he appeared on television on *The Billy Cotton Show* and *The Black and White Minstrel Show*. Between 1960 and 1968, he was a regular presenter on *Crackerjack* before becoming the face of Stork SB Margarine in the 1970s. He also starred in *The Leslie Crowther Show* (1971) and appeared in the comedy *My Good Woman* (1972–73) as well as touring on stage with Bernie Winters playing Chesney Allen and Bud Flanagan.

Suzanne Danielle (1957–) was a regular face on television during the 1980s appearing in *Give Us a Clue, Blankety Blank, Doctor Who, Morecambe and Wise* and *Tales of the Unexpected*. She was born Suzanne Morris on 14 January 1957 and also appeared in various movies including *The Stud* (1978), *The Wild Geese* (1978), *Long Shot* (1978), *Carry On Emmannuelle* (1978), *Arabian Adventure* (1979), *The Golden Lady* (1979), *Sir Henry at Rawlinson End* (1980), *Flash Gordon* (1980) and *The Boys in Blue* (1982). She was the girlfriend of actor Patrick Mower before marrying the golfer Sam Torrence.

Sharron Davies (1962–) was born on 1 November 1962 and represented Great Britain in the Olympics and European championships as well as competing in the Commonwealth Games. In 1978, she won two gold medals at the Commonwealth Games in Edmonton and later in 1980 won a silver medal in the 400-metre individual medley at the Olympics in Moscow. She made regular appearance on television in the 1980s appearing in *Sporting Superstars* (1981), *On Safari* (1982), *Cheggers Plays Pop* (1983), *Children in Need* (1983), *Punchlines* (1981–84), *Bullseye* (1985), *French and Saunders* (1987), *3–2–1* (1987) and *Blankety Blank* (1985–90).

Peter Davison (1951–) became the fifth Doctor Who, following Tom Baker, in 1981. He was born Peter Moffett on 13 April 1951. He was already well known on television for playing Tristan Farnon in *All Creatures Great and Small* (1978–90). Other roles in the 1980s included *Sink or Swim* (1980–82), *Holding the Fort* (1980–82), *The Hitchhiker's Guide to the Galaxy* (1981) and *A Very Peculiar Practice* (1986–88). He was formerly married to actress Sandra Dickinson and is the father-in-law of David Tennant, the tenth Doctor Who.

Bobby Davro (1959–), a comedian, writer and impressionist, was born Robert Nankeville on 13 September 1959. During the '80s, he appeared on television in *Live at Her Majesty's* (1983) before going on to appear in *Copy Cats* (1985–1986), *Bobby Davro on the Box* (1986), *Bobby Davro's TV Annual* (1986) and *Bobby Davro's TV Weekly* (1988) as well as making guest appearances on many other popular shows.

Anne Diamond (1954–) hosted *Good Morning Britain* for TV-am with Nick Owen in 1983. She formerly worked at Butlin's as a redcoat and chalet maid. When she left, she began a career in journalism working for the *Bridgwater Mercury* and *Bournemouth Evening Echo*. Her broadcasting career began at BBC West in Bristol before she joined ATV Today in 1979, working as a reporter and newsreader. When ATV became Central Television in 1982, she was teamed up with Nick Owen and together they presented the new *Central News*. She left *Central* and joined ITN before rejoining the BBC as a reporter on their flagship programme, *Nationwide*. When Anna Ford and Angela Rippon left TV-am, Greg Dyke asked Nick Owen to present the programme and Owen suggested Anne Diamond as his co-host. She left the show in 1990 to work full time on TVS's *TV Weekly*. She teamed up with Nick Owen again in 1992 and presented the BBC daytime show, *Good Morning with Anne and Nick*. It ran for four years until 1996.

Michael Elphick (1946–2002) made his debut in *Fräulein Doktor* (1968) followed by appearing as Captain in Tony Richardson's version of *Hamlet* (1969). He also appeared in Lindsay Anderson's *O Lucky Man!* (1973) and

The First Great Train Robbery (1979) as well as playing Phil Daniels's father in the movie *Quadrophenia* (1979), playing a night porter in *The Elephant Man* (1980), Pasha in *Gorky Park* (1983) and the poacher, Jake, in *Withnail & I* (1987). He is well remembered for a series of appearances in various television programmes throughout the 1980s including *Private Schulz* (1981), *Auf Wiedersehen, Pet* (1983), *Pull the Other One* (1984) and Boon (1986–92).

Ben Elton (1959–) first appeared on television doing stand-up on the BBC1 youth and music programme, *The Oxford Road Show*. At twenty-three, he had his first television success as co-writer of the television comedy, *The Young Ones*, in which he also sometimes appeared. Between 1983 and 1984, he penned Granada Television's sketch show *Alfresco*, in which he also appeared. The show featured early appearances by Stephen Fry, Hugh Laurie, Emma Thompson and Robbie Coltrane. In 1985, he wrote his first solo script for the BBC. The comedy series *Happy Families*, starred Jennifer Saunders and Adrian Edmondson. Soon afterwards, he reunited with Rik Mayall and Ade Edmondson together with Nigel Planer for the showbiz sitcom *Filthy Rich and Catflap*. In 1985, Elton began writing with Richard Curtis and together they wrote *Blackadder II*, *Blackadder the Third* and *Blackadder Goes Forth*. Also during the decade, he appeared in *Comic Relief* (1986–89), *Lenny Henry Tonite* (1986) and *Saturday Live* (1986).

Harry Enfield (1961–) first appeared on Channel 4's *Saturday Live* where he appeared as several characters which he had created with Paul Whitehouse. These included Stavros, a Greek kebab shop owner and Loadsamoney, and later as the Geordie 'Bugger-All-Money'. In 1988, he played both Loadsamoney and Bugger-All-Money at the Nelson Mandela Birthday Tribute Concert at Wembley Stadium. In 1989, Enfield appeared in *Norbert Smith – a Life*, a send-up of the many British theatrical knights slumming in the film industry. He also created many of the voices for *Spitting Image* as well as starring as Dirk Gently in the BBC Radio adaptations of *Dirk Gently's Holistic Detective Agency* and *The Long Dark Tea-Time of the Soul*.

Gregor Fisher (1953–) is best known for his role as Rab C. Nesbitt, a character in a comedy series first broadcast in 1988. The show was a spin off from the popular BBC2 show *Naked Video*. Another of Fisher's characters from the show, 'Baldy Man' regularly appeared in adverts for Hamlet cigars. During the 1980s, he also appeared in *Crown Court*, *Boon*, and *Scotch & Wry*. More recently, he has appeared in the movies *Love Actually*, *Lassie* and *Wild Target*.

Russell Grant (1951–) His broadcasting career began on Yorkshire Television's show *Extraordinary,* in which he discussed astrology, in 1979. During 1980 and 1981, he became the regular astrologer on Granada Television's *Live from Two.* Between 1983 and 1986, he appeared on BBC's *Breakfast Time* where he presented the *Your Stars* section. In 1986, he joined TV-am and became their resident astrologer appearing on *Good Morning Britain* and *After Nine* until 1990. From 1992 until 1995, he was the regular astrological expert on *This Morning with Richard and Judy.* During this time, he also wrote magazine columns, books and made records with the Starlettes.

Hale and Pace met at teacher training college before becoming successful comedians. Gareth Hale (1953–) and Norman Pace (1953–) first appeared on Radio 4 before finding fame on television in *The Entertainers* (1984), *Pushing Up Daisies* (1984) and *The Saturday Gang* (1986). They appeared in BBC sitcom *The Young Ones* three times, in the episodes *Flood*, *Nasty* and *Time*. After completing a one-off special for London Weekend Television in Christmas 1986, they were given their own series in 1988, which went on to win the Silver Rose of Montreux as well as the Press prize. Their series continued for the next ten years. Their most famous comic creations were The Two Rons (based on the Kray Twins) and the ever-smiling and colourfully dressed children's television presenters Billy and Johnny.

Jools Holland (1958–) played as a session musician before finding fame with the band Squeeze. When Channel 4 was first introduced, he became the regular presenter, alongside Paula Yates, on the popular music show *The Tube.* During 1987, he formed the Jools Holland Big Band, which included Gilson Lavis from Squeeze. This eventually became the 18-piece Jools Holland's Rhythm and Blues Orchestra. Between 1988 and 1990, he performed and co-hosted two seasons of the music programme *Sunday Night* on NBC late-night television.

Bob Holness (1928–2012) became famous as the host of the popular game show *Blockbusters*. He began his career in 1955 presenting *Late Night Extra*, first on the BBC Light Programme and later on Radio 1 and Radio 2, alongside Terry Wogan, Michael Parkinson and Keith Fordyce. In 1956, he played James Bond in a radio production of *Moonraker*. He began his television career in 1962 as the host of the game show *Take a Letter* and was the relief host of Thames Television's magazine programme *Today* in 1968. From 1983 until 1994, he presented the British version of *Blockbusters*, for which he was best known. He also appeared in *Catchphrase* (1988).

Henry Kelly (1946–) had been a writer and journalist before embarking on a television career. In 1981, he became a co-presenter on London Weekend Television's primetime show *Game for a Laugh*. He remained with the show until 1983 when he joined TV-am presenting the Saturday edition of *Good Morning Britain* with Toni Arthur. He left TV-am in 1987 to present the daytime show *Going For Gold*.

Matthew Kelly (1950–) had his first major television break appearing in the ITV sitcom *Holding the Fort* (1980–82). He also appeared as a panellist on the game show *Punchlines* (1981–84) which was hosted by Lennie Bennett. He was also a regular presenter of *Game For a Laugh* (1981–85) alongside Jeremy Beadle, Henry Kelly and Sarah Kennedy. He appeared in many light entertainment shows over the years including *Kelly's Eye* (1985).

Sarah Kennedy (1950–) began her radio career with the British Forces Broadcasting Service in Singapore in 1973. In 1977, she joined BBC Radio 2 as a newsreader and continuity announcer as well as presenting *Family Favourites*. Her television career began with her reading the news on Southern Television's *Day by Day*. She gained nationwide fame as one of the hosts of *Game for a Laugh* between 1981 and 1984. She was also involved with the short-lived BBC current affairs programme, *60 Minutes*, (1983–84). She later presented the ITV game show *Busman's Holiday* (1985–93) and co-hosted *The Animals Roadshow* and *Animal Country* with zoologist Desmond Morris. She later became a regular presenter on Radio 2 and also published a novel *Charlotte's Friends*.

Timmy Mallett (1955–) began his career working on the student radio station, Radio Warwick before joining BBC Radio Oxford. He later moved to Centre Radio (now Leicester Sound) before becoming a presenter on Radio Luxembourg and Manchester's Piccadilly Radio. At Piccadilly, he hosted *Timmy on the Tranny* which was broadcast between 8pm and 11pm. In 1983, he hosted *Summer Run*, the Saturday morning section of the new breakfast television station, TV-am. In 1984, he became a presenter of *Wide Awake Club*, a Saturday morning children's show on TV-am, which he co-presented with Michaela Strachan, James Baker, Arabella Warner and Tommy Boyd. After *Roland Rat* moved to the BBC, TV-am asked Mallett to present their new Saturday morning show called *Wacaday* which began broadcasting in 1985.

Rik Mayall (1958–2014) with Ade Edmondson found fame at *The Comedy Store* in the early 1980s. They performed as a double act, *20th Century Coyote*, while Mayall developed solo routines, which included the character Kevin Turvey as well as a pompous anarchist poet called Rick. Mayall, Adrian Edmondson and *Comedy Store* compere Alexei Sayle as well as other upcoming comedians including Nigel Planer, Peter Richardson, Dawn French, Jennifer Saunders, Arnold Brown and Pete Richens, went on to set up their own comedy club which they called The Comic Strip. Mayall appeared regularly as Kevin Turvey on the television show *A Kick Up the Eighties* (1981). He also appeared as Rest Home Ricky in Richard O'Brien's *Shock Treatment*, a sequel to *The Rocky Horror Picture Show*. Mayall's appearances as Kevin Turvey led to a mockumentary being made which was entitled *Kevin Turvey – The Man Behind The Green Door* (1982). On stage, he continued his partnership with Edmondson appearing regularly as 'The Dangerous Brothers'. Channel 4 offered the Comic Strip group six short films, which became known as *The Comic Strip Presents...* The first film was shown in 1982. Soon after, the BBC commissioned *The Young Ones*, which was written by Mayall and his then-girlfriend Lise Mayer together with Ben Elton. Mayall appeared in many shows throughout the decade, most notably *Whoops Apocalypse* (1982), *The Black Adder* (1983), *Saturday Live* (1986), *Blackadder II* (1986), *Filthy Rich & Catflap* (1987), *The New Statesman* (1987–94) and *Blackadder Goes Forth* (1989).

Mike Morris (1946–2012) was well known as a television presenter and journalist particularly as a presenter on TV-am's *Good Morning Britain*. He was originally a sports correspondent on TV-am before becoming presenter of *Good Morning Britain's* Saturday programme. In 1987, he became a chief weekday presenter alongside Anne Diamond, Kathy Tayler, Maya Even and Lorraine Kelly. He was the first broadcaster on British television to conduct a live interview with Nelson Mandela shortly after his release from prison. Morris stayed with TV-am until the station lost its ITV franchise towards the end of 1992.

Nick Owen (1947–) began his career as a graduate trainee at the *Doncaster Evening Post* before moving on to the *Birmingham Post*. In 1973, he was employed by *Radio Birmingham* as a news producer and sports editor. He joined ATV in 1978 as a sports reporter, commentator and presenter for ATV news. He also did the voice-over for the first series of *Bullseye* and appeared on the programme in 1983 throwing darts for charity. At the beginning of 1982, when ATV became Central TV, Owen and Anne Diamond were chosen to present the new *Central News East*. However, neither presenter was ever seen on screen due to an industrial dispute. Owen left the station in January 1982 and joined TV-am as a sports presenter. When Greg Dyke became director of programmes, he made Owen the main presenter of *Good Morning Britain* in April 1983, and soon after he was joined by Anne Diamond until 1986 when he left TV-am to become a presenter for ITV Sport.

Andi Peters (1970–) His broadcasting career took off after appearing as a presenter on Children's BBC alongside Edd the Duck. Previously, he had presented *Freetime* on ITV but reached a far wider audience presenting alongside Edd the Duck and Wilson in 'The Broom Cupboard' section on Children's BBC. He appeared regularly from May 1989 to September 1993.

Su Pollard (1949–) found fame in the BBC sitcom *Hi-de-Hi* (1980–88) playing chalet maid Peggy Ollerenshaw. Previously, in 1979, she played Flo in the BBC sitcom, *Two Up, Two Down*. During 1981, she was a presenter on the children's magazine show, *Get Set for Summer*. While appearing on Hi-de-Hi, she reached number two in the UK Singles Chart in 1986 with the song 'Starting Together', which was the theme from the BBC Television documentary series *The Marriage*. Previously, she had released a single, *Come To Me (I Am Woman)* but it only reached number seventy-one in the charts. Her LP, *Su*, reached number eighty-six in the UK Albums Chart in November 1986. During 1987, she toured the country with *The Su Pollard Show* and also co-hosted *It's a Royal Knockout*. Shortly after *Hi-de-Hi!* had ended, she was chosen by writers David Croft and Jimmy Perry to play Ivy Teasdale in their new sitcom *You Rang, M'Lord?* (1988–93). The show also starred her *Hi-de-Hi!* co-stars Paul Shane and Jeffrey Holland. In 1989, she presented the game show *Take The Plunge* as well as voicing the lead character in the BBC children's television show, *Penny Crayon* (1989–1990).

Vic Reeves (1959–) first appeared on television in December 1986 on Channel 4 Television's *The Tube*, taking part in a comedy game show segment called *Square Celebrities*. He later appeared on the comedy chat show *One Hour with Jonathan Ross* as part of a game show segment called *Knock Down Ginger*.

Anneka Rice (1958–) began her broadcasting career as a trainee working for the BBC World Service before moving to Hong Kong, aged nineteen, where she read the news on the English language television station, *TVB Pearl*.

In 1982, she landed her first major television role alongside Kenneth Kendall in *Treasure Hunt*. It became one of Channel 4's most popular shows and was nominated for a BAFTA in 1986. In 1988, she left *Treasure Hunt* and was replaced by Annabel Croft. Rice went on to host alongside Sir Trevor McDonald and Zoë Ball in the ITV programme *Extinct*.

Selina Scott (1951–) made her television debut on Grampian Television's evening news programme, *North Tonight*. Several months later, she was employed by ITV as a newsreader on *News at Ten*. The BBC engaged her to present their new morning show *Breakfast Time* in 1983, which she co-presented with Frank Bough until 1986. She later presented *The Clothes Show* (1986–88) for the BBC and was a stand-in host on the chat show *Wogan*. In the mid-1980s, she moved to America where she hosted a chat show for CBS.

Carol Vorderman (1960–) found fame on Channel 4's game show *Countdown* appearing on the programme between 1982 and 2008. During her time on *Countdown,* she also presented various other television shows including *Better Homes* and *The Pride of Britain Awards* for ITV, as well as guest hosting shows including *Have I Got News for You*, *The Sunday Night Project* and *Lorraine*. She first appeared on *Countdown* alongside Richard Whiteley and later with Des Lyman and Des O'Connor.

Wincey Willis (1948–) was born Florence Winsome Leighton in Gateshead, County Durham. She started her career as a radio host before presenting the weather spot on Tyne Tees Television. In May 1983, she was employed by Greg Dyke on the then struggling TV-am. She took over the weather section of the programme from Commander Philpott and also presented other segments on the show, mainly involving animals and pets. She became very popular and later joined the cast of *Treasure Hunt* in 1985, with Kenneth Kendall and Anneka Rice. In 1987, she left TV-am focusing her career on helping animal charities.

Paula Yates (1959–2000) found fame on television presenting Channel 4's pop show *The Tube* alongside musician Jools Holland. She later regularly appeared on *The Big Breakfast* interviewing celebrity guests, the best remembered being an interview with INXS frontman Michael Hutchence. In 1982, she recorded the Nancy Sinatra song *These Boots Are Made for Walkin'* and in 1987 made a spoof mockumentary about Bananarama with her friend, Jennifer Saunders. She was the long-time partner of Bob Geldof and later had a relationship with Michael Hutchence.

Acknowledgements

Thanks to Tina Cole and Tilly Barker for all their help putting this book together. Thanks also to Dan Gilson for letting me use the photo of him as a boy in his Knight Rider car. It's much appreciated.

Bibliography

Books
A 1970s Childhood by Derek Tait (History Press 2011).
Best Movies of the 80s by Helen O'Hara (Portable Press 2018).
Cars We Loved in the 1980s by Giles Chapman History Press 2014).
Remember the 70s by Derek Tait (Pen & Sword 2017).
Remember the 80s by Richard Evans (Portico 2008).
You Know You're a Child of the 1980s When... by Charlie Ellis (Summersdale 2016).

Websites
80s Nostalgia at www.80snostalgia.com
Simply 80s at www.simplyeighties.com

Photo credits
Saturn Robot (Derek Tait), Action Man (Derek Tait), Rubik's Cube (Derek Tait), Knight Rider car and boy (Dan Gilson), Annabel Croft (AIB London), Atari (Evan-Amos), BBC Micro (Stuart Brady), Commodore 64 (Bill Bertram), Cadbury's Creme Egg (Evan-Amos), *Challenger* explosion (NASA Public Domain), *Columbia* (NASA Public Domain), Berlin Wall (Wikipedia), *Happy Days* (ABC Television/Public Domain), Jim Bowen (Wikipedia), Live Aid (Wikipedia), Margaret and Denis Thatcher (The National Archives), Michael Douglas (ABC TV/Public Domain), Michael Foot (Marcel Antonisse/Anefo), Michael J Fox (Alan Light), Noel Edmonds (Lawson Speedway/Public Domain), Video Recorder (Wikipedia), Ronald Reagan (Public Domain), Oliver Stone (Wikipedia), Michael Hutchence (Derek Tait), Frankie Goes to Hollywood (Jane McCormick Smith), Sony Walkman (Esa Sorjonen), Sylvester Stallone (Alan Light), Sylvester McCoy and Sophie Aldred (Wikipedia), Margaret Thatcher portrait (public

domain), New Romantic shirt (Wikipedia), Reagan and Gorbachev (public domain), Reagan assassination attempt (public domain), ZX Spectrum (Bill Bertram), Cadbury's Flake (Evan-Amos), Princess Diana (Nick Parfjonov/ Public Domain), John Travolta and Diana (Public Domain).